SAN DIEGO

California's Cornerstone

SAN DIEGO
California's Cornerstone

Iris Engstrand

Sunbelt Publications
San Diego, California

San Diego: California's Cornerstone

Sunbelt Publications, Inc.
Copyright ©2016 by Iris Engstrand
All rights reserved. First paperback edition 2005
Second edition 2016
Printed in the United States of America

Photography Editor: Allen Wynar
Copy Editor: Cynthia van Stralen
Cover, maps and book design: Allen Wynar
Project management: Deborah Young

Sunbelt Publications, Inc.
P.O. Box 191126
San Diego, California 92159-1126
(619) 258-4911, fax: (619) 258-4916
www.sunbeltpublications.com
19 18 17 16   4 3 2 1

"Sunbelt Cultural Heritage Books"
A Series Edited by Lowell Lindsay

Library of Congress Cataloging-in-Publication Data

Names: Engstrand, Iris Wilson, author.
Title: San Diego : California's Cornerstone / by Iris Engstrand.
Description: Second edition. | San Diego, Calif. : Sunbelt Publications,
    2016. | Includes bibliographical references and index.
Identifiers: LCCN 2016016726 | ISBN 9781941384244 (softcover : alk. paper)
Subjects: LCSH: San Diego (Calif.)--History.
Classification: LCC F869.S22 E543 2016 | DDC 979.4/985--dc23 LC record
    available at https://lccn.loc.gov/2016016726

All photos were taken by the author unless otherwise credited.
Front cover: San Diego skyline at night.
Insets: Louis Bank of Commerce, California Tower, *Star of India*, Chicano
Park, Petco Park.
Back cover insets: Padre Dam, Serra Museum, Casa de Estudillo.

Dedication

To Madison, Ryan, James, Trevor, Kensington,
Declan, Grayson, Avery, Paislyn, and Wyatt,
who will help shape San Diego as a global city.

Early surfers Charlie Wright and Faye Baird Fraser, Mission Beach, December 28, 1926. *Photo ©San Diego History Center.*

Acknowledgements

First, I would like to thank my students in California history at the University of San Diego who have, through the years, researched many of the subjects included in this book. They have been especially helpful on recent events and giving insight into what they deemed to be important. A number of people must work together to make any book a reality and, it is hoped, a success. I owe a debt of gratitude to my book designer, Allen Wynar, who has spent many hours enhancing the quality of the photographs, designing their placement, and remaining patient while making many little changes. I would also like to thank my previous book designers, Stephanie and Tom Gould, who designed the 2005 edition.

I am deeply appreciative of my colleagues and fellow historians who read various drafts of the final chapter. I am grateful to Roger Showley for a helpful reorganization of topics and valuable insights into events of the past ten years. I also wish to thank Robert Price both for his constant encouragement and for giving thoughtful criticism of content and emphasis over several drafts. Logan Jenkins was particularly helpful in the overall inclusion of topics. My copy editor and good friend Cindy van Stralen read and improved numerous copies of the manuscript with the utmost care and thoughtfulness.

My colleagues Molly McClain, University of San Diego; David Edick, World Affairs Council; Bill Lawrence, executive director, and Matthew Schiff, marketing director, San Diego History Center; and Peggy Gartin, web designer, all helped make the final chapter flow more smoothly. Thanks go to Heather Keil of the USD History Department for updating the index to include the final chapter.

I would like to express my gratitude to Diana Lindsay and Lowell Lindsay, publishers, and Debi Young, editor and project manager, Sunbelt Publications, for their enthusiasm from the beginning and thorough reading of the manuscript. Their helpful suggestions have made the book a better product. To all those who have dedicated time and effort to this revised edition, I am grateful.

TABLE OF CONTENTS

San Diego County

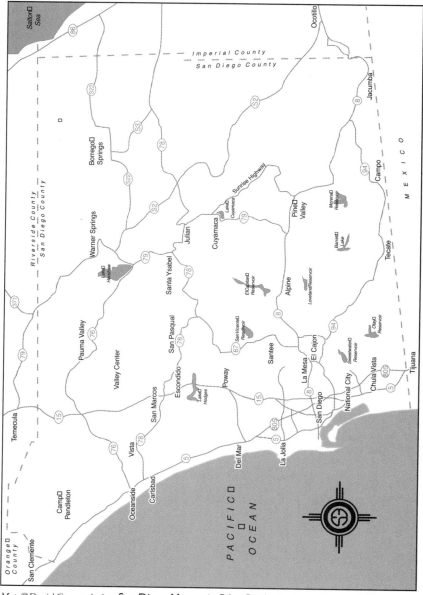

Map ©Daniel Greenstadt, from San Diego Mountain Bike Guide, *Sunbelt Publications* 1998.

INTRODUCTION

Tracing its heritage to Native Americans as well as to European newcomers, San Diego's history and this book begin with these distinct peoples. Initial contact between original inhabitants and Spanish colonizers produced long-lasting changes. Native American culture—much affected by missions and ranchos—has continued to the present day. Understanding the origins of Spanish institutions transported to California sheds light on San Diego's complex history, while these factors and later immigration contribute to an understanding of its dynamic present.

In these days of international travel, globalization of the Internet, and instant communication, it is difficult to realize that the Iberian Peninsula, like San Diego County, was at one time geographically isolated. Spain's position at the extreme west of the Mediterranean Sea and the extreme south of the European continent had a significant effect in shaping her historical destiny. The Pyrenees Mountains stand high along the French border, and the rest of Spain, surrounded by Atlantic and Mediterranean waters, is further protected by a coastal perimeter of mountains. Her temperate climate and fertile land have, nevertheless, attracted a host of invaders.

San Diego, in a similar manner, is also isolated. Fronting on a great expanse of ocean, it is backed by mountains and desert. These natural barriers have given the region a distinct identity. Geographic remoteness shaped the life of its aboriginal inhabitants and established the settlement pattern of later colonizers. From the beginning, communication by sea, moderate temperatures, and available fertile land made living close to the ocean desirable and San Diego became the cornerstone of the area's development.

Early settlers stayed along the coast even though rainfall was erratic. Prevailing westerly winds, low clouds, and frequent fogs provided important sources of moisture for the land. Spanish padres with Indian workers built the first dam in the 1780s. As more people entered the area, availability of water became a significant factor in the promotion of agriculture and urban settlement. After the American conquest, water continued to be a major consideration in the growth of the San Diego region and remains so at the present time.

It is also important to understand the impact of American settlement on the Native Americans. During the early American period, agriculture and ranching continued to dominate the economy in southern California while the 1849 Gold Rush dramatically altered the lives of those living in the central and northern parts of the state. So great a population surge had a serious impact on Indians of the Sierras and left San Francisco as California's major city and port. Sacramento became the state capital.

In San Diego, Spain's influence was still very apparent. The conversion of many Native Americans to the Roman Catholic faith, the widespread use of Spanish placenames, a "mission revival" style of architecture during the early 1900s, and the popularity of Mexican cultural traditions kept the influence of Spain and Mexico alive. On the other hand, widespread immigration from the eastern United States during the 1880s and a great influx of population resulting from World Wars I and II, which included a number of African Americans, transformed the San Diego community into a blend of cultures and styles. The arrival of a new wave of immigrants in the post-Vietnam era, making San Diego the state's second largest city by 1980, again changed the city's economic and cultural outlook. Its future in the twenty-first century remains to be seen.

This is an updated edition of my previous books that were based upon works including *San Diego: California's Cornerstone* (Continental

San Diego skyline, 2005. *Photo by Steven Schoenherr.*

Heritage Press, 1980; Sunbelt Publications, 2005) and *Gateway to the Pacific* (Pioneer Publications, 1992). Now out of print, these have been standard reference works for many students of San Diego history. The previous editions saw San Diego's entry into the new millennium with modern residential skyscrapers, the expansion of the Convention Center, the development of the Gaslamp District as a center for tourism, the unexcelled growth of North County, new homes being built to the south and east, the success and expansion of the San Diego Trolley, and the opening of a new downtown ballpark for the San Diego Padres.

Changes do not come smoothly and San Diego has been no exception. There have been some challenges along the road and different choices could have been made, but that is always the benefit of hindsight. Soaring housing costs, crowded freeways, droughts, fires, flash floods, and pollution have caused many to seek other places in which to live. Nevertheless, an almost "perfect sun," a beautiful bay, a myriad of recreational and cultural activities, nationally renowned institutions of higher learning, a viable group of Native Americans, and hardworking residents have made San Diego what it is today. Historians can point out the forces and events that have shaped this city, indicating what avenues remain open and can best be chosen for improved future development. But the future is up to the next generations who take the lead.

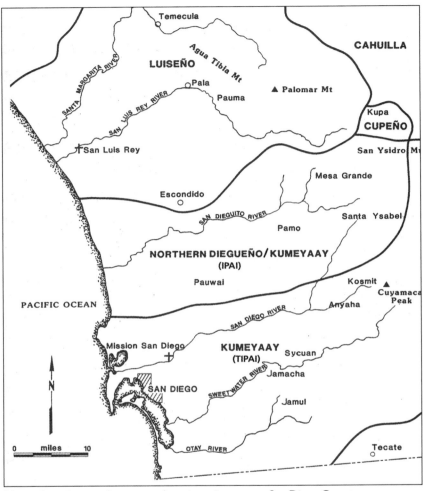

Native American settlements and territory in western San Diego County.
Courtesy Richard Carrico.

Chapter I

THE LAND AND ITS PEOPLE

The Changing Coastline

San Diego's recorded history is but a moment in geologic time. About 80,000 years ago, a slightly curving coastline protected an area considerably different from today. Point Loma stood as a separate island, and Crown Point to the north formed a bar across the mouth of ancestral Mission Bay. The mainland consisted of a broad mesa continually cut deeper and deeper by the San Diego River. Finally, a canyon 500 feet deep and 2,000 feet wide separated Linda Vista from Mission Hills. Throughout many centuries, the river carried mud and debris into the open sea, building up a delta to tie Point Loma to the mainland, closing off Mission Bay from San Diego Bay and creating a flat area at the base of Presidio Hill. Farther south, storm winds, nearshore north-moving currents, and an eddy on the lee side of Point Loma caused sediment from the Río Tia Juana (now called the Tijuana River) to build up long sandy spits, forming North Island and South Island to create Coronado and enclose San Diego Bay. Thus the area took on essentially its present shape, with the river wandering between San Diego and Mission Bay.

Modern commercial and military demands have seen San Diego's port grow into a modern harbor where towering cruise liners and the world's largest warships can dock. By extensive dredging, two new "islands"—Shelter and Harbor—have been created for human use. Much of the area in Mission Bay, once silted up and clogged by sediments, has been made into a recreational park. Still, natural forces never cease to alter the landscape. Savage storm waves and constant winds work away at the jagged shoreline, eventually to carve new rocky inlets, form irregular sandbars, and erode the long, white beaches. Secluded coves become imperceptibly larger; and sometimes the soft, overhanging cliffs, no longer finding support, tumble and fall into the sea—carrying human creations with them. Both nature and man give and take.

The Sandy Shore

Northerly from the Mexican border, the sandy shoreline rims a long coastal plain from which the natural harbor is cut. The coastal strand of Coronado with its characteristic dunes offers a number of woody perennials—shore sandbur, white-leafed saltbush, and iceplant. Gulls, snowy plovers, and many tiny invertebrates such as sand crabs and sand fleas call this home. To the north, Sunset Cliffs and La Jolla feature surf-beaten beaches where reefs and rocky formations extend from the shore and form tidepools.

Along the entire San Diego coastline, there are surf grasses, seagulls, and an infinite variety of marine life. Farther north, the white beaches are broken by a shelf of sandstone that forms sculptured promontories and shallow caves near the water's edge. Where seasonal and small rivers empty into the sea, a number of tidal lagoons and salt marshes are formed. These include mudflats with low herbs or shrubs such as sea blite, salt grass, and cord grass. The clapper rail, common egret, snowy egret, black brant, marsh hawk, Savannah sparrow, western sandpiper, least tern, and other shorebirds find a home along with saltmarsh mosquitoes and the saltmarsh fly. Butterflies hover and sail; mice and rats scurry about.

Inland Hills and Mountains

But not all of San Diego is coastline. Much of the county consists of chaparral and oak-covered hills and mountains. The word "chaparral"

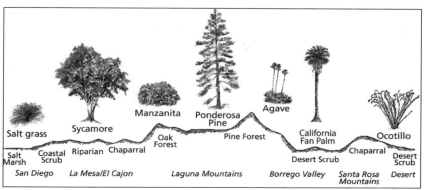

Biotic communities of San Diego and Imperial Counties go from salt marsh to pine forest to desert scrub. *Illustration by Joanne Crosby.*

comes from the Spanish **el chaparro** meaning the evergreen scrub oak. Spanish riders wore leather pants or **chaparajos** (chaps) to protect their legs from the dense prickly cover that was an effective barrier to ground travel by humans and large animals. These brush-covered hills and mountains—dissected by branching arroyos that contain running water only during the rainy season—rise higher and higher toward the east and culminate in elevated areas where scattered forests of live and deciduous oaks, incense cedar, yellow pine, sugar pine, California juniper, and other coniferous trees grow. To the northeast, Mount Palomar is 6,138 feet high and in the southeast, Cuyamaca Mountain reaches an elevation of 6,515 feet. This part of the Peninsular Province mountain mass is still being uplifted. The Palomar, Volcan, and Laguna mountains are thought to be upraised fault blocks.

The characteristic bushy growth of the hillsides and mesas is relieved by riparian woodlands of alder, cottonwood, oak, sycamore, and maple along rivers such as the San Luis Rey and Santa Margarita. In addition to what people consider natural vegetation, San Diego features two human-created biotic communities with a coastal orientation—cismontane urban and cismontane rural. The first includes a great variety of introduced trees, most of which are today considered a part of the natural landscape. Olive, eucalyptus, many palms, jacaranda, bougainvillea, acacia, and others from Africa, Australia, South America, Asia, and various parts of the United States abound. Private and public landscaping, dependent upon the use of water imported from long distances outside the county, have made luxuriant gardens out of areas where formerly only scrub oak could survive.

Desert Lands

Beyond the mountains, the Colorado Desert contains the present below-sea-level Salton Sea, a great brackish inland lake. Its ancestral waters were at times connected with the Gulf of California. The Colorado River in ages past brought down and deposited vast amounts of silt that formed the rich soils of the Imperial Valley, a part of San Diego County until 1907. The Anza-Borrego Desert State Park to the north produces a spectacular wildflower show each spring. It is also the home of the endangered desert bighorn.

Cultivated Lands

In rural areas, cultivated croplands; pastures; fruit orchards of lemons, oranges, and avocadoes; truck gardens; vineyards; and fields of flowers have provided important revenues and new beauty throughout San Diego County. These areas are inhabited not only by humans but by opossums, gophers, rats, skunks, coyotes, rabbits, mice, and several kinds of snakes. Planted areas host a seemingly insurmountable number of garden snails. Doves, quail, hawks, pigeons, sparrows, finches, mockingbirds, blackbirds, starlings, and hummingbirds grace the skies, while ladybugs, butterflies, and sowbugs are also well-known residents.

Changes in the Natural Environment

San Diego's first inhabitants, few in number, changed the natural environment very little. Subsequent generations altered the landscape to provide for themselves and their families. Today the region maintains a balance between old-timers and newcomers, urban dwellers and rural farmers, those who prefer the natural setting in contrast to those who like green lawns and landscaped gardens.

Palm Canyon in Anza-Borrego Desert State Park. *Photo courtesy of San Diego Convention & Visitors Bureau.*

Recurring drought cycles and increased population pressures have forced those in charge of planning to reevaluate future land uses.

The byword for landscaping adopted during the latter part of the 1980s was xeriscape derived from the Greek word **xeros** meaning dry. The warm climate of San Diego and available native or imported low-water-use plants slowly changed the concepts of those used to an expanse of green lawn. San Diegans, along with other Californians, became educated in conserving water, and by the winter of 1991–92 had more than indicated their ability to meet the water crisis. Fortunately, spring rains of 1992 eased the problem somewhat, but San Diego County's two million plus population and limited water resources made "xeriscape," a popular and necessary idea. Unfortunately, continued dry spells created an extremely dry backcountry that erupted into devastating firestorms in late October 2003. Heavy rains in October 2004 once again encouraged significant undergrowth.

The Native Inhabitants

Prior to European contact, San Diego's natural food supply provided for a relatively larger Indian population than in other areas of the United States. Although natives in the region never reached the dense numbers that existed in central Mexico and Peru, estimates generally run from 18,000 to 20,000. These were divided between two major linguistic groups. In the extreme south and east, including adjacent areas of Baja California and Arizona, the majority of Native Americans belonged to the Hokan family. Yuman is a subfamily of this group, which include the Kumiái, who are divided into the Kamia toward the east, and northern and southern Kumeyaay divided into Tipai/Ipai (or Diegueño as they were named by the Spaniards) toward the coast.

These modern Indians displaced two prehistoric cultures—the San Dieguito dating from at least 8000 BCE and the La Jolla from about 5000 BCE. A migration of Yuman-speaking peoples around the year 500 CE brought new artifacts and created the cultural complex that eventually interacted with the Spaniards. In north county the Native Americans belonged to the Uto-Aztecan family, linguistically (but distantly) related to the Aztecs of Mexico. Its Takic subfamily (earlier called Shoshonean), reached southern California about 2,000 years ago and included the Luiseño, Cupeño, and Cahuilla whose descendants still live on the same lands.

By the mid-eighteenth century, despite their linguistic differences, most of the region's Native Americans shared common cultural characteristics. They were generally an attractive, healthy, and peaceable people who had a highly specialized hunting and food-gathering economy based upon vast ecological knowledge. The staple food supply, the acorn, was rather elaborately ground, leached, rinsed, and prepared into a kind of gruel to which seeds, berries or other fruits were added for variety. They also consumed currants, wild plums, bulbous roots, seeds of sage, stalks of agave and yucca, and different kinds of rushes. Deer, rabbits, ground squirrels, quail, and ducks provided game. Coastal Indians ate shellfish and caught bay and ocean fish in nets fashioned from milkweed, nettles, or a kind of fiber called **ixtle**. Nets from yucca fiber were also used to snare rabbits and other small game. Roasted grasshoppers were a delicacy for the Cupeños in the grassy valley of San Jose near today's Warner's Ranch.

Stone bowls from the La Jolla Complex ca. 4000 BCE taken from a site approximately 1,000 yards from the La Jolla shore under the direction of Scripps Institution of Oceanography. *Photo courtesy of James Moriarty.*

Native Material Culture

Because of the moderate climate and limited building materials, Indian lodgings consisted of pole frames covered with bark, brush, willow, cattails, or other woven grasses in the shape of a dome. Usually their villages, or **rancherías** as they were called by the Spaniards, consisted of as many as 40 dwellings for sleeping purposes. These were semipermanent during the winter, and scattered at intervals of a few miles; some near today's downtown, others flanking Mission Valley and several more along the coast. Inhabitants of different villages quarreled over food sources when supplies were scarce and retaliated for the kidnapping of women.

Clothing was minimal; the men usually wore nothing and the women favored a kind of double woven skirt tied at the waist. In winter all wore cloaks around their shoulders made from sea otter, rabbit, or deerskins. Fiber sandals were preferred for long journeys. Men tied up their long hair while women let it hang freely. Both sexes practiced tattooing with vertical lines or simple patterns, although the women exhibited more elaborate markings.

The women were skilled basket makers and wove a variety of designs. Baskets served for carrying goods, storage, cooking, plates, and many other uses. Pottery making was not widespread although some had apparently learned it from Indians living in the Colorado River region. Men made fishing and hunting nets from local fibers, shaped knives and arrowheads from stone, and carved bows from willow, alder, or ash. Coastal dwellers built simple rafts from cattail reeds and other bouyant material.

Social Life

All Indian groups enjoyed recreation. Their games often involved batting a wooden ball about with a curved stick, guessing where a particular nut or stone was hidden, or tossing carved rings in the air and catching them on a stick. Village ceremonies concerned significant transitional periods in the life of the individual—puberty, marriage, and death. Coming-of-age rites were often the most elaborate. For girls, the celebration centered upon preparation for marriage and childbearing. Boys often drank jimsonweed potion to envision future achievements. Special songs were sung by the elders and taught to the young people. Religious beliefs varied in complexity throughout the region but usually included ideas about life after death, a God-creator, and supernatural forces.

The marriage ceremony was important and brought families together for several days of feasting. Nevertheless, if the marriage failed, new partners could be found for the couple. If a partner died, a new spouse was generally sought within the family group. The Kumeyaay had a general idea of a soul and when questioned about the death of a relative, one individual answered, "He went to the stars." Because spirits of the dead were believed able to return to make requests or occasionally do evil things, proper funeral rituals had to be conducted. The body was cremated the day after death and later the deceased's possessions were burned. Some evidence for prone burial has come to light through excavation of very early western Kumeyaay sites, but cremation was the general practice. The concept of amassing material possessions or leaving an estate did not exist.

Trade Networks

Although needs were limited primarily to food, clothing, weapons, and ceremonial items, an economic network based upon the barter

Kumeyaay village drawn by William Crocker.

system functioned in the area. The Cahuilla supplied the Kumeyaay with roots, bulbs, cattail sprouts, yucca leaves, mescal, pine nuts, manzanita berries, and mesquite beans. The Cahuilla received gourd rattles from the Quechan and basketry caps from the Chemehuevi. The Kumeyaay supplied acorns, tobacco, baked mescal roots, yucca fibers, sandals, baskets, carrying nets, and eagle feathers to the Kamia and Cocopa, and acorns to the Mojave. In turn, the Kumeyaay received salt from the Cocopa, gourd seeds from the Mojave, vegetables and salt from the Kamia. The Cupeño and Los Coyotes Cahuillas often exchanged goods through the use of shell money.

The Spanish and Mexican Periods

Despite their political disunity, the Native Americans of southern California had a wide range of contacts and lived in an active, orderly, and self-sufficient manner. During the period of Spanish and Mexican occupation, about one-fifth of California Native Americans were incorporated into missions, where a large number died from disease. Others, however, learned new skills and a knowledge of the Spanish language. A substantial number of these later worked on ranchos and in towns (see Chapters 2 and 3). The discovery of gold at the end of the Mexican period further disrupted the orderly progression of Indian life, especially in northern California.The natural evolution of the Native Americans' lifestyle, interrupted by European contact, left them with three options—to resist, to withdraw, or to cooperate. Each was tried with varying degrees of success, but their goal was always the same—the preservation of their own political sovereignty and cultural integrity. Despite occupation of the San Diego area by non-Native Americans for more than 200 years, these first arrivals never lost their foothold.

Native Americans During the American Period

The 1860 census for San Diego County listed 2,807 Native Americans living in San Diego County. The census did not include all of the Indian inhabitants of the period since only 25 of the 45 known villages were included, so a figure of 4,000 would be closer to the actual number. Of the 98 whose occupations were indicated, there were 42 laborers, 20 servants, 22 vaqueros, 7 washerwomen, 4 cooks, and a gardener, woodcutter, and shepherd. In general, those who were working could find only low-paying jobs. Judge Benjamin Hayes, writing in 1861, commented that the Indians had suffered a hard fate and there were "too many influences now working against any sensible improvement of their condition."

Their descendants presently exceed some 20,000 in the county, more than the estimated 18,000 at the time of Spanish arrival, and control 118,000 acres of federal land. They not only survived secularization of the missions under Mexico, the American conquest, and ensuing problems of the 1850s and 1860s, they attracted congressional support as early as 1873 when John G. Ames investigated the state of former mission Indians and others residing in the eastern and northern areas of San Diego County. Described by Ames as "homeless wanderers who have been dispossessed of their lands by settlers," they retained their separate identity. In 1874 when there remained probably fewer than 3,000 Native Americans in the area, special commissioner Charles A. Wetmore toured the county and

Luiseño Indian boys at San Antonio de Pala Mission School in the early 1900s.
Photo ©San Diego History Center

recommended the foundation of several small reservations and the reestablishment of Roman Catholic missionary work.

Indian Reservations

As a result, in 1875, President Ulysses S. Grant by executive order set aside land for nine Indian reservations: Portrero, Cahuilla, Capitan Grande, Santa Ysabel, Pala, Agua Caliente, Sycuan, Inaja, and Cosmit. In the 1880s, additional lands were set aside for Indian use by the executive orders of Presidents Rutherford B. Hayes, Chester A. Arthur, Grover Cleveland, and Benjamin Harrison. On various occasions, however, these same presidents issued other executive orders that restored portions of these lands to the domain.

After the appearance of Helen Hunt Jackson's *Century of Dishonor* and her immensely popular novel *Ramona* during the 1880s, efforts were made to create permanent reservations for these Indians. In 1891, the federal Mission Indian Relief Act was passed, empowering the secretary of the interior to appoint three commissioners to select a reservation for each group of Native Americans residing in

Kumeyaay store in Old Town San Diego State Historic Park.

California. In 1893, trust patents were issued for the Campo, Cuyapaipe, La Jolla, La Posta, Laguna, Manzanita, Pala, Rincon, and Pauma-Yuima reservations. Subsequently, patents were also issued for the Santa Ysabel, Inaja, Cosmit, Barona Ranch, Viejas, and Los Coyotes reservations. The federal government purchased some 3,438 acres to add to the Pala reservation in 1903 to accommodate Indians who had been displaced from Warner's Ranch. In 1910, the San Pasqual reservation was also patented.

New Legislation for Native Americans

In the final quarter of the nineteenth century, the federal government began to pass special laws to aid Native Americans throughout the country. Homestead law provisions were extended to Indians in 1875, and the Dawes Severalty Act of 1887 provided for the allotment of land after 25 years to individual Indians with citizenship. During the early twentieth century, additional special acts were passed. A statute of 1919 gave citizenship to all Native Americans who had received an honorable discharge from service in World War I. In June 1924, all remaining non-citizen Native Americans living within the territorial limits of the United States were awarded citizenship.

Additional special legislation authorized the bringing of suits against the United States for its Indian wrongs. Pursuant to an act

The modern Sycuan Casino in East San Diego County.

passed in May 1928, a federal Court of Claims awarded the California Indians $5 million in 1944. Two years later, Congress passed the Indian Claims Commission Act, a comprehensive act aimed at settling Indian claims once and for all. As a student, I worked for the California Indians. They received an award of $29 million in 1965 for the taking of their lands and other damages. The hopes of resolving old conflicts by this legislation, however, were too great. Even though some Indian claims have been since settled, additional claims against the United States and other entities relating to Indian land and water rights were still pending in 2015. The one area in which Native Americans have made unprecedented progress, however, has been in the establishment of gaming casinos throughout San Diego County.

Indian Gaming

Although the state of California operates a state lottery, permits pari-mutuel horse-race betting, and allows bingo games for charitable purposes, in 1984 the voters approved Article IV Section 19(e) to the California Constitution. It provides that "the legislature has no power to authorize and shall prohibit casinos of the type currently operating in Nevada and New Jersey." Gaming, sponsored by tribal governments on a large-scale basis, started in early 1980. The Cabazon and Moronga Bands successfully challenged the right of the state of

California and Riverside County to interfere with or regulate bingo and other card games conducted on their reservations. The litigation reached the United States Supreme Court, which, in 1987, held that the state law and county ordinance regulating bingo and card games "impermissibly infringes on tribal government." (*California v. Cabazon Band of Mission Indians.* 1987: 480 US 202, 222.)

Repeated efforts in Congress to regulate Indian gaming had failed, but on October 7, 1988, in the wake of the Cabazon decision, Congress enacted the Indian Gaming Regulatory Act (IGRA). The act sought to balance the competing interests of the federal government, state governments, and Indian tribes by giving each a role in the regulatory scheme. IGRA divides gaming into three categories and intensifies the level of regulatory oversight depending on the category of gaming:

Class I gaming includes social games with prizes of minimal value, as well as traditional forms of Indian gaming, and is subject to exclusive regulation by Indian tribes.

Class II gaming includes bingo and card games explicitly authorized or not explicitly prohibited by the state, but does not include any banking card games or slot machines. In banked or percentage card games, players bet against the "house" or the casino. Class II gaming includes non-banked card games, that is, games that are played against other players rather than against the house. Class II gaming is subject to joint regulation by the federal government and tribal authorities.

Class III gaming is defined as all forms of gaming that do not fall under Class I and Class II. It includes pari-mutuel horse-race betting, lotteries, banking card games, slot machines, and all games with non-Indian origins. Class III gaming is lawful on Indian lands only with (1) approval by the governing body of the tribe and the chairman of the National Indian Gaming Commission (NIGC); (2) permission by the state in the sense that the state permits "such gaming … for any purpose by any person"; and (3) existence of a Tribal-State Compact that is approved by the secretary of the interior.

The Tribal-State Compact, the key to Class III gaming under IGRA, allows the federal government to cede its primary regulatory oversight to states and Indian tribes. In this way, they may develop joint regulatory schemes through the compacting process. The state gains civil regulatory authority while the tribe gains the ability to offer Class III gaming.

On March 8, 1998, California Governor Pete Wilson signed the so-called "Pala Compact." It met with so much disapproval by the Indian community that thirty-two of the thirty-nine gaming tribes rejected it. On November 3, 1998, the voters approved Proposition 5, which was sponsored by the tribes. It contained a model compact designed to overcome positions taken by the Wilson administration in its negotiations. The California Supreme Court declared Proposition 5 invalid in August 1999 because it was contrary to the 1984 constitutional amendment prohibiting Las Vegas-type gaming.

On September 10, 1999, Governor Gray Davis approved fifty-seven Class III gaming contracts on behalf of the state of California. The tribes met the three conditions that allowed the contracts to become effective. First, the state legislature ratified them along with approval of subsequent identical compacts in 1999. Second, on March 7, 2000, voters approved Proposition 1A, which added Article IV Section 19(F) to the state constitution. It permitted the governor to negotiate such compacts in accordance with IGRA despite the 1984 constitutional prohibition of Las Vegas-style gaming. Third, on May 5, 2000, the compacts were approved by the secretary of the interior.

Sixty-two tribes have approved contracts and thirty-nine operate casinos with Class III-type gaming. Lawsuits in state and federal courts (*Flynt v. California Gambling Control Comm.* [2002] and *Artichoke Joe's California Grand Casino v. Norton* [2003]) challenged the validity of the compacts. They were unsuccessful and both courts upheld the compacts. The practical effect is that Indian tribes with state compacts enjoy a monopoly in California over Class III-type gaming.

Indian government gaming generated $12.7 billion in 2001 (36 *University of San Francisco Law Review* 1034:2002). David Valley, in his

Barona Tribal Museum and Cultural Center. *Photo courtesy Barona Tribal Museum.*

book *Jackpot Trail: Indian Gaming in Southern California* (2003) summarized the effects of Indian gaming: "The Indian gaming business, though only in its first decade, is growing rapidly. It is literally changing the landscape in many areas. The extent of its growth and development will likely exceed expectations." The author described the 22 casinos operating on ex-mission Indian reservations in southern California. There are 9 casinos in San Diego County including Pala, Pauma, Rincon, Valley View Casinos, the La Jolla slot arcade, Barona, Viejas, Sycuan, and Golden Acorn. The reservations have expanded into the hotel business, golf resorts, and RV parks. Sycuan has purchased Singing Hills Golf Course, US Grant Hotel in downtown San Diego, and Borrego Springs Bank. Viejas owns a successful factory outlet mall.

Tribal management of these enterprises has resulted in sufficient income for increased health care, housing, education, and retirement pensions. The Barona Band has completed a cultural center and museum with a collection of over 2,000 ancient items dating as far back as 10,000 years. Because of gaming, Indians of San Diego and Imperial Counties have been able to restore their pride and guarantee a better future for their members.

Chapter II

OLD AND NEW WORLD BACKGROUNDS

Although the history of San Diego begins with the region's indigenous peoples, the arrival of Europeans forever changed the course of Native American development. The year 1492, which we celebrate as the "discovery" of America, was a turning point not only for the New World, but for Spain just prior to the voyage of Christopher Columbus. In 1492, certain fundamental events took place that reflected the changing role of the Spanish people and the new directions their lives would be taking. On January 2, the last Moorish stronghold of Granada fell to the Catholic monarchs Fernando and Isabel; the war against the Muslims was over. The victory climaxed seven centuries of effort to establish Christian hegemony in Spain. The Reconquest had created fervent religious crusaders and zealous military leaders among the Spanish people, and it had also created a nation based upon racial, if not religious, tolerance.

For seven centuries Muslims and Christians lived side by side, often in peace and harmony, and there was considerable cultural exchange between the two major peninsular groups. As a result, Muslim laws, customs, institutions, and architecture became an integral part of Spanish society, and in turn, were used in the colonization of America. Spain's meticulously organized rules for New World administration had roots in both Roman and Muslim law. Tolerance and even encouragement of intermarriage with converted Native

Americans followed the customs of the Iberian Peninsula. Spanish
laws reflected the religious zeal of a crusading Christian nation.

Spain in 1492

With the final expulsion of the Moors, Isabel could turn much of the
energies of Castile to new projects. The queen alone sponsored
Christopher Columbus in his initial voyage of discovery. This
marginally equipped expedition, which set sail from southern Spain
on August 3, 1492, was perhaps the most daring venture in Western
history. In that undertaking a handful of men, impelled more by their
dreams than by the winds that filled their sails, embarked upon the
navigation of alien waters to search for new means to better their
economic condition. The territories that they discovered became part
of Castile, the province ruled by Isabel. Other sailors might have
touched the shores of America before the Spanish expedition, but
Columbus provided the first permanent link between the Old World
and the New. In reality, the epochal meaning of his discovery eluded
the famous navigator; he called the new land "the Indies" because
he thought he had found a new route to India.

Spain gave to the New World a curious blending of medieval
civilization and Renaissance ideas. The Reconquest had kept the
crusading spirit and the idea of a universal church firmly alive in
Spain, along with a strong belief in all mythical elements known to
the realm of fable and romance popular during the Middle Ages.
Some of the Spanish conquerors were Renaissance men in their
fondness for adventure, wealth, and fame; but there exists a greater
continuity between medieval developments and the early institutional
and cultural life of the Ibero-American colonies.

Medieval Legends of Wealth

Columbus, the spiritual heir of Marco Polo, was not so much the
first of modern explorers as the last of the great medieval travelers,
inspired more by legends of fabulously rich islands off the coast of
Asia than a desire to colonize new lands. Even while navigating

French map showing California as an island engraved in 1656.

through the Caribbean and along the American mainland, he thought he was visiting islands depicted in medieval maps at the end of the Orient in the vicinity of Cathay. But most poignantly medieval of all was the conviction of Columbus on his third voyage (1502) that he had found the site of the Terrestrial Paradise. He showed the Orinoco Delta on the Venezuelan coast to be the mouths of the four rivers of Genesis, which proceed from the Tree of Life. His description of the fabulous wealth of Paradise did nothing to lessen the notions of subsequent explorers that somewhere in America would be found all the mythical beings, monsters, griffins, Amazons, gilded men, and golden cities known to the medieval world.

California, especially, was surrounded by legend. In fact, one of the most significant forces that propelled Spanish explorers into the Pacific was the idea that somewhere an island called California held a host of hidden marvels, of unsolved mysteries. Spaniards of the sixteenth century, inspired by golden legends and novels of chivalry, searched the most unlikely corners of the American continent in their quest for riches. Even the natives, so erroneously called Indians, became a principal mystery that perplexed the Spanish nation. Speculation ran from suppositions that they had descended from the lost Ten Tribes of Israel to an idea that somehow the Indians were an offshoot of the Welsh nation. Fact had to be sorted from fiction before the desire of the Indians for Christianity and European civilization, or the lack thereof, could be understood and the Spanish church could determine what kind of relationship should be established with them. Spaniards had little experience with people of totally different social and cultural values.

The Spanish "Right of Conquest"

Also in 1492 Alexander Borja, a Spaniard, was elected Pope. This gave Fernando and Isabel a strong ally in Rome and, at the same time, established the nature of Spanish control in America. The Papal Donation of 1493, by which Pope Alexander VI divided the New World between Spain and Portugal, gave dominion over the Indies to the Crown of Castile and imposed upon it the obligation to spread Christianity throughout the new land. Each Spaniard, made to feel individually responsible for conversion of the natives, was forced to question the basic nature of the Indian to determine how he could best be Christianized and brought to a "civilized" or European, Roman Catholic way of life.

Conquistadors asked whether conversion should be attempted by peaceful persuasion or whether just war could be waged to compel Indians to serve God and the king. Priests asked how natives could be made to change from what they were to what Christianity dictated they ought to be. Among the documents of the conquest are opinions

Fernando of Aragon and Isabel of Castile were the ruling monarchs of a united Spain in 1492. The laws of Castile applied in the New World.

on all these questions, together with numerous, and sometimes curious, proposals for the protection and welfare of the American Indians. Spanish legal scholar Francisco de Vitoria, 1492–1546, is considered a significant contributor to the theory of just war.

Among the major European colonizing nations, mainly the Spaniards, legalistic and fervently Catholic, asked these questions with such general and genuine concern. The pattern was set by Queen Isabel who, to the day of her death, regarded the welfare of the American natives as Spain's major responsibility in the New World. Unfortunately, many practices by ruthless conquerors were never envisioned by the humanitarian goals of Isabel and the Catholic church. The criticisms of Bartólome de las Casas of the cruel practices perpetrated upon many of the Native Americans during the early sixteenth century would not soon be forgotten.

A Castilian Grammar

Another historic event of the year 1492 was the publication of Antonio de Nebrija's Castilian *Gramatica*, the first grammar of a modern European language. This book marked the clear supremacy of Castile and its language not only in Spain, but assured its dominant position in America. The book's immediate significance remained beyond the grasp of even Queen Isabel, who, when inquiring as to its use, was told by the Bishop of Avila, on behalf of the author: "Your Majesty, language is the perfect instrument of empire." In the end, Spain imposed her language on great territories and a vast population far exceeding those of the home country.

Thus, the fifteenth century was Spain's greatest hour. By 1492 she stood at the pinnacle of her destiny; she exerted herself to create the golden moment—no other nation was in such a perfect position to profit from the discovery of a New World. Spain was able to follow through and become, for a time, a decisive factor in Western history. All the elements were present: the political and religious solidarity achieved by the marriage of Fernando and Isabel; the military and religious energies released by the final expulsion of the Moors; the crusading and colonizing zeal encouraged by both church and state; the fortunate accident of Isabel's faith in Columbus; and the intense pride, courage, and spirit of the Spaniard himself.

Patterns of Conquest and Settlement

These circumstances set the pattern of New World conquest, and from them resulted the kind of settlement that Mexico and finally California would experience at the first European hands.

By the middle of the sixteenth century, Spain as a power began to decline. While daring navigators were conquering new lands and fabulous galleons returned laden with treasure and spices, the Spanish nation lived on New World successes. But this atmosphere of enchantment was eventually destroyed by excessive national pride, frivolity, and indifference. Spanish armies overran Europe while the common people lived in poverty; half the population of Spain consisted of nobles while the rest were beggars and vagabonds. As a result, Spanish predominance became more the reward of chance and the fruit of inheritance than the product of legitimate effort. In 1588 the humbling defeat of the Spanish armada at the hands of a rising English nation dealt a crucial blow.

Spanish stamp celebrating the bicentennial of the death of Carlos III (1788–1988).

But at the same time Spain was losing force as a world power, her literary expression achieved such a peak as to be called Spain's Golden Age—an era exemplified by Miguel de Cervantes's classic novel *Don Quijote*. This masterpiece of satire offered a wealth of insight into the extravagances of the sixteenth century Spanish gentlemen— *Don Quijote* himself neglected the management of his estate and sold many acres of land to buy books on chivalry. Cervantes, with irony and humor laid open the Spanish soul, and with subtle, piercing criticism, exposed Spain's impossible dreams. Just one more period of greatness interrupted the downward trend of Spain's colonial period.

Revival under the Bourbon Monarchy

During the latter half of the eighteenth century, the Spanish nation experienced a reawakening under the Bourbon monarchy of Carlos III. Revitalized, Spain renewed her contributions to the New World through administrative and economic reform. As a result, her capable ministers successfully effected the long-delayed settlement of California, the first stop being San Diego. For another half century,

Spanish leadership, laws, and institutions would set the pattern for colonization of the Pacific Coast of North America.

In her American adventure, Spain gave birth to a score of nations that, through the ages, have risen and prospered. Whatever the effect of her later role in world progress, Spain's arrival in the Americas caused the greatest impact yet felt upon the history of mankind. It shifted the center of gravity of the known world and turned the eyes of civilization from the crusades of the East to the conquest of the West. Historian John Crow has aptly summarized the significance of Spain's unprecedented contribution:

"It was the end of the dark, the mystical, the inward life; the start of a forward motion which has not yet been arrested.... Men of action and enterprise replaced men of birth as leader in deed and thought. America was at first an illusion, later a hope, and when the great cities of gold did not materialize, the experience of the conquistadores (worth more than gold itself) made possible the creation of new empires beyond the sea. These men turned their gaze from the classic truths of antiquity toward the future and its promise of a fuller and richer life."

Early Spanish Exploration

Columbus founded Santo Domingo, the first permanent settlement in the New World and present-day capital of the Dominican Republic, on the southern shore of Hispaniola in 1496. Discovery of some placer gold nearby destined it to become the earliest important city and seat of Spanish rule in America. The island of Hispaniola became a base for further expansion in America. Between 1508 and 1511, the Spaniards settled the islands of Jamaica, Cuba, and Puerto Rico; expeditions were sent along the coasts of Florida, Mexico, and northern South America. Columbus's dream to find a route to India, still zealously pursued, received welcome encouragement when Vasco Nuñez de Balboa crossed the Isthmus of Panama in 1513 to find el Mar del Sur (the South Sea), a great uncharted ocean lying apparently due south. This discovery inspired other Spanish explorers to seek

Aztec offerings to Hernán Cortés and Doña Marina. *Codex Lienzo de Tlaxcala.*

a way into the new ocean from the Atlantic, because they were certain that once they sailed through or around the giant American land mass, they could at last head for Asia.

Ferdinand Magellan, a Portuguese navigator sailing for Spain, first entered the fierce, stormy strait that bears his name at the southern tip of South America in 1520, and experienced waters so dangerous that he called the peaceful ocean that greeted his exit the "Pacific." Magellan successfully crossed the Pacific Ocean to the Philippines, where he was killed in a skirmish with the natives. The arrival of his ship in Spain after sailing around the world increased interest in the search for a still shorter route to Asia—for some North American passage that would save the long journey around Cape Horn or through the difficult strait named for Magellan.

The Conquest of Mexico

The conquest of Mexico, perhaps more than Balboa's momentous discovery or Magellan's courageous voyage, is first in the direct chain of events that led to the discovery and settlement of California. Reports of substantial Indian wealth existing inland from the Mexican gulf coast inspired Diego de Velásquez, governor of Cuba, to outfit some ships under Hernán Cortés, a man he thought ambitious and brave enough to tackle the Aztec Indians of central Mexico.

Cortés's expedition faced unparalleled dangers, but reaped greater rewards than any the Spaniards had yet known. Its success, like that of its leader, resulted from the combined elements of luck, cleverness, and courage.

The battle with the Aztecs lasted two years and it was not until August 1521 that the conquest was ended. Cortés, despite heavy losses, became master of the ruined Aztec capital of Tenochtitlan. He proclaimed Spain's authority, banned human sacrifices, destroyed pagan temples and idols, and took over the Aztec treasury. By defeating the powerful Aztec nation, which held political, economic, and military control in central Mexico from the Gulf to the Pacific and as far southeast as Guatemala, the Spaniards were able to spread their victory over a large, densely populated area. Cortés's group of 400 to 450 soldiers initiated the thrust whereby the Spanish empire extended its control over an estimated fifty million Indians in central and southern Mexico. For three years after the fall of the capital, Cortés devoted himself to rebuilding Tenochtitlan. He established municipalities, appointed officers, promoted agriculture, and issued general ordinances affecting all lines of activity.

Expansion of the Empire

The gold, silver, and jewels of the Aztec empire naturally led the Spaniards to believe that other areas of Indian wealth must lay to the south and north of the Mexican capital. By 1522 Cortés reached the Pacific at Michoacan and founded the port city of Zacatula. He ordered construction of four ships for northward exploration, but a lack of supplies and skilled labor slowed progress. Essential European items such as ironwork and rigging had to be transported slowly overland from Vera Cruz. Four ships were nevertheless completed by 1527—just in time to comply with a royal order sending three of them to the Moluccas to strengthen Spanish claims in the East Indies.

As early as 1524, royal authority was strengthened as the king's officers assumed financial control of Mexico. In 1527 the Crown established the Royal Audiencia, a judicial body that served as a court

Vasco Nuñez de Balboa (left), who reached the Pacific Ocean in 1513; Hernán Cortés (center); and a Spanish explorer (right) of the late sixteenth century drawn by José Cisneros. *Reproduced courtesy of Texas Western Press, El Paso.*

of appeals and, in the absence of an executive, as a committee of government. It governed Mexican affairs until 1535, when the Kingdom of New Spain became a viceroyalty and was placed under a high-ranking personal representative of the king. Antonio de Mendoza, the first viceroy of New Spain, expanded upon the general features of Spanish colonial policy as first introduced on the island of Hispaniola.

Since the Spanish sovereign claimed exclusive possession of the Indies, the king became absolute proprietor of all new lands, and sole political and religious head of all provinces created from them. Every privilege and position—economic, political or religious—came from him. The prominent role of the church also characterized Spanish policy. The crown relied heavily upon ecclesiastical authority in questions pertaining to salvation of Indian souls, distribution of native lands and labor, settlement of disputes between Spaniards and Indians, and general transmission of all the elements of Spanish civilization that would make the Indians as much a part of the Spanish empire as if they were born in Spain.

Further Exploration into the Pacific

In his exploration of the Pacific, it is thought that Cortés hoped to find both the famous golden island of the Amazons and the long-sought Northwest Passage or Strait of Anián somewhere to the north of the Mexican coast. Diego Hurtado de Mendoza commanded two new ships that sailed from Zacatula in 1532 to pursue those objectives, but the expedition ended in mutiny. Cortés outfitted a second venture in his effort to penetrate the mysterious Pacific under his distant cousin Diego de Becerra, a haughty and disagreeable man who was put to death by his crew.

Fortún Jiménez, first pilot and leader of the mutiny, took over command. Sometime in late 1533 or early 1534 he reached what he thought was an island, but was instead the peninsula of today's Baja California. Jiménez anchored in a bay, which he named La Paz, and the Spaniards went ashore. A sudden attack by hostile Indians brought the death of Jiménez and twenty of his men; the rest escaped to the Mexican west coast port of Jalisco. The survivors reported that the natives of their newly discovered island were primitive savages, but they had collected an abundance of pearls. Pearls alone gave Cortés sufficient incentive to plan his own expedition. He was joined by volunteers who knew the captain's reputation for finding wealth.

Three vessels reached the Bay of La Paz on May 3, 1535. Cortés named the "island" Santa Cruz and founded its first settlement on the dry, rocky coast. Native hostility and a lack of food made it necessary for two ships to return to the mainland for supplies—one of these was wrecked in the Gulf of California—then called the "Red Sea of Cortés." On a second attempt to obtain supplies, only the ship that Cortés himself commanded made it back across the treacherous, stormy waters to La Paz. In the meantime, twenty-three of his men died of starvation on Baja California's inhospitable shore. Cortés took the one remaining vessel and returned to Mexico to get further relief. Finally, toward the end of 1536, prospects of success seemed so remote that Cortés sent ships to pick up the surviving colonists. Thus ended the first in a long succession of attempts to settle California.

The Ulloa Expedition

In 1539 Cortés issued instructions to the final expedition that, under his direction, would hopefully pierce the mysteries of the north.

Typical Spanish galleon of the sixteenth century.

Three vessels commanded by Francisco de Ulloa sailed from the port of Acapulco in July of that year; one, the tiny *Santo Tomas*, was wrecked in the stormy waters of the Gulf of California before reaching La Paz. Ulloa's fleet, reduced to the 120-ton *Santa Agueda* and its flagship, the *Trinidad*, a 35-to-40-ton vessel not more than forty feet in length, left La Paz and headed across the choppy Red Sea of Cortés to the mainland shore. Ulloa cruised northward to the port of Guaymas, which he named Puerto de los Puertos (the Port of Ports), and further on expected to find a passage around the California "island." Instead, the ships encountered violent tides caused by the Colorado River descending into the sea at the head of the narrow gulf. The bleak shoreline—a lonely desert broken by stark mountains—offered few prospects for golden cities, so Ulloa turned southward, the first to know that Baja California was not an island.

Ulloa took possession of the land he found and then sailed along the eastern shore of the peninsula until again reaching La Paz. He tried to round the southern tip at Cape San Lucas, but for eight days violent winds and tempestuous rains kept his ships beating up and down the gulf coast. Finally the two vessels rounded the cape by the end of January 1540, then sailed up the western shore as far north as the Isla de Cedros (Island of Cedars) so named because, according to Ulloa, "on the tops of the mountains therein, there grows a wood of these Cedars being very tall, as the nature of them is to be." After three months Ulloa sent the larger *Santa Agueda* home and continued his explorations northward in the *Trinidad* to perhaps Point San Antonio, just south of latitude 30 degrees.

Ulloa's revelation that Baja California was a peninsula aroused little attention and the "island" of California persisted on maps as late as 1784. His expedition, the last with which Cortés had any official connection, faced severe storms to explore both the eastern and western coasts of the peninsula. Ulloa's discovery of an island of cedars compensated little for expected cities of gold. Disappointment was great and Cortés, angered at his lack of authority and frustrated by Viceroy Mendoza's constant opposition, sailed for Spain in 1540. Cortés argued his claims before the royal court, but his lawsuits dragged on before an untouched officialdom. Years of effort gave him little satisfaction and finally, in 1547, death claimed the unhappy Cortés, first of the Spanish explorers to open the way to California.

The Coronado Expedition

While Ulloa's voyage was still in progress, Viceroy Mendoza organized a vast, two-pronged land and sea expedition to find the fabulous Cíbola, a city of gold somewhere in the interior of the continent, and claim the area for Spain. Led by the able Francisco Vásquez de Coronado, the land procession was launched in February 1540, from Compostela, near Tepic, with some 200 horsemen, 70 foot soldiers, and nearly 1,000 Indian allies and servants. So great were the expectations of wealth that Coronado invested his entire personal fortune in the venture and Mendoza authorized its eager volunteers to be equipped at royal expense.

For the sea detachment, three vessels commanded by Hernando de Alarcon left Mexico in May 1540, with instructions to explore the upper part of the Sea of Cortés (Gulf of California) and make overland contact with Coronado's soldiers. During August and

Cabrillo's *San Salvador* as an early galleon. *Courtesy of Melbourne Smith.* Inset: Juan Rodríguez Cabrillo.

September, Alarcon explored the lower Colorado River, but a narrow canyon forced him to return downstream at a point south of Yuma, just short of touching California soil.

Coronado moved his main army slowly northward through the Yaqui River Valley and in September, before entering the barren lands of New Mexico, dispatched Melchior Díaz, an experienced frontier soldier, to look for Alarcon at the head of the gulf. While Coronado searched on for Cíbola, Díaz reached the mouth of the Colorado and followed its course to the point where Alarcon had given up. Finding a cross and Alarcon's letter explaining his return, Díaz decided to continue up the river. Contemporary accounts indicate that after five or six days' travel, the party reached an area possibly near present-day Blythe, California. They crossed the Colorado in Indian basketlike rafts, made watertight with pitch, and journeyed into the inhospitable Colorado Desert. Forced back by lack of water, Díaz and his men seem to have crossed the sand dunes of Imperial Valley on a shortcut to Yuma. Hostile Indians harrassed the group in their trek to reach Sonora. Díaz, while chasing a greyhound, accidentally impaled himself on his own lance. The intrepid explorer died of wounds twenty days later on January 18, 1541. Even though Díaz left no statement of his discovery, it seems certain from supporting journals that he was the first Spaniard whose expedition reached Alta California and whose death directly resulted from his penetration into the territory. Had he lived, Díaz may well have been claimed as California's "discoverer."

Viceroy Mendoza, disillusioned by the meager results of Coronado's effort, resolutely turned to the sea with yet another plan to find the elusive Strait of Anián. Pedro de Alvarado, governor and captain-general of Guatemala, appeared at the port of Acapulco in 1540 with a fleet of thirteen vessels and offered his services to the Crown for Pacific exploration. Close to Alvarado's right hand during the conquest of Guatemala stood Juan Rodríguez Cabrillo, shipbuilder, horseman, captain of crossbowmen, and eventual discoverer of Alta California at the site of San Diego. When Alvarado became captain-general of the province stretching from southern Mexico to the boundary of Panama, Cabrillo was appointed admiral of its fleet.

The Cabrillo Expedition

New details on the background and early life of Juan Rodríguez Cabrillo have come to light from a deposition found in the Archives of the Indies in Seville in mid-2015. In a nine-hundred page document concerning the wrongdoing of a Spaniard known to Cabrillo in Guatemala, Cabrillo listed his place of birth as Palma de Micer Gilio, now known as Palma del Río, in the province of Córdoba in southern Spain. Previously described as "a Portuguese navigator sailing under the flag of Spain," most descriptions of Cabrillo's career seemed to begin on the California coast. His original 1542 journal of exploration has not been found, but other documents, including a later copy of the journal describing his voyage, can also be found in the Archives of the Indies in Seville. Documents in the Royal Audiencia section give information about Cabrillo's service to Spain, his family and estates in Guatemala, his relationship with the Sanchez Ortega family, and his later activities.

Port of Navidad on the west coast of Mexico.

The record of Cabrillo's life in America begins in Panama, where he arrived in 1514 with Governor Pedrarias. He then travels to Cuba where, as a young crossbowman, he is sent by Governor Velásquez to travel with Panfilo de Narváez to return the defiant Cortes to Cuba. Hearing of the governor's plan, Cortés left part of his army under Alvarado at Tenochtitlan, and returned to Vera Cruz to face the new threat from his home base. Defeating the Spanish force in a surprise move, Cortés won the soldiers to his side with promises of gold and prepared them to attack the Aztec island capital.

Cabrillo thus became a part of Cortés' reinforced army and, because Alvarado had failed to contain the Aztecs, served through the bloodiest battles of the conquest. Bernal Díaz del Castillo, writing forty years later, recorded that Cabrillo "was a good soldier in the Mexican campaign...who later, as a resident of Guatemala, was a very honorable person, and was captain and admiral of thirteen ships on Pedro Alvarado's behalf, and he served his majesty well in everything that presented itself to him."

Juan Rodríguez Cabrillo first engaged in farming and mining in Guatemala on the estates granted to him by Alvarado. In 1536 he was charged with the construction of a fleet of ships capable of exploring the most dangerous and remote areas of the Pacific. Assembling materials for such ships was so difficult that Cabrillo established headquarters in Honduras to get supplies by sea from the Atlantic. At a great sacrifice of lives, thousands of Indians then transported the heavy metalwork, rigging, and other equipment across swamps and mountains to the Pacific coast at Acajutla in present-day El Salvador. Construction of Alvarado's fleet proceeded slowly as tools were scarce and Cabrillo insisted upon high standards of quality. Thirteen ships were finally completed by 1540, although one, the *San Salvador,* was built by Cabrillo at his own expense. When the vessels were ready to sail, Alvarado asked his master shipwright to join the expedition in his own *San Salvador* as admiral of the entire fleet. Cabrillo agreed and the ships reached the Mexican port of Navidad, near Colima, on Christmas Day 1540.

Viceroy Mendoza and Alvarado entered into a partnership for Pacific exploration that, incidentally, included the use of Cabrillo's own ship. They planned to divide the fleet into two parts: one to investigate islands as far west as the East Indies, and the other to explore the North American Pacific coast "until its end and secret were sighted." Just before departure, however, Alvarado left his ships in charge of Cabrillo while he fulfilled the viceroy's request to help put down an Indian uprising known as the Mixton War. This battle, in 1541, ironically cost Alvarado his life—he was crushed to death by a falling horse. Viceroy Mendoza took possession of Alvarado's fleet and, showing high regard for Cabrillo, commissioned the Guatemalan admiral to sail the galleon *San Salvador* and *La Victoria* northward along the Pacific Coast in search of the Strait of Anián. The remaining vessels were dispatched to the Philippines.

Because of the untimely death of Alvarado, Cabrillo's expedition set sail from the port of Navidad on June 27, 1542. With three of the vessels of Alvarado's fleet, they were to explore the remote, uncharted areas of California and the North Pacific. The goal that had inspired so many before them—finding the Northwest Passage and a shortcut to Oriental riches—propelled these Spanish

Statue of Juan Rodriguez Cabrillo at the Cabrillo National Monument on Point Loma. San Diego sunset with Coronado Islands in background. *Photos by Robi Olson.*

adventurers into unknown waters further to the north than any yet sailed by European ships.

The *San Salvador, La Victoria,* and *San Miguel* cruised northward along the west coast of Mexico, crossed the Sea of Cortés, and proceeded up the Pacific side of what Cabrillo knew as the California peninsula. The name California was already in use by 1542, but its first application, and by whom, remains a mystery. It came into existence sometime after Ulloa's expedition of 1539, but the exact time and, indeed, the exact reason, for its appearance are still speculative. Most likely the name was taken from the mythical island of California featured by Ordoñez de Montalvo in his novel *Las Sergas de Esplandían* that described the beautiful Amazon Queen Calafia who, with her all-female army, ruled with weapons of gold over her Island of California.

The Name of California

The name California has also been attributed to other possible origins. It may have been a combination or derivation of Spanish or other European words. *Calida* meaning hot or *cal* for limestone may have been joined with *forno* (an old Castilian or Catalan form of *horno*) meaning oven, because the burning desert lands of the peninsula resembled a hot oven, or the abundance of limestone suggested a limekiln. Further possibilities are *kalifon*, Hispano-Arabic for "large province;" *Calafia*, a female form of Caliph; cala, Spanish for "cove" and fornix, Latin for "vault" or "arch;" and finally, the name may have been chosen "because an Irishman, who was traveling, said that the island looked like the one where Calpurnius (Califurnio), the father of Saint Patrick was born." Until more definite proof of the word's origin is found, all these choices have merit. Nevertheless, the name selected by Ordoñez for his island of Amazons (near the Garden of Eden) still holds the most widespread support.

Cabrillo's three ships entered the Bay of Ensenada, Baja California, on September 17, 1542. The expedition remained in port five days and then continued on, covering a daily fifteen to twenty miles. Within three days they sighted the three Coronado Islands, called by Cabrillo *Las Islas Desiertas* (Deserted Islands) and placed at 34 degrees latitude (nearly 2 degrees, approximately 140 miles north of their actual location). From these waters the Spanish seamen noticed the smoke of coastal Indian fires and, as they approached the mainland, saw a promising green valley backed by high mountains. On September 28, 1542, Cabrillo headed his ships into San Diego Bay, dropped anchor on the lee side of Point Loma, and formally discovered Alta (upper) California—as distinguished from Baja (lower) California.

Cabrillo's San Miguel

The Spaniards stepped ashore and were greeted by friendly Indians whom Cabrillo described as "well built" and clothed in animal skins. The admiral bestowed the name of San Miguel Arcangel (St. Michael Archangel) upon his newly discovered "closed and very good port," but it was changed sixty years later by Sebastian Vizcaíno, the Spanish navigator who chose instead to honor San Diego de Alcalá.

Three Indians timidly approached Cabrillo's ship, indicating by signs that they knew of other similarly dressed white men, carrying crossbows and swords, traveling far inland. Cabrillo understood from their gestures that these strangers (probably a detachment from Coronado's expedition) wielded lances from horseback and had killed many Indians. For this reason the California natives were afraid, but the Spaniards gave them presents and calmed their fears. When Indians wounded three seamen on a night fishing party near the shore, Cabrillo ordered his crew not to fire on them but to win their confidence. Spain's first visitors to San Diego, called "Guacamal" by the natives, set a precedent of friendly treatment that was followed with few exceptions during the entire Spanish occupation of the territory.

Sailing from San Diego after six days' rest, the expedition sighted the Channel Islands of San Clemente and Santa Catalina. Off Catalina the Spaniards saw numerous Indians dancing and shouting on the shore, making signs for them to land. Cabrillo reported: "Launching a fine canoe containing eight or ten Indians, they came out to the ships. These were given some beads and presents.... The Spaniards afterwards went ashore and both the Indian men and women and everybody felt very secure."

Misfortune Befalls Cabrillo

The *San Salvador* and *La Victoria* headed toward the mainland and Cabrillo sighted the bay of San Pedro (his "Bay of Smokes"); they continued a course along the coast, visiting an Indian fishing village that Cabrillo called *Pueblo de Canoas*. Heavy winds from the northwest near Point Conception forced the ships to anchor in a small port (Cuyler's Harbor) of San Miguel Island. On this island, which they named *Isla de la Posesión*, misfortune marred their enviable exploring record. While going ashore, Cabrillo fell and broke his arm on the rocky beach. Ignoring his wound, Cabrillo ordered his men to continue their mapping and coastal explorations. Despite winter storms, they reached an area near San Francisco Bay by mid-November. Here they turned southward and set their course for the safety of San Miguel.

By the end of December gangrene had complicated Cabrillo's injured arm and internal injuries finally caused his death on January 3, 1543. The crew buried their leader on one of the windswept Channel

Islands, possibly San Miguel or, according to more recent evidence, the north end of Catalina Island. Shifting winds and sands have covered all traces of the grave. Cabrillo's final words reflected the spirit of the early Spanish explorers. He instructed his chief pilot, Bartolomé Ferrer, not to give up their projected reconnaissance of the northern coast. The two ships again sailed into the open sea and made their way northward against heavy gales. Finally driven dangerously near the shore at a point somewhere near the Oregon boundary, they prayed for protection and were saved by a sudden change of wind. The expedition's journal describes few recognizable landmarks, making their exact course difficult to follow, but leaves no doubt about their courage in facing the perils of unknown waters.

Cabrillo's crew, weakened from exposure and scurvy, responded gratefully to Ferrer's order that the *San Salvador* and *La Victoria* return home. They reached the port of Navidad on April 14, 1543, with the sad news of Cabrillo's death and the discouraging results of their discoveries. They had found no Strait of Anián, no fabulous Indian civilization, no weapons of gold from an island of Amazons—nothing to enrich or even excite the expectant viceroy of New Spain. Mendoza closely guarded the charts of the explorations, and Cabrillo's own journal, kept a secret, as yet has not been found.

Replica of the *San Salvador* heading toward San Diego Bay in 2015. *Photo by Jerry Soto.*

Chapter III

THE SPANISH PERIOD: 1769–1821

Cabrillo's failure to find the passage to India, plus Spain's need for expanded trade, brought renewed efforts to conquer the Philippines. Discovered by Ferdinand Magellan in 1521, the islands nominally belonged to Portugal by the Papal Donation of 1493. Ruy López de Villalobos had taken possession of the Philippines for Spain in 1542 but, unable to overcome native hostility, was eventually captured by the Portuguese. None of the explorers, however, had found a successful return route across the Pacific to New Spain. Vessels sailing eastward from the islands were quickly becalmed; the only certain way was around Africa to the Atlantic. Clearly a return route and a port on the coast of California would have to be found.

Sixteenth Century Spain

Philip II (1556–1598) inherited the Spanish empire at the time of its greatest extension but was also left with its most serious problems. While New World viceroys strengthened Spain's hold in the Indies, the home country lagged behind the rest of Europe. As the Protestant movement gained force, Spain doggedly clung to its dream of a Catholic Europe and spent its vast resources on futile battles. She subsidized an enormous priesthood for many who wished mainly to avoid hard work. Philip II expelled the last of the Moors, enlightened and industrious subjects, to achieve total Catholic unity, and carried on a religious "cold war" with much of Europe. The constant financial drain upon the country caused by foreign enterprises, and heightened by frequent English raids on the Spanish treasure fleet, made new sources of income vital. Philip II ordered New Spain's Viceroy Luis de Velasco (1551–1564) to outfit an expedition for Pacific conquest.

The crucial navigational problems of the Philippine route were entrusted to Andres de Urdaneta, an Augustinian monk. Philip II thought Urdaneta, an experienced mariner, indispensable to the voyage so appointed him chaplain of the expedition. The Philippine fleet reached the islands in February 1565, and about 400 ground troops under Miguel López de Legazpi began their conquest on Cebu. Urdaneta, after studying the winds and currents, took three vessels and headed northward to the Japanese currents. He plotted a great circle route reaching the Pacific coast at about Cape Mendocino; when the vessels sighted California they turned southward and sailed for Acapulco. Urdaneta received credit for discovering a feasible, although long and difficult, trade route that opened the way for Spain's famed Manila Galleons. In the meantime, Legazpi's troops occupied Cebu, overcame native and Portuguese resistance, and eventually took over Luzon. Legazpi, given authority by Viceroy Velasco of New Spain, founded the town of Manila in 1571.

A regular trade route by means of one or two annual galleons was opened between Manila and Spain via Mexico. The ships, usually not larger than 500 tons, carried a crew of about 115 men; they were fitted out at royal expense and commanded by an officer of the king. Profits were high, but miserable conditions on board ship caused heavy losses by death and desertion. The inadequate water supply often turned brackish and even the vermin-invested food ran out before shore was reached. Provisions were sacrificed for trade goods— silks that were made into Spanish shawls and gowns, velvet, gold and silver brocades, jewelry, perfumes, exotic preserves of orange and peach, cedar chests, fine thread, ornaments of all kinds, and the highly-prized pepper and other spices—in great demand for the preservation and palatability of meat.

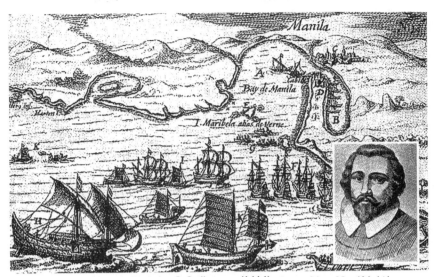

Engraving of the Bay of Manila by G. Spilbergen (1616). *Courtesy Museo Naval Madrid.*
Inset: Sebastián Vizcaíno.

Prices for these commodities from Asia were so high, bringing as much as $25,000 profit to the captain on a single trip, that Spanish seamen endured incredible hardships if given permission to carry a small share of goods. English pirates such as Sir Frances Drake in 1579 and Thomas Cavendish in 1587 captured Manila Galleons and looted Spanish ports on their journeys around the world. Sebastián Vizcaíno, one of the persons held captive by Cavendish from the galleon *Santa Ana*, would end up on the shore of Baja California in 1595. Vizcaíno later led the second Spanish expedition to enter the port of San Diego.

The Vizcaíno Expedition

Because of the success of the Manila Galleon trade, it was nearly 60 years before the Indians of the area called Guacamal (San Diego) again received European visitors. During the early seventeenth century, however, a new viceroy, Gaspar de Zuñiga y Acevedo, the fifth Count of Monterey, believed it would be a good idea to find a safe anchorage for the galleons along the California coast. Sebastián Vizcaíno, merchant and survivor of the Manila Galleon trade with the Philippine Islands, sailed from Acapulco on May 5, 1602. He commanded the *San Diego, Santo Tomás, Tres Reyes,* and a small auxiliary ship. His company of 200 men included a cosmographer and three Carmelite friars.

Vizcaíno entered San Diego Bay on November 10, noting its good anchorage and abundant natural resources. "On the 12th of said month, which was the day of the glorious San Diego [de Alcalá], almost everyone went ashore; they built a hut, said mass and celebrated the feast of San Diego." Since the Spaniards did not recognize the area as Cabrillo's San Miguel, they named the port after Diego, a Spanish Franciscan brother who had performed his labors in Alcalá de Henares near Madrid during the mid-1400s. He was canonized upon the urging of Philip II as Saint Didacus in 1588. Spanish playwright Lope de Vega wrote a play entitled *San Diego de Alcalá,* first performed in 1653.

According to the Carmelite Father Antonio de la Ascensión, about 100 Indians with bows and arrows appeared on a nearby hill, "but did nothing until the Spaniards, with offerings of presents, assured them of friendship." At the crest of Point Loma, Father de la Ascensión recorded the discovery of "another good port"—present-day Mission Bay. Here the land was fertile, the variety of fish numerous, and gold pyrites were abundant along the water's edge. The Indians conducted Vizcaíno and others to their *rancherias* where women, dressed in animal skins, were cooking food in pots.

After a visit of ten days, the expedition sailed on November 20, stopping briefly at Catalina Island, where Cabrillo had visited for a short while, and then sailed on through the Santa Barbara Channel. On December 16, 1602, Vizcaíno anchored in the bay on which they would bestow the name of Monterey to honor the viceroy of New Spain. Vizcaíno's unqualified praise of Monterey as the best port that could be found and one that was sheltered from all winds resulted in its selection as Spain's first capital of California. Unfortunately, the infrequency of these ideal weather conditions made the port unrecognizable by California's first overland explorers in 1769.

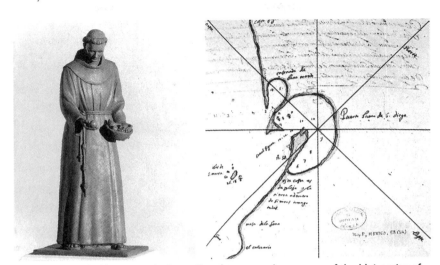

San Diego de Alcalá—statue by Jesus Domínguez on the campus of the University of San Diego. First map of San Diego Bay drawn by Enrico Martínez from the Vizcaíno expedition in 1602. *Map courtesy of the Archivo de Indias, Sevilla.*

After sailing as far north as Cape Mendocino, the explorers returned southward early in 1603. Vizcaíno sailed into Acapulco on March 21, 1603, with his glowing reports about Monterey and was at first well received. Viceroy Monterey was impressed with Vizcaíno's report but his successor, the Count of Montesclaros, did not favor the idea of a California port and discouraged further exploration.

Settlement of California

Although Alta California continued to attract attention for a possible Manila Galleon port, no further attempts to explore or colonize the area were made during the next 166 years. Instead, Spain maintained her interest in the region of northern Mexico and established presidios and missions throughout the Southwest. The Jesuit mission chain in Baja California, begun in 1697 at Nuestra Señora de Loreto, extended from the southern tip to the northern portion of the peninsula. Alta California, however, remained solely occupied by Indians until the late eighteenth century when expulsion of the Jesuits, threatened Russian expansion into Alaska, and an availability of funds combined to provide the impetus for northward penetration.

Actual colonization and settlement of San Diego resulted from the efforts of several individuals. The driving force was *Visitador General* José de Gálvez, a powerful and energetic representative of Spain's King Carlos III who had since 1765 carried out a number of governmental reforms in Mexico. Gálvez developed the plan for occupation of Alta California while surveying the west coast port of San Blas in 1768. He selected the personnel and wrote out lengthy instructions to leaders of four separate expeditions—two by sea and two by land—designed to reach San Diego in 1769. He gained viceregal approval of his plan and then sailed to La Paz to supervise operations. With unusual insight, Gálvez appointed Baja California's Governor Gaspar de Portolá, a well-qualified army officer from Lérida, Spain, to head the military force. He placed Father Junípero Serra, Order of Friars Minor (OFM), president of Franciscan (formerly Jesuit) missions in Baja California, in charge of religious conversion.

Fray Junípero Serra, OFM

Father Serra, born Miguel José in Petra on the Spanish island of Mallorca in 1713, first reached America with a party of missionaries in 1749. Having given up a prestigious career as professor of theology in Palma de Mallorca to labor among the Indians of the New World, he served with great success for nine years among the Pame Indians in the Sierra Gorda region of eastern Mexico. Gálvez chose him to lead the Franciscans who replaced the expelled Jesuit priests in fourteen missions of Baja California. Serra, canonized in September 2015, was a hardworking missionary who, despite poor health and a lame leg, never wavered in his goal to bring Christianity to those he believed needed salvation.

The maritime branch of the Alta California expedition prepared the way for overland occupation. Two ships, the *San Carlos* under Vicente Vila and the *San Antonio* commanded by Juan Pérez, left from La Paz on January 9 and February 15, 1769, carrying supplies and about 100 persons. Contrary winds, strong currents, and faulty navigational information caused considerable delay, especially for the

Serra Museum designed by William Templeton Johnson in the architectural style of Mission Revival. Statue of Father Junípero Serra by Jesús Domínguez on the campus of the University of San Diego.

San Carlos. Both ships reached the port of San Diego in late April with a majority of crew members suffering from scurvy or a deadly communicable disease. More than 60 men died on the beach in a makeshift hospital tent near today's Dead Man's Point during the first few months. A third ship, the *San José*—scheduled to deliver needed supplies—disappeared at sea.

Two overland parties left the northern peninsula in March with equipment, food, animals, and Indian personnel from the former Jesuit missions. The first, led by Captain Fernando de Rivera y Moncada of the Loreto presidio, with Mallorcan Father Juan Crespí as diarist, successfully blazed the trail for the second party, headed by Portolá with the spiritual guidance of Father Serra. All reached San Diego by July 1, 1769, and set up an encampment on a nearby hill. Indians of a local village called Cosoy helped the newcomers find a source of water. Even though sickness had taken its toll, there were still enough soldiers to continue the march northward in search of Monterey.

On July 14, Portolá led the overland expedition to the north along the coast, turning inland where San Juan Creek reaches the ocean. They passed the sites of present-day Santa Ana (where they experienced their first earthquake), San Gabriel, and Los Angeles. After reaching the La Brea tar pit area, they turned east, crossing the mountains into the San Fernando Valley, where they encountered friendly Indians. They reached the coast again near Ventura and continued their search for Monterey, the port Vizcaíno thought appropriate for the capital of California. Failing to recognize that port, they finally came upon the expansive San Francisco Bay on November 1, 1769. Father Crespí recorded their discovery and the party returned to San Diego in early spring without having achieved its original goal.

Founding of Mission San Diego de Alcalá

Two days after Portolá's departure, the four Franciscan fathers— Junípero Serra, Juan González Vizcaíno, Fernando Parrón, and Francisco Gómez—blessed a site on Presidio Hill with the name of San Diego de Alcalá, the first mission in Alta California. They built a brush chapel and within a short time began construction of a small adobe church. Their early days were spent caring for the sick and dying Spaniards and, after some minor skirmishes, continuing their friendship with the local Indians.

Finally, in March 1770, the *San Antonio* arrived with needed supplies from Baja California. Plans were made for further settlement. This time the search for Monterey proved successful, and Father Serra officiated at the founding of the presidio of Monterey and Mission San Carlos Borromeo on June 3. When the news reached Mexico City, cathedral bells rang out in honor of Spain's success.

Life in San Diego proceeded at a slow pace while soldiers and missionaries struggled to cultivate the land. Some of the married families lived in brush huts within the presidio complex and the children learned their catechism from the priests. In 1772 members of the Dominican order took over the missions of Baja California, freeing a number of Franciscans for service in the newer missions of Alta California. A boundary line south of today's international border marked the division between Alta and Baja California for missionary purposes.

Among the Franciscans who served San Diego were Father Luis Jaume (1771–1775), a native of Mallorca, and Father Vicente Fuster (1773–1777) from Aragon. Both were in residence in August 1774,

Postcard of the San Diego Mission from a painting by H.M.T. Powell done in 1850.

when poor soil and lack of water forced reestablishment of the mission six miles inland. The new site, where the mission stands today, was close to the San Diego River and included the Kumeyaay village of Nipaguay. Despite their slow beginning, the Franciscans baptized more than 100 Indians during the first five years, and about 97 made their home at the mission.

Spain continued to strengthen her claims over the north Pacific regions with the 1774 voyage of Juan Pérez to parallel 54°40' just north of the Queen Charlotte Islands, and by recruiting colonists for the California settlements. During that year, Juan Bautista de Anza opened a 2,000-mile overland trail from the presidio of Tubac, Arizona, to Mission San Gabriel. This linked California with the Spanish Southwest. Dominican fathers laid the foundations for Mission Nuestra Señora del Rosario, south of Ensenada, in March 1774. By January 1, 1775, the presidio at San Diego, commanded by Lieutenant José Francisco de Ortega, reached its largest number: a sergeant, one corporal, and 23 soldiers. In addition, a corporal and four soldiers formed the mission guard.

Presidio rations were scarce. Married women obtained extra food for their families by making tortillas and preparing meals for bachelor soldiers in exchange for additional corn and beans. New crops were planted at the mission in hopes of more abundant provisions.

Revolt at Mission San Diego

After a record baptism of 60 Indians in October 1775, events suddenly took an abrupt turn at Mission San Diego. Some of the Kumeyaay, unhappy about the mission's location at Nipaguay, resentful of Spanish intrusion and changes in their lifestyle, decided to revolt. Encouraged by native leaders, they planned a simultaneous assault on both mission and presidio. On November 5, 1775, approximately 600 natives burned the mission buildings and cruelly killed Father Luis Jayme. Two other Spaniards died and many suffered wounds, but the presidio escaped attack. The Indians gave up their efforts after their unsuccessful attempt to destroy the mission. They feared the soldiers' reprisal and abandoned further plans for destruction. Slowly they returned to the mission as converts.

Fathers Fermín Francisco de Lasuén, a Spanish Basque from Vitoria, and Gregorio Amurrio from Calahorra joined Father Fuster, the surviving missionary at San Diego, in December 1775. The Franciscans moved to Presidio Hill with their converts and resumed construction of the chapel at the entrance to Mission Valley.

During early 1776, Governor Rivera and Lt. Colonel Anza both made tours of Kumeyaay villages. They reported no apparent unrest. Father Serra arrived in San Diego aboard the *San Antonio* in July and supervised the mission's reconstruction at the Nipaguay site. The mission was slowly rebuilt with the help of Indians and sailors from the *San Antonio* who made adobe bricks, dug trenches, and gathered stone. Mission San Juan Capistrano was founded in November and the Franciscans baptized their first convert at the new Mission San Diego de Alcalá on December 8, far removed from events that had taken place in Philadelphia since July 4, 1776.

Final Days of Spanish Control

Peace and agricultural development typified the final days of Spain's control over California from 1776 to 1821. Father Lasuén, who succeeded Serra as father president of the missions, served at San Diego

Sketch of Mission San Luis Rey by the French explorer Duhaut-Cilly in 1826.
Photo courtesy of the Bancroft Library.

from 1777 through 1784. During this period the mission took the form of a large quadrangle surrounding a spacious courtyard. Lasuén's annual report to Serra in 1783 described the church as 30 varas (yards) in length by 5½ in width (84 by 15 feet) "with walls two adobes thick, its large beams of pine, with corbels of oak and over that eleven unpolished beams of alder and poplar" supported by the same to form the roof, which was covered by tule and dried mud as a precaution against fire. The passageway extending along the south side was nearly ten feet wide, with pillars and brackets of oak. "The entire aspect, especially the interior of the church and sacristy, is attractive, clean, and pleasing, because of the excellent ensemble achieved by the skill of the workers in using the resources of the mission. Thanks be to God."

Indians worked in the gardens, orchards, and fields to produce the necessary beans, chickpeas, lentils, corn, wheat, and barley for themselves and their livestock. Because of a shortage of water and lack of prime soil, the harvest at San Diego was generally less abundant than at other missions. Nevertheless, by 1783, the Franciscans had performed 966 baptisms and supported a live-in population of about 800. Since the number of Indian deaths from diseases spread within the mission complex, many Indians in the back country preferred to maintain their original lifestyles.

Southern California Development

The role played by members of the San Diego presidial company in developing the Pueblo of Los Angeles in 1781 was significant. Several served as guards for the fledgling town and others patrolled the area in between. The first three *rancheros* in the Los Angeles area (and also in California) were Juan José Dominguez, Manuel Nieto, and José Maria Verdugo of San Diego who were granted three large ranchos for cattle raising in 1784. A few retired soldiers chose to stay near the presidio to grow vegetables, raise some chickens, and herd two or three milk cows. Since large scale cattle ranching was restricted to outlying areas, several others eventually moved to Los Angeles. The population at the San Diego presidio in 1791 included 112 men and 85 women. Fifteen local Indians worked there as servants.

San Diego remained relatively isolated until 1793 when British captain George Vancouver visited the harbor on his return from the Pacific Northwest. He reported to London that the fine port was poorly defended and could be better protected from Point Loma. Any country able to take over the area would have an excellent potential for trade with the Orient. The Spanish forces, taking heed of the guarded threat, built Fort San Joaquin, nicknamed Guijarros, located at today's Ballast Point near the entrance to the harbor.

The Battle of San Diego

The little brig *Betsy* became the first American ship to enter San Diego Bay when it took on wood and water in 1800. Word of abundant sea otter and the high price of their fur in China had spread throughout the East Coast after several Americans visited the Pacific. In 1803 Spanish authorities prevented the ship *Alexander* from smuggling 500 otter skins out of the port. Later that year, the brig *Lelia Byrd* was stopped for the same reason. Fired upon from Fort Guijarros, the *Lelia Byrd* answered with a few shots. The Battle of San Diego was

Padre Dam built by Kumeyaay Indians ca. 1813 to irrigate mission lands.

the only instance in which harbor defense guns were put into action. Before long, other ships manned by "Boston-men" entered into trading activities on the California coast.

Regional Development

Indian converts at Mission San Diego spent their days cultivating fields and tending livestock. The padres directed the building of a dam upstream in Mission Gorge to provide a more adequate water supply for irrigating crops. Nevertheless, Mission San Luis Rey de Francia, founded in 1798, became the agricultural center for the region. The opening day ceremony, presided over by then Father President Lasuén, brought together a multitude of nearby Indians, and 54 children received baptism. Father Antonio Peyri, a native of Tarragona, witnessed the mission's establishment and remained there as senior priest for 34 years. His wisdom, energy, and architectural talent created buildings well known for their beauty and utility, and the mission fields stretched far inland.

Father Peyri founded Mission San Antonio de Pala as a branch or *asistencia* of San Luis Rey in 1816. Standing in a pleasant river valley in the foothills east of today's Pala Mesa, the building is still in active use as a parish church for the local Indians. During the Spanish period, it served the large and cooperative Indian population working the grain fields of the area. The *asistencia* grew rapidly to rival the mission in importance and at its peak embraced more than 1,000 converts. Both Mission San Luis Rey and its sub-mission furnished agricultural produce to other areas and carried on brisk trading activities.

During construction of Mission San Diego's fourth church, a great earthquake on December 8, 1812, shook the buildings and caused structural damage. Fathers Fernando Martin and José Sanchez concluded that flared wings should be added to the facade as buttresses against future tremors that rolled on a north-south axis. They worked on the church during the next year and held dedication ceremonies for the building completed in its present form on November 12, 1813. Five years later, in 1818, the *asistencia* of Santa Ysabel was founded 60 miles east of San Diego to serve a group of 250 Indians who lived in the picturesque valley. Although it remained small, the permanent adobe buildings included a chapel, a granary, and some houses; the number of Indians reached 450.

Mexico Takes Over

Until 1821, when revolutionary troops in Mexico succeeded in overthrowing Spain's government, San Diego remained essentially a religious and military outpost. When word of independence reached the distant port settlement, San Diegans raised the Mexican flag on April 20, 1822, amid appropriate festivities and swore allegiance to their new leaders. The only sadness was experienced by soldiers who had to cut off their long braids—symbols of the old regime. Spanish control over San Diego ended as it had begun—quietly and without violence. The cross and the sword, however, had left a permanent impression. The name San Diego de Alcalá; conversion of a significant group of Native Americans to the Catholic faith; and interaction of Spaniards and Indians in agriculture, architecture, and arts and crafts all marked the beginning of a different way of life.

Chapter IV

UNDER MEXICAN RULE: 1821–1846

The changeover from Spanish to Mexican control affected San Diego and the province of California in various ways. The most important change was the removal of the capital from Monterey to San Diego, a point more centrally located between Alta and Baja California. The presidial soldiers and their families who lived on the hill, released from Spanish royal restrictions, began to think in terms of a permanent civilian town as founded in Los Angeles.

It is thought that the first person who moved down to the flat area below Presidio Hill was Captain Francisco María Ruiz, a native of Loreto in Baja California. Ruiz served as the last Spanish-appointed commandant of the presidio. He started a garden and helped lay the foundations for several houses on the present site of Old Town. In 1823 he received the first private land grant in San Diego County—*Rancho de Los Peñasquitos*. Captain Ruiz represented the new trend—less emphasis upon military matters and more interest in town building and ranching. The presidio literally began to crumble.

The Pico Family

One of the most famous residents of early San Diego was Pío Pico, the last Mexican governor of California. His family typified those living in the southern region during the years that spanned three epochs—Spanish, Mexican, and American control. The Picos were involved in all aspects of political, military, social, and religious life. Pío's father, José María, was of mixed Spanish, Indian, and African ancestry. He came to San Diego from Sinaloa, Mexico, accompanied by his Sonoran-born wife, María Eustaquia, to join other presidio families in 1782. Their eldest son, José Antonio, was born on the hill in 1794 while Pío was born at Mission San Gabriel in 1801. Seven daughters and son Andrés, born in San Diego in 1810, completed the Pico family.

Because the elder Pico died in 1819 and José Antonio was in the service, Pío took charge of the household in San Diego. When they moved into the pueblo during the early 1820s, several other families had built houses in the area west of the plaza to the north and south. Pío opened up a small store where he sold liquors, provisions, chairs, and shoes. He frequently traveled to Los Angeles, to the missions, and to the frontier of Baja California to sell goods and bring back cattle and other products. He also gambled. Brother Andrés preferred the military and achieved a reputation as "brave, reckless, jovial, kind-hearted and popular." He never married although his sisters all found husbands locally. Pío's brothers-in-law included members of the Ortega, Carrillo, Alvarado, and Argüello families. His wife, María, was an Alvarado.

The Carrillo Family

Closely associated with the Pico family were the Carrillos. Joaquin Carrillo, founder of the most numerous branch, came up from Baja California sometime after 1800. His cousin Guillermo had arrived earlier with Father Serra's entourage in 1769. The Carrillo house (now on Calhoun Street) may have been San Diego's first. Joaquin's daughter Josefa eloped in 1829 with American sea captain Henry Delano Fitch, causing quite a stir in the conservative Catholic pueblo. Since Fitch's rival for Josefa's hand was Governor José María Echeandía, the man mainly responsible for moving California's capital to San Diego in 1825, the couple's hasty departure for Valparaiso, Chile, without a proper church wedding was the talk of the town. Nevertheless, Josefa's

Maria Anita Alvarado, Leonora and Pío Pico, with niece Trinidad Ortega.
Photo ©San Diego History Center.

family finally forgave her, and in time, Henry became a prosperous merchant and trader in San Diego, dealing with the many Boston ships that frequented the port. Their large family occupied the Carrillo home, and Fitch later served as a justice of the peace.

Governor Echeandía's problems during his six-year term from 1825 to 1831 involved a number of issues more serious than a lost sweetheart. These included the proposed secularization of the missions, for which he offered a plan of voluntary freedom with education, unrest among soldiers and non-mission Indians, and the arrival of foreigners by sea and land. Relaxed regulations had allowed French, British, American, Dutch, and Russian ships to put in at San Diego for trade and supplies, but they often avoided paying customs duties through various smuggling activities.

Jedediah Smith—Mountain Man

A more serious threat, however, was the arrival of the first overland party from the growing United States—a group of mountain men led by Jedediah Smith of Missouri's Rocky Mountain Fur Company. Governor Echeandía rightly feared that once given an opening wedge, Americans would soon be coming to California in large numbers. He refused Smith and his men permission to stay. When James Ohio Pattie arrived in San Diego in 1829, with his father, Sylvester, and a party of trappers from New Mexico, they were housed in the local jail. Although Pattie gained his freedom by helping vaccinate people against smallpox, further warnings were issued to overland parties seeking entrance.

After 1831—following Echeandía's ouster during a period of political unrest—Mexican policy was relaxed to allow Americans or other foreigners to enter the province and become naturalized Mexican citizens. This required conversion to Catholicism if they wanted to remain. Many men did so during the 1830s and married into local families. This also made it possible for them to apply for a land grant.

San Diego Becomes a Pueblo

San Diego fought to keep the capital in the south. But as political fortunes vacillated between centralists and federalists in Mexico, repercussions were felt in California. Pío Pico and others supported Carlos Carrillo for governor, and Pico himself actually served twenty days in the post in 1832. Nevertheless, the southern group lost. When Brigadier General José Figueroa arrived as governor of California in January 1833, the capital was officially returned to Monterey. Residents of San Diego—then numbering 432—appealed to the legislature assembled there that San Diego be granted official *pueblo* or town status, complete with municipal officers.

Approval of a new civilian government was granted on June 4, 1834, and put into effect on January 1, 1835. Elected officials were Juan María Osuna, first alcalde (mayor); Juan Bautista Alvarado and Juan María Marrón, councilmen; and Henry Fitch, city attorney. They were installed by presidio commandant Santiago Argüello who agreed to supply Osuna with an inventory of documents in the "archives of San Diego."

The Bandini and Estudillo Families

By the mid-1830s, a recognizable town was beginning to take shape in San Diego. The Juan Bandini home southeast of the plaza was a center for political discussions and social activity. Juan's father, José,

110 — Marriage Place of Ramona, Old Town, San Diego, California.

The house of José Antonio Estudillo from a postcard ca. 1915. *Author's collection.*

a native of Spain, had migrated to Lima, Peru, where his children were born. Juan, a merchant, arrived in California in 1818 and in 1822 married María Dolores Estudillo. They became the parents of five children. After María's death, Juan married Refugio Argüello, and they also had five children. The large Bandini house, originally one story, had fourteen rooms and elegant furnishings. A kitchen and two storerooms were separated from the main house by an arcade.

The Estudillo house across the path contained twelve rooms surrounding a spacious courtyard. Its builder, José Antonio Estudillo, was a native of Monterey, well educated, and congenial. His wife, María Victoria Domínguez de Estudillo, whom he married on March 1, 1824, was one of the most gracious and charitable women in early San Diego. Her roots were from Mexico and Spain, and she had inherited the concept of family in the fullest sense. Her great uncle, Juan José Domínguez, was one of the soldiers who accompanied Father Serra to San Diego in 1769.

María Victoria was born within the presidio walls in 1805 and grew up in and around the presidio. After her marriage to José Estudillo, the couple had five sons—José María, Salvador, José Guadalupe, José Antonio, and Francisco—and six daughters—María Antonia, Francisca, Rosa, Concepción, María de los Reyes, and

Dolores. Although her husband received a grant of Rancho Janal, María Victoria preferred the house in town with her friends and neighbors. In 1851, after her daughter and son-in-law died, she took in their four children. That same year, her widowed sister died, leaving five more children in María Victoria's care. She also adopted several Indian children whose parents were dead. Then, in 1852, her husband died. But she kept the family together through her strong will and determination. She continued to live in Old Town always caring for others. Five days before she became bedridden with her final illness in October 1873, she visited a sick friend to offer help. She died at the age of 72, still elegant and stately.

Richard Henry Dana

Richard Henry Dana, visiting California from Boston aboard a hide and tallow trader, saw San Diego in the summer of 1835 with shipmate Jack Stewart. Dana later recalled in his best-selling book *Two Years before the Mast* that San Diego was decidedly the best place in California for landing and taking on board hides. Because the harbor was small and landlocked, vessels could lie within a cable's length of the smooth, sandy beach. Dana and Stewart paid a visit to the "old ruinous presidio" overlooking the small settlement of "about forty, dark-brown looking huts, or houses, and two larger ones, plastered" belonging to the Bandini and Estudillo families. They noticed that wood was scarce, and few trees grew in the area. For recreation they visited the local grogshop, then rented some horses to ride out to the mission. There they ate "baked meats, frijoles stewed with peppers and onions, boiled eggs, and California flour baked into a kind of macaroni" which, "together with the wine, made the most sumptuous meal" they had eaten since Boston.

Dana enjoyed his stay in California but his strict puritanical background showed up frequently. He liked the violin and guitar playing but thought the men "thriftless, proud, and extravagant, and very much given to gaming.... The women had but little education and a good deal of beauty."

Machado Silvas adobe house ca. 1880s in Old Town San Diego. *Photo ©San Diego History Center.*

What Dana may not have appreciated, among other aspects of California living, were the difficulties in building an adobe house. The three-foot-deep walls of the typical one-room shelter of the Spanish and Mexican adobes required about 1,000 mud blocks. These were shaped in a rude mold to an average size of sixteen inches in width and twenty in length. Blocks were generally three to six inches thick and weighed from twenty to forty pounds. Straw was preferred as binding for the adobe substance, but inferior strengtheners such as shells, sticks, birds' nests, and reeds were often necessary. The more prosperous homes were L-shaped or U-shaped around an interior courtyard. The use of wood for flooring was practically unknown before 1835; the earth on the site was stamped to a degree of smoothness and occasionally hardened by watering. Glass was rare, and the lack of building timber prevented the addition of a second story. Two-story dwellings came later when lumbering operations began.

Dana's companion Jack Stewart married Rosa Machado, daughter of prominent San Diego resident José Manuel Machado. Machado and his wife, María Serafina Valdéz, parents of twelve children, provided at least three adobe houses near the plaza for their various offspring. (The Machado Stewart and Machado Silvas adobes have been restored.) Daughter Juanita, whose first husband, Damasio Alipaz died in Sonora in 1835, later married first American settler

Thomas Wrightington of Fall River, Massachusetts. Wrightington had left the brig *Ayacucho* in 1833 to remain in San Diego. He kept a general store featuring liquors, dry goods, shoes, bread, and fruits. The Machado families have many descendants in San Diego today.

Secularization of the Missions

A major change occurred in California with secularization of the 21 Franciscan missions during Governor José Figueroa's administration. The missions had been designed as temporary institutions, and local officials pointed out that they had long since fulfilled their obligations of conversion and training. The priests thought that the Indians were not yet ready for assimilation and objected to any change. But those with an eye on the extensive and prosperous mission lands thought otherwise. Authorities in Mexico City agreed that the time had come for a change and approved a general decree of secularization in August 1833.

Effective in California the following year, the governor's decree placed Mission San Diego under civilian control on September 30, 1834, with a portion of the land going to the Indians. Joaquin Ortega became administrator of mission properties in April 1835, at a salary of $50 per month, to be paid from proceeds of mission products. Pío Pico took over the secular administration of Mission San Luis Rey that same month, but, according to his memoirs, "considered that all this property belonged by right and justice to the Indians." He received some 15,000 sheep, but all the cattle were wild and scattered since Father Antonio Peyri had departed the year before to retire in Spain. The Christianized Native Americans of San Luis Rey had not favored his departure, but Father Peyri did not want to remain through the secularization period.

Although some mission administrators were well intentioned, the task of supervising Indians removed from the rigid mission discipline was enormous. Little by little, individual Indians—because of a lack of protection, training, and/or motivation—lost or gave up lands assigned to them. Soon private ranchos took the place of

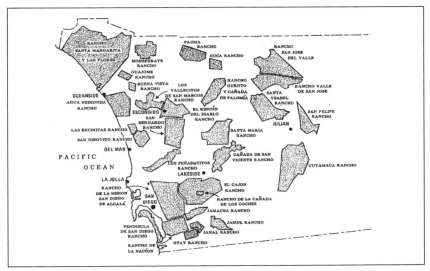

San Diego County ranchos based on a map dawn by W.J. Hermiston for Richard Pourade and the Copley Press.

mission farm and grazing lands. Some Native Americans found work on these ranchos, but many were forced into the backcountry without visible means of support. Some of the Indians organized a little pueblo called San Dieguito in November 1835, with 34 ex-mission families, while others searched for work as artisans in the pueblo.

Rancho Grants

Of the local residents who received grants of land for ranchos during the early Mexican period, some had been military men while others were prosperous merchants. All were well connected politically and had sufficient means at their disposal to qualify for a minimum grant of four square leagues (4,436 acres per square league). Santiago Argüello, whose father and brothers had been governors, received in 1829 Rancho Tía Juana, a sizable rancho extending from south of San Diego Bay to the site of present Tijuana in Mexico. Argüello and his wife Pilar Ortega also needed room to raise their 22 children. Other ranches granted by Governor Echeandía that year included Jamul (8,926 acres) to Pío Pico; Janal (4,436 acres) to José Antonio Estudillo; and Otay (6,637 acres) to Magdalena Estudillo.

Because of frequent changes in the governorship, and the problems
of secularization, few grants were made during the 1830s. Many of
the former mission holdings and other lands of San Diego County
were granted to private owners by Governor Manuel Micheltorena
during the period from 1841 to 1844. One of the largest was Rancho
Santa Margarita y Las Flores—133,440 acres stretching along 35
miles of coastline from Oceanside to Orange County and inland to
Fallbrook. It was rented and later granted to Pío and Andres Pico in
1841 and 1844. Some 300 Indians lived within the grant at Las Flores,
a village founded in 1822 around an *asistencia* of Mission San Luis
Rey. The smallest was Cañada de los Coches, a 28.33-acre hog farm
within present-day El Cajon, granted to Doña Apolinaria Lorenzana,
a devout woman who had been brought to California as an orphan
to Villa de Branciforte north of Monterey in 1800. Because of her
charitable deeds, she was called *La Beata* (the Devoted One). She had
previously been given Rancho Jamacha (8,881 acres) as a reward for
her services.

Other ranchos granted by Micheltorena included 8,824 acres
called San Dieguito (later known as Rancho Santa Fe) to Juan María
Osuna; Agua Hedionda (13,311 acres including much of today's
Carlsbad) to Juan María Marrón; Las Encinitas (4,431 acres) to Andres
Ybarra; Rincon del Diablo (today's Escondido—12,653 acres) to Juan
Bautista Alvarado; Los Vallecitos de San Marcos (8,877 acres) to José
María Alvarado; Rancho San Bernardo (17,763 acres) to British sea
captain Joseph F. Snook, husband of María Antonia Alvarado; and
Santa María, now the site of Ramona (17,708 acres), to British sea
captain Edward Stokes, husband of Refugio Ortega. Stokes and his
father-in-law, José Joaquin Ortega, also received Rancho Santa Ysabel
(17,719 acres) a year later. The 13,309-acre Pauma Rancho deep in
Cupeño Indian territory was granted to José Antonio Serrano.

The area that became known as Warner's Ranch resulted from
the combination of two prior grants. Silvestre de la Portilla received
Rancho Valle de San José (17,634 acres) in 1836. A grant of 26,688
acres to José Antonio Pico in 1840 was called Rancho San José del

Santa Margarita ranch house by James Walker. *Photo courtesy of the Seaver Center, Natural History Museum of Los Angeles County.*

Valle and included the Indian *ranchería* of Agua Caliente. Both Pico and Portilla abandoned their ranchos because of Indian attacks. Jonathan Trumbull Warner—a native of Connecticut who had come to California in 1831 from Santa Fe, New Mexico—had passed through the valley and noticed its fertility. He became a Mexican citizen and in 1837 married Anita Gale, a ward of Pío Pico's widowed mother, Doña Eustaquia. Warner applied for both ranchos in 1844, citing their abandonment, and received a grant of the entire San José Valley. He built an adobe house and trading post four miles south of Agua Caliente and encouraged the Indians of the hot springs settlement to work for him.

Pío Pico as Governor of California

Shortly before the end of the Mexican period, Pío Pico finally realized his dream of becoming governor and established his headquarters in Los Angeles. During his term of office from February 22, 1845, to August 10, 1846, he did not forget his friends in San Diego and granted a number of sizable ranchos. One of the largest was Rancho El Cajon—48,799 acres given to María Antonia Estudillo de Pedrorena, wife of Spanish-born Miguel de Pedrorena, a merchant and trader who held several local offices. The grant included present-day El Cajon, Lakeside, Santee, Bostonia, and land east to El Monte

Park. The Pedrorena family built a large adobe home near the center of Lakeside and a smaller one near the eastern end of Mission Gorge. Among the smaller grants was Cuca Rancho of 2,174 acres near Pauma Valley granted to María Juana de los Angeles Soberanes. It remained for some years in the hands of her daughter, wife of Gregorio Trujillo.

Other grants made by Governor Pico during 1845 included much of the county's agricultural and grazing lands, but these did not remain for long in the hands of their original owners. Many of the activities associated with these lands are of a later period. Rancho Cañada de San Vicente y Mesa del Padre Barona (13,316 acres) was granted to Juan Bautista López but deeded to Domingo Yorba in 1850. The southern part of the tract became the Barona Indian Reservation, named for Mission Father Joséf Barona. The 2,219-acre Rancho Guajome (near Vista), given to Indian brothers Andrés and José Manuel, was in turn sold to Abel Stearns of Los Angeles. It later passed into the hands of Stearns's sister-in-law, Isadora Bandini, and her husband, Cave J. Couts.

Pico also granted nearby Rancho Buena Vista to Felipe Subria, a Luiseño Indian who had served as *alcalde* of the rancheria at Buena Vista. He gave it to his married daughter, Maria La Gradia Dunn, wife of William B. Dunn, a private with the regiment of Dragoons under Stephen Watts Kearny who reached California in 1846. By the summer of 1851, Dunn had left Maria and it became clear to Felipe that Dunn had no intention of returning the valuable wedding present. Felipe and his daughter protested but were unsuccessful in regaining the land. Its 1,184 acres were also acquired by Cave Couts.

The expansive Cuyamaca Rancho of 35,501 acres was granted to Agustin Olvera, an early resident of Los Angeles whose family gave Olvera Street its name. Olvera only visited the ranch occasionally and allowed several squatters to make their homes there. Rancho Guejito y Cañada de Palomia (13,298 acres near Lake Wohlford), was granted to José María Orozco, a justice of the peace in San Diego who hosted countless fiestas at his large adobe ranch house.

Carrillo House still standing near Old Town with historical marker.

Governor Pico granted San Diego's *alcalde* Pedro C. Carrillo and his wife, Joséfa Bandini, a 4,185-acre tract called Peninsula de San Diego, the site of today's Coronado and the Silver Strand. It lacked water and turned out to be unsuitable for grazing cattle. Even though Pedro won his battle with the pueblo over the rancho's boundaries, he decided to unload his barren land to Captain Ebenezer Simmons of the American ship *Magnolia* for $1,000 in 1848. Simmons did much better in a later transaction.

On the mainland side of the bay, Rancho de la Nación (26,631 acres of presidio grazing lands) was granted to Pico's brother-in-law John (Juan) Forster of Liverpool, England. Forster's holdings also included Rancho Santa Margarita y las Flores, which he purchased from Andrés and Pío Pico and is the present site of Camp Pendleton, and Rancho San Felipe near the Banner Grade crossing in the Laguna Mountains toward Julian. Forster resided near San Juan Capistrano and in 1865 sold La Nación, the ranch that would later embrace National City and Chula Vista.

The 9,972-acre Rancho San Felipe was originally granted to an Indian, Felipe Castillo, who transferred it to Forster. The 13,322-acre Monserrate Rancho was granted to Ysidro María Alvarado who built a small adobe home on the north side of the San Luis Rey River and carried on some ranching activities. A smallpox epidemic took the lives of many in the area during the 1860s, although son Tomas Alvarado lived there with his family until the late 1870s.

Ex-mission Lands

The final area disposed of during the Mexican period was Rancho de la Misión San Diego de Alcalá—58,875 acres stretching from the pueblo boundaries to El Cajon and from National City to today's Clairemont. It included present-day Linda Vista, Miramar, Mission Gorge, Allied Gardens, Del Cerro, San Carlos, Kensington, San Diego State University, La Mesa, Encanto, and Lemon Grove. Pío Pico turned over the choice land to Santiago Argüello "in consideration of past services," and the deed was drafted June 8, 1846, in Los Angeles. Argüello was to pay the mission's debts, support the priests, and maintain religious services. A death knell for the mission was sounded, however, when American troops occupied the mission buildings during the American conquest of San Diego.

The U.S.-Mexican War brought changes to San Diego, and the arrival of so many newcomers in California gradually transformed the way of life. In many ways, the changeover was peaceful and the adoption of new customs merely a continuation of the influence exerted by a number of non-Mexicans such as Philip Crosthwaite, a young Irishman who reached California in 1845. Crosthwaite—having lost the toss of a coin for the only berth on an eastbound ship—decided to stay in San Diego permanently. He married María Josefa López, settled in the pueblo, and leased the ex-mission ranch lands from Argüello in 1848.

Philip Crosthwaite joined Henry Fitch, Abel Stearns, Edward Stokes, Jonathan (Juan José) Warner, Joseph Snook, and others who tried to help San Diego manage a smooth transition from Mexican to American rule. Inevitably, life in southern California would never be the same, although the Old Town area, preserved as Old Town San Diego State Historic Park, can take visitors back to the days when San Diego was a part of Mexico.

Chapter V

YANKEES ARRIVE: 1846–1870

The changes that the US-Mexican War of 1846–1848 brought to San Diego forever altered the course of its history and significantly modified the structure of its society. Although never directly involved in the mainstream of the war, San Diegans felt the repercussions of events taking place on distant fronts. In the spring of 1846, American troops under Captain John C. Fremont camped near Monterey to survey "topographical features" of the nearby landscape. José Castro, captain of the presidio, thought they presented a threat and asked them to leave the province. These problems occurred while more serious disagreements were taking place on the border between Texas and Mexico.

Prelude to War

Mexican suspicions in California had been aroused ever since Americans under Commodore Thomas ap Catesby Jones had captured Monterey in 1842 under the mistaken belief that the United States was then at war with its neighbor to the south. After Castro's warning, Fremont's troops headed toward Oregon—only to return to Sutter's Fort in Sacramento in June 1846 to support a group of American immigrants who had risen independently against Mexican control to establish the Bear Flag Republic. Since war against Mexico had been officially declared over problems in Texas the previous month, the three-week-old republic ended when the United States Navy raised the American flag over Monterey on July 9. Northern California fell to the invaders in short order.

On July 29, 1846, the USS *Cyane* under Commander Samuel F. Dupont sailed into San Diego Bay bringing John Fremont, the scout Kit Carson, and a battalion of California volunteers to secure the southland. Lieutenants Stephen C. Rowan (United States Navy) and William A. Maddox (United States Marine Corps) went ashore with a marine guard and raised the American flag in the plaza near the Estudillo house. For a time, there was little opposition. Dupont stayed in the home of Juan Bandini and commented that his host had long been a friend to the Americans and was ready for the change. There was music and dancing every night and, according to Dupont "Don Juan (Bandini), although over sixty, is the most indefatigable and active of the dancers, saying it is *muy inocente*. His son-in-law, Don Pedro Carrillo, was educated in Boston and speaks English well. Don Miguel Pedrorena also speaks it fluently. These people are all intelligent and make it a much more agreeable place than Monterey...."

John Fremont was especially impressed by San Diego's surrounding countryside and wrote in his memoirs: "Among the arid, brush-covered hills south of San Diego we found little valleys converted by a single spring into crowded gardens, where pears, peaches, quinces, pomegranates, grapes, olives, and other fruits grew luxuriantly together, the little stream acting upon them like a principle of life. This southern frontier of Upper California seems eminently adapted to the cultivation of the vine and the olive. A single vine has been known to yield a barrel of wine, and the olive trees are burdened with the weight of fruit."

Ten days after the American flag was raised in the plaza, Fremont rode north with his battalion on a beautiful sorrel horse given to him by Juan Bandini. Other Mexican residents of San Diego—including members of the Osuna, Carrillo, Cota, Marrón, and Machado families—failed to follow the appeal of Bandini and Santiago Argüello not to resist the Americans. They were not convinced that California's

Cosmopolital Hotel. Inset: Mormon soldier. *Photo ©San Diego History Center.*

separation from Mexico was inevitable and that a new government would bring protection and stability. The Estudillos remained neutral. When San Diego was left virtually undefended after Fremont's departure, a number of loyal Californians again flew the Mexican flag. Finally, Albert B. Smith, a sailmaker, nailed the Stars and Stripes permanently to the plaza flagpole. In November 1846, Commodore Robert Stockton of the Pacific Squadron arrived in San Diego aboard the 60-gun USS *Congress* to assure American control. He posted a garrison on the hill near the presidio and called the encampment Fort Stockton.

The Battle of San Pasqual

In addition, General Stephen Watts Kearny's Army of the West had been marching overland from Santa Fe to reinforce American troops in California. Guided by Kit Carson, the Kearny column of 110 officers and men reached Warner's Ranch on December 3 after covering some 1,000 miles of rugged terrain since September 25. They rested at Warner's Ranch while messengers were dispatched to Fort Stockton at San Diego. Meanwhile, 200 California lancers under Andrés Pico prepared to intercept the American invaders. On the night of December 5, Kearny marched to a position above the San Pasqual Valley.

Early on the morning of December 6, they made a premature and disorganized attack on the Californians. This engagement—known as the Battle of San Pasqual—was fought approximately five miles east of present-day Escondido and several hundred yards southeast of today's battlefield marker. The Americans suffered 31 casualties, including eighteen dead, while the Californians escaped unharmed. On December 7, the battered Kearny column camped on a nearby hill. Constantly harassed by the lancers, they were forced to burn their baggage and eat their remaining mules. The campsite became known as Mule Hill. Kit Carson and Navy Lieutenant Edward Fitzgerald Beale finally slipped out of camp and made their way to San Diego to get help. Two hundred United States Marines and sailors arrived from San Diego on December 11 to escort Kearny's column to the southern port. The Californians withdrew and were finally defeated when Fremont returned from the north. Andrés Pico capitulated at Cahuenga Pass near Los Angeles on January 13, 1847, and the war in California was essentially over.

As a result of the war with Mexico, San Diego was infiltrated by newcomers from the military forces of the United States. Major William H. Emory, Kearny's chief of staff, wrote that San Diego consisted "of a few adobe houses, two or three of which only have plank floors... the rain fell in torrents as we entered the town, and it was my singular fate here...to be quartered in a miserable place of one room." Dr. John Griffin, Kearny's medical officer who spent most of his time caring for the wounded men, lamented that the houses were ill-ventilated and that their first Christmas in California was a solemn affair.

The Mormon Battalion

When the Mormon Battalion under Lieutenant Philip St. George Cooke arrived from Fort Leavenworth via a long march from Santa Fe, they were too late to participate in the war for which they had volunteered. Instead, they hired themselves out to the townspeople

California soldier in stained glass at the San Pasqual Battlefield State Park in Escondido.

of San Diego. They made a whitewash and used it to brighten up the houses. They also built a bakery, fired bricks, built log pumps, dug wells, did blacksmithing, and repaired carts. The wife of Captain Jesse Hunter of the Mormon group gave birth to the first American child born in San Diego. Called Diego in honor of his birthplace, the boy was cared for by local Mexican women when his mother died a short time later. Captain Hunter served as Indian agent at Mission San Luis Rey; his orders were to protect the Indians from local residents. Lieutenant Robert Clift became San Diego's justice of the peace from June 1847 until March 1848.

Most of the Latter-day Saints preferred to move on to Salt Lake City, Utah, but Colonel Jonathan D. Stevenson, in command of a regiment of New York volunteers, asked that they stay on in California. Seventy-eight of the Mormons remained at Fort Stockton while others went north. Those staying behind were joined by Company I of Stevenson's men who had made the former San Diego Mission their headquarters and barracks. The soldiers at the mission conducted the first American census and listed 248 white residents, 483 converted Indians, 1,550 wild Indians, three Negroes, and three Sandwich Islanders (Hawaiians).

On February 2, 1848, the Treaty of Guadalupe Hidalgo was signed, ending the war between Mexico and the United States. An international boundary commission under John B. Weller and Pedro Garcia Conde was set up to survey the new line from Texas to the Pacific coast. After some delay, they began to work in San Diego.

Gold Discovery near Sacramento

To complicate matters, James Marshall's discovery of gold on the American River near Sacramento in late January 1848 had, by mid-March, become known throughout the state and had touched off the migration of numerous gold seekers. Many passed through San Diego on their way to northern mining areas. The *Daily Alta California* reported in December 1849 that the port of San Diego had "taken quite a start. Quite a number of Americans have gone down there recently and established themselves in business for the winter. A number of frame houses are in the process of erection and many others are being shipped from this port (of San Francisco). The town is represented to us as being quite a bustling, lively, little place."

Several military men including Cave J. Couts, John Bankhead Magruder, Samuel P. Heintzelman, Thomas W. Sweeny, Thomas D. Johns, Edward Murray, Edward H. Fitzgerald, and John E. Summers had purchased property in La Playa or near the plaza. Couts married Juan Bandini's daughter Isidora and later acquired Rancho Guajome near former Mission San Luis Rey. Couts also owned the Colorado House, a hotel on the plaza, and took an active part in local affairs. H.M.T. Powell, an artist from New Mexico who had arrived in 1849, made several sketches of the town and port and at Couts's request drew one of the area's first maps.

Powell described the heart of San Diego as a place of bullfighting, gambling, and drinking. Although such activities no doubt took place, life around the plaza consisted generally of children playing, families gathering, and normal socializing. Washington Plaza, as it was sometimes called, hosted caravans with trade goods and vendors who often sold their wares from stands in the square. A town well

Model of Old Town San Diego State Historic Park by Joe Toigo.

sunk at the eastern end near the Estudillo house had a windmill for drawing water. The Americans introduced a Fourth of July celebration in 1847 and continued to celebrate that date each year with firecrackers, marching bands, speeches, and much singing and dancing.

San Diego Becomes a City

An act to incorporate the City of San Diego was passed on March 27, 1850. The first elections were held on June 16, and Joshua H. Bean, a former soldier, was chosen as the first mayor. An act had also been passed the previous February 18 dividing California into 28 counties in anticipation of entry into the Union. San Diego's boundaries included all of today's Imperial and much of Riverside and San Bernardino counties. First county officers elected by voters at the two precincts of San Diego and La Playa on April 1 were: assemblyman, Oliver S. Witherby; county judge, John Hayes; county clerk, Richard Rust; county recorder, H.C. Matsell; treasurer, Philip Crosthwaite; sheriff, Agoston Haraszthy; assessor, José Antonio Estudillo; district attorney, William C. Ferrell; surveyor, Henry Clayton; coroner, John Brown; and county attorney, Thomas W. Sutherland. Also serving as treasurer for a time was Juan Bandini.

The first term of the District Court of San Diego was convened on May 6, 1850, with Oliver S. Witherby as presiding judge. The first grand jury included Charles Haraszthy, Ramon Osuna, James Wall, Loreto Amador, Manuel Rocha, J. Emers, Bonifacio López, Holden Alara, Seth B. Blake, Louis Rose, William H. Moon, Cave J. Couts, José de Jesus Moreno, Cristobal López, and José Antonio Aguirre. The total population given for the county was 798, with the city listed at 650. Assessment rolls of the city totaled $374,260, divided among Old Town, $264,210; New Town (a settlement by the bay), $80,050; and Middletown, $30,000.

New San Diego

The new arrivals in San Diego helped transform the little Mexican community into a growing commercial center. New businesses were started and more homes were built. One man, however, thought that the town's location was poor for shipping. William Heath Davis— once called "Kanaka Bill" because of his Hawaiian parentage—First saw San Diego in 1833 and never forgot it. In 1850, Boundary Commission surveyor Lieutenant Andrew B. Gray interested him and several others—including Miguel de Pedrorena, José Antonio Aguirre, and William C. Ferrell—in investing in 160 acres by the water's edge.

Davis laid out a 32-square block area between present-day Broadway and Market streets, purchased lumber, bricks, and some prefabricated houses for his New Town, but people did not settle there. Davis gave some land to the United States government for an army post and the "San Diego Barracks" served for a number of years as the army supply depot for southern California. A shaky city began to assemble around a plaza called Pantoja Park, and several stores were opened. Davis spent $60,000 on a wharf, constructed a warehouse, and built his own residence on State Street. When the new site failed to develop, it became known as Davis' Folly. As founder of New San Diego, Kanaka Bill was ahead of his time.

Another proposed development called Middletown (a similar bay

Robinson-Rose House ca. 1850s. Old Town San Diego State Historic Park.

tract) was laid out between Old Town and New Town at the same time. A grant of 687 acres was made to Davis' brother-in-law José Maria Estudillo and others including Oliver Witherby, Cave Couts, Agoston Haraszthy, and Juan Bandini. This site also failed to attract settlers for many years. So for the first decades of the American period, what became known as Old Town continued to be the heart of San Diego.

Changing San Diego

As Easterners and Europeans brought in their ideas of architecture, the houses around Old Town's Washington Plaza began to take on a different appearance. Louis Rose, a native of Germany, arrived in 1850 via New Orleans and entered into several businesses. He opened a tavern on the first floor of the Robinson-Rose Building. During the 1850s, a single-story adobe—built by Juan Rodriguez and called Tienda California—became the Exchange Hotel run by Juan's son-in-law George Tebbetts. In 1855 Maurice and Lewis Franklin, Jewish merchants from Liverpool, England, obtained the property and constructed the first three-story building—the Franklin House. The hotel housed a meeting hall, barber shop, offices, and quite a variety of activities.

Another structure to experience an American evolution was a four-room, single-story adobe occupied after 1847 by two African

Americans, Richard Freeman and Allen B. Light, former fur traders. New proprietors in 1857 covered the adobe with board siding and created the American Hotel. The building included a saloon, billiards, and bowling. Maria Lorenza Silvas and George Smith were married there in 1860. The newlyweds inherited the Machado-Silvas adobe and retained its original design. Over the years it served as a home, rooming house, restaurant, art studio, and even a community church.

The Garra Uprising

All did not go smoothly in San Diego during the 1850s. Sheriff Haraszthy attempted to collect taxes from the Indians in the backcountry. In November 1851, Antonio Garra, chief of the Cupeños, incited his people to fight against white settlers. He had the help of some San Diegans but was caught after a few scattered attacks. William Marshall and Juan Verdugo were executed in the plaza for their part in instigating the Indian uprising. Garra was shot by a firing squad on January 10, 1852. Few other Indians attempted to fight back against unjust taxes. Sheriff Haraszthy, a native of Hungary, left San Diego in 1852 when he was elected to the California legislature. He later gained fame as one of the founders of California's commercial wine industry.

Edward Fitzgerald Beale was appointed Indian agent for San Diego but little provision was made for these Native Americans at this time. They were subjected to frequent abuse, including the rape of Indian girls and women. Prostitution among native women became a serious problem as economic conditions for Indians worsened. The law prohibiting the sale of liquor to Indians was virtually unenforceable; so much of the degradation of natives living near white population centers could be traced to poor treatment and the availability of liquor.

The Press in San Diego

Journalism came to San Diego with John Judson Ames who carried a printing press to Davis' New Town in 1851 to start publication of the weekly San Diego *Herald*. As New Town's prospects temporarily

House of Lt. George Derby and later Lt. George Pendleton in Old Town San Diego.

dimmed, Ames moved his press to quarters fronting on Old Town's plaza and there ran into army engineer and humorist Lieutenant George Horatio Derby.

Although Derby successfully directed construction of a dike to turn the San Diego River into False (later Mission) Bay to halt the silting of the harbor, he is perhaps better remembered for his humorous writings as John Phoenix or the venerable Squibob. Ames, a staunch Democrat, asked Derby to take over the *Herald* while he was in San Francisco for a visit. Derby, a Whig supporter, reversed the paper's politics with a touch of good humor. Although Derby was basically a humorist, he objected to the ill treatment of Indians and wrote about the fact that whites accused of killing Indians were rarely brought to trial or convicted. Derby's writings have since been reprinted in numerous anthologies. Ames operated the *Herald* until April 7, 1860, when he closed up shop. More than eight years passed before another paper—*The San Diego Union*—began publication.

Transportation Development

With completion of the Gadsden Purchase in 1853, talk of a transcontinental railroad was frequently heard in San Diego. Secretary of War Jefferson Davis had ordered a number of cross-country surveys, and a southern route seemed to be the most practical. Residents of Old Town organized the San Diego & Gila, Southern Pacific & Atlantic Railroad Company, but they failed to build a railroad from San Diego to Yuma.

James Birch opened a stage line between San Diego and San Antonio, Texas, in 1857 to provide passenger and mail service. Birch died soon after, but the company lived on for four years as the Jackass Mail Line. John Butterfield, organizer and first director of the American Express Company in 1850, opened a stage route from Tipton, Missouri, to San Francisco, California, on September 16, 1858, providing 25-day service. The new line, called the Butterfield Overland Mail, carried passengers and mail along the Birch route from Texas into East County but bypassed San Diego by turning northward through Warner's Ranch. It passed through the Carrizo Corridor, Vallecito, the San Felipe Valley, Warner's, and Oak Grove. Since San Diego was never on the main route of travel, it continued to rely heavily on ships for transportation and communication. The outbreak of the Civil War ended any hope for a transcontinental railroad through the South as plans and surveys made after 1862 were for a northern line.

The Whaley House

During the late 1850s, despite the lack of easy communication with the East, San Diego moved slowly forward. Thomas Whaley, a native of New York, began construction of his two-story brick home and store on May 6, 1856. The Whaley House was a beautiful and spacious structure complete with wall-to-wall carpeting—something little seen in southern California. The north room, originally a granary, was extensively remodeled for a county courthouse in August 1869. Just two years later, promoters of Alonzo Horton's New Town wanted to move the county records and courthouse to Sixth and G Streets. There was a hearing on the county's obligation to Whaley, but before

The house of Thomas Whaley ca. 1870s. The Whaley House was the first brick structure built in Old Town during the early 1850s. *Photo ©San Diego History Center.*

it was fully settled, the newly appointed county clerk and recorder,
and a few helpers, forcefully removed the records one night and took
them to the downtown location. Whaley lost the fight for their return
but insisted the county should pay rent on the courthouse or
compensate his loss. The county never got around to paying Whaley,
and he never forgot. He officially died in 1890; some say he still stalks
around muttering about the unfairness of it all and is one of the
several ghosts thought to haunt the Whaley House.

Yankee Jim Robinson, said to be another prominent ghost, was
hanged on the premises in August 1852 for stealing a boat. The
scaffold stood somewhere between the parlor and the music room.
The ghost of Yankee Jim began making his presence felt with noisy
footsteps and other creaks when a theater group decided in the early
1960s to put on a play, *The Ballad of Yankee Jim,* based upon the
execution. Apparently Robinson has good reason to haunt the place.
He was wounded during his capture and left unconscious during
most of his trial. Even the scaffold was so poorly constructed that
he strangled for fifteen minutes before actually dying.

The last Whaley to live in the house was Corinne Lillian, youngest
of the Whaley's six children. She died in 1953 at the age of 89. A
group of San Diegans who saved the house from demolition in 1956
saw to its complete restoration and reopening as a museum. John J.

Lamb's *San Diego Specters* gives detailed information about the ghosts said to inhabit the Whaley House, including a small spotted dog, several children, and Anna De Lannay Whaley, who married Thomas in 1853.

Old Town Residents

Near the Whaley House stands the former home of George Pendleton, a native of Virginia and classmate of Cave J. Couts at West Point. Pendleton, who arrived in 1855, was the nephew of Colonel John Bankhead Magruder, one of the town's first lawyers. Pendleton married Concepción B. Estudillo and served as county clerk and recorder from 1858 to 1870. George Derby stayed in the Pendleton house while temporary editor of the San Diego *Herald*. The home was moved in 1962 from its original location to the lot adjoining the Whaley House.

José Antonio Aguirre gave an adobe structure to the Catholic Church in 1858 for a chapel. It was located near El Campo Santo Cemetery. The walls were covered with board siding and the interior remodeled. Blessed as the Church of the Immaculate Conception, it served as the center for Catholic activities. Certain Protestant denominations used portions of various other buildings around the plaza. Although there had been schools conducted at the presidio and in a number of San Diego homes, the first schoolhouse was not built until 1865 at the corner of Congress and Mason Streets. It was moved to make room for a two-story building in 1872, but has now been restored and returned to Old Town as a historic structure.

Mary Chase Walker from Manchester, New York, taught there in 1865, but was forced to resign for befriending a young African American woman. Mary Walker later recalled, "My school was composed mostly of Spanish and half-breed children with a few English and several Americans. Many American soldiers and some sailors had come to San Diego in the early days and married pretty señoritas." Walker married Old Town lawyer and businessman Ephraim Morse shortly afterwards. Morse, who would later move to

The reconstructed house of Sheriff James McCoy in Old Town San Diego State Historic Park.

New Town, lamented the fact that the old presidio had fallen into ruin after most of the roofing and tiles had been used in building homes below. Even the church walls had been carried away.

During the 1860s, life in San Diego seemed to remain at a standstill. There was a general drought, and many of the cattle were dying on the nearby ranches. The rancheros made fewer visits to the town center to purchase luxuries. The Civil War had disrupted communication with the East, and the promised railroad had never arrived. Ephraim Morse summed up the state of affairs: "I'm still keeping store here but not making money. There is but little business here, the place not being so large as it was ten years ago...there are only two men in San Diego that don't occasionally get drunk and they are James McCoy, the sheriff, and myself." McCoy had one of the most elegant houses in town, just off the plaza and surrounded by a white picket fence.

The San Diego Union Begins Publication

One bright spot was the arrival in San Diego of newspaper publisher William Jeff Gatewood from San Andreas. Gatewood had married Philip Crosthwaite's sister and settled in northern California. After

The San Diego Union Museum in Old Town San Diego State Historic Park.

the gold rush, Crosthwaite induced the family to move to the southern community and start a paper. Gatewood, with J.N. Briseño and Edward W. Bushyhead, set up their equipment in the frame building owned by José Antonio Altamirano. It was next door to Altamirano's wife's family home, the adobe house of Miguel de Pedrorena. The first *San Diego Union* paper came off the press on October 10, 1868, but Gatewood did not remain long at the helm. By May 1869, he had become president of the San Diego, Gila & Atlantic Railroad Company and had sold out to Bushyhead and Charles P. Taggart. That first newspaper office still stands on its original site, fully restored, with an adjoining historical museum. Soon, however, Old Town would no longer house the newspaper. Times were beginning to change.

Chapter VI

NEW TOWN IS BORN AGAIN: 1870–1889

Even though the economic situation had contributed to a slowdown of activities around the Old Town Plaza, the arrival of a Connecticut Yankee by the name of Alonzo Horton was the most significant factor in the decline of San Diego's original settlement. Born in 1813 as one of seven children, Alonzo had moved with his family to New York. After running a small shipping business between Oswego and Canada, Horton moved west in 1836 to Milwaukee and speculated in land. At the close of the US-Mexican War, he founded a small town called Hortonville about 20 miles from Oshkosh, Wisconsin.

Alonzo Horton

In 1851, Horton sold his interests for $7,000 and headed for California. He returned to the East Coast and married Sarah Wilson Babe in Jersey City in 1860. After several business ventures, he settled with his wife in San Francisco and opened a store at Sixth and Market Streets. One night early in 1867, Horton heard a speaker talk about the wonderful opportunities in San Diego, one of the healthiest places with one of the best harbors in the whole world. He was then 54 years of age—a little beyond what people thought of as "prime" in those days, but the same age Father Serra had been when he received his call to California 100 years before. Just the thought of San Diego's possibilities kept Alonzo Horton awake all night.

On April 15, 1867, the steamer *Pacific* brought Horton and a small group of passengers up the bay to the foot of present-day Market Street. Since nothing but a few pilings remained of Davis' Wharf, the passengers were rowed ashore and helped to dry land. While Horton was awaiting a buckboard to take him to the plaza, he looked around at the harbor. He thought it "must be a Heaven on Earth...the best spot for building a city he ever saw." But when he saw Old Town, he commented that he would not give five dollars for the whole thing. "It doesn't lie right. Never in the world can you have a city here." Horton knew that even though others like Davis had failed, the harbor site was the only logical choice for building a new town.

Horton contacted county clerk George Pendleton to see about electing a board of trustees who could sell pueblo lands. He met Ephraim Morse and the two became fast friends. Morse showed him the land that was available, and Horton's Addition soon became a reality. Horton attended church at the Adobe Chapel and struck up an acquaintance with Father Antonio Ubach, the resident priest. Ubach helped the eager newcomer to find appropriate trustees for the land auction. Sheriff James McCoy served as auctioneer on May 10, 1867, and Horton purchased 960 acres for $265 or 27½ cents an acre. The trustees gave Horton a deed to the land on May 11, and he registered as a voter in San Diego. He returned to San Francisco on the next steamer with a promise to be back. And back he came— New Town was born again.

The Seeley Stables

In the meantime, Alfred Seeley, owner of Old Town's Seeley Stables, purchased the house of Juan Bandini, added a story, and converted it into the Cosmopolitan Hotel. He remodeled the Franklin House as a stage depot for his San Diego-Los Angeles line. Seeley confidently announced to his fellow residents around the plaza, "Old Town is *the* town, the real San Diego; your mushroom town...will soon peter out, and all the people who want to travel will have to come to Old

New Town San Diego ca. 1870s. *Photo ©San Diego History Center.*

Town to take the stage." But even Thomas Whaley and his partner Philip Crosthwaite were selling out cheap for cash. By 1870 *The San Diego Union* reported that they were fitting out the first floor of Horton's Hall for a store. "One by one the leaves are falling from Old Town, and the old place looks desolate. Nothing will be left there in a short time but a few saloons and lawyers."

New Town Becomes the New Center

The final blow came in 1870 when the county board of supervisors answered the cry of New San Diego residents and ordered removal of all county records from the Whaley House in Old Town to the Express Building in New San Diego. A posse was organized in Old Town and placed in front of the Whaley House. *The San Diego Union* reported: "Old Town has seceded.... They have nailed their flag to the staff in the Plaza...the watchword is Old Town—Now and Forever—One and Inseparable." Then *The San Diego Union* moved to its new headquarters downtown. The removal of the records was finally carried out quietly in April 1871, and the historic pueblo took second place. A disastrous fire swept through the area in 1872 and sealed Old Town's fate. Nevertheless, a number of residents remained and one observer in 1873 wrote that "Old Town has the finest school house in the Pueblo, with an average attendance of 75 pupils.... The residences of our citizens are generally comfortable even if not of the highest style of architecture."

City Park

Alonzo Horton may have been blessed with Yankee ingenuity, but a significant key to San Diego's development was its Hispanic heritage —not because of its missions, presidios, and ranchos but because of its pueblo lands. When San Diego's Chamber of Commerce was formed by a small group of citizens in January 1870 it could point with pride to some eleven square leagues or 47,324 acres of municipally-owned lands—its inheritance from Spain's practice of preserving ample lands for city purposes and the common benefit of all settlers. Fortunately, Horton, the chamber's first treasurer, and certain Old Town residents knew what they had. With a farsightedness hardly equaled by today's most ardent planners, they set aside 1,400 acres for a public park.

Horton first talked about the idea of a public park in 1867 when he asked trustees Joseph S. Mannassee, Thomas H. Bush, and Ephraim Morse to consider two 160-acre tracts as park sites. Some thought a 320-acre park more than sufficient for a town of 2,310 people. Morse—perhaps thinking of his native Boston Common— felt that since the city had 40,000 acres available, they should reserve nine tracts or 1,440 acres. He suggested the land bounded by Sixth, 28th, Ash, and Upas.

Before the final resolution was passed by new trustees José Guadalupe Estudillo, Marcus Schiller, and Joshua Sloane in May 1868, 40 acres to the south between Ash and Date were sold. Strenuous attempts were made to reduce the amount of park land, but trustee Estudillo, joined by James McCoy and Matthew Sherman, requested that the state legislature approve the transfer of the land to park purposes. It was done on February 4, 1870. The final amended federal survey of San Diego's pueblo grant was not completed until 1872, but the 47,324 acres of the Fitch survey was confirmed by the United

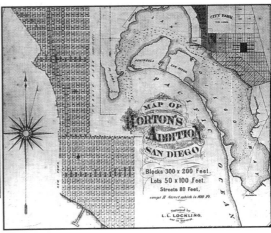

Alonzo Horton. Map of
Horton's Addition. *Photo ©San
Diego History Center.*

States in 1874. Eighteen years later, in 1890, 83 percent of the land
was gone, having been conveyed by the city to private interests. The
park (a portion of the 8,000 acres still owned by the city) remained
a wilderness area covered by dense chaparral and a few patches of
yellow, white, and blue flowers of wild adenostema, sagebrush,
Spanish violets, shooting stars, milulas, and white popcorn.

The Chamber of Commerce

Workmen broke ground on the first day of January 1870 for the
grand Horton House Hotel, a magnificent structure planned to
grace the heart of the city. The newly formed chamber of commerce
had first met at David Felsenheld's store at Sixth and F Streets the
same month. They elected Aaron Pauley as president and Horton
as treasurer. They discussed the need for better transportation to
San Diego, especially a railroad, and planned harbor improvements,
a new courthouse, a library, schools, and churches. Their first
brochure reflected the optimism and broad horizons of these early
residents when they predicted San Diego would be "the natural
commercial center of a vast scope of country, rich in mineral and
agricultural wealth" embracing all of the Southwest and northern
Mexico. All the city needed was for Congress to approve the building

of a railroad to the Pacific so that "the bulk of traffic between the States east of the Mississippi and the Asiatic ports" would pass through San Diego.

The men were wrong about the railroad, but were undaunted in their spirit. On the positive side, a minor rush to the backcountry had occurred with the discovery of gold by rancher Fred Coleman, an African American who had escaped slavery in the South. He lived simply with his Indian wife and children north of the Cuyamacas. In February, shortly before Washington's birthday, another major discovery was made of gold-bearing quartz; the George Washington Mine was soon opened. Among those in the area at the time were Drury, James, and Frank Bailey and their cousins Mike and Webb Julian, all from Georgia.

Gold Strike in Julian

Drury Bailey had homesteaded much of the land because of its scenic beauty and founded Julian City in honor of his cousin Mike. In August a new discovery was made by Julian's assayer Louis Redman, who marked the spot with an American (some say Confederate) flag. This "banner" gave its name to the spot, now at the foot of Banner Grade on Highway 78. A number of other mines were opened but within a few years the quantity and quality of gold declined. One by one the mines closed, leaving Julian a picturesque but quiet town in the heart of apple country. Another black family achieved prominence as the builders of the Robinson Hotel in Julian. Albert and Margaret Robinson built the hotel in 1887 and operated it for 28 years until Albert's death in 1915. Margaret later sold it for $1,500. Today, renamed the Julian Hotel, it is the oldest continuously operated hotel in southern California.

New Town Development

By June 1870, residents of San Diego thought a bank would be appropriate since anyone of substance either had to buy a safe, hide his money, or ship it to San Francisco. On June 9, the Bank of San

Horton House, built in 1870 on D Street (Broadway). *Photo ©San Diego History Center.*

Diego was officially formed with a capitalization of $100,000 and officers Alonzo Horton, president; James M. Pierce, vice president; and Bryant Howard, treasurer. *The San Diego Union* hailed the bank's formation and later that same month moved its offices to Fourth and D Streets. In less than a year, the paper became a daily with 400 subscribers. Western Union opened a telegraph line in August.

The palatial 100-room Horton House held its gala opening on October 10, 1870. The building—construction was supervised by Horton's brother-in-law William W. Bowers—was one of the most sumptuous of the times. All rooms were richly carpeted and boasted marble-top tables and washstands. They were connected to the desk by a bell. The 360-degree view from the hotel's observatory was breathtaking. Water from a 55-foot-deep well supplied a 7000-gallon tank that could provide 2,000 gallons of water per hour. The $150,000 hotel took its place beside the Grand in Paris, the Astor in New York, the Cosmopolitan in San Francisco, and the Pico in Los Angeles. Horton set aside a half block across the street as a plaza so his guests would have a place to sit in the sun.

The hotel's first clerk was a young man just turned twenty—George White Marston. His family had known the Hortons in Wisconsin and there learned about San Diego. George stayed at the hotel for six months and then went to work in merchandising. In three years, Marston and Charles S. Hamilton bought out Joseph Nash and started a store of their own. San Diego had a sizable

Hispanic population, and Horton House guests included travelers from all parts of the world, American soldiers from Arizona, miners from Baja California, and the usual number of adventurers.

As 1870 closed, prospects for San Diego looked bright. Assessed valuation of real estate in the city was $2.28 million with a population of about 3,000. There were 915 occupied houses and 69 business buildings. The San Diego County Medical Society was founded in 1870 and the area boasted 73 physicians and 11 dentists by 1872. New Town and Old Town struggled to see which would become the civic center. When Old Town defender George Pendleton died in March 1871, the board of supervisors appointed Chalmers Scott to his offices of county clerk and recorder. The board then leased a part of Horton's Express Building at Sixth and G Streets and turned the first floor into a courtroom with the clerk's office upstairs. County judge Thomas Bush had vigorously opposed moving San Diego's records to the new location, but he accepted the inevitable without further protest. On April 14, the South San Diego or New Town post office became the San Diego post office. The fire that devastated Old Town in 1872 further sealed the fate of the city's first center.

With the official move of the county seat, the board of supervisors accepted Horton's offer of a site for a new courthouse at D (later Broadway) and Front Streets. When the cornerstone was laid in August, speaker E.D. French said he "hoped the ill feeling...between Old and New San Diego might be buried in the stone." The elegant courthouse was completed in June 1872, and, with three additions, served for 90 years as courtroom, jail, and most county offices. With this building occupied, Horton had succeeded in doing almost all he had set out to do. There was one major exception—no railroad seemed to be on the horizon.

Waiting for the Railroad

In 1868 Frank and Warren Kimball from New Hampshire had purchased the 26,632 acres of Rancho de la Nación for $30,000 from a financial firm in San Francisco on behalf of themselves and brother

Frank Kimball and his home in National City built in 1868. *Photo by Steven Schoenherr.*

Levi. Hoping that a railroad would soon be coming to San Diego, they cleared and laid out a 100-foot-wide thoroughfare six miles long and marked out a town they called National City. The Kimball brothers also built a wharf and competed with San Diego for the terminus of the southern railroad. The northern transcontinental line had been completed May 10, 1869. So far the steamer *Orizaba* had brought most newcomers to San Diego. Its skipper, Henry James Johnston, purchased 65 acres in what became Mission Hills. His daughter eventually built Villa Orizaba overlooking the harbor.

In the spring of 1871, Congress passed a bill approving construction of the Texas & Pacific Railroad. Speculation was rife when Colonel Thomas Scott, president of the company, came to the Horton House to check over possible depot sites. The offer of enough open land and town property assured location of the terminus on San Diego Bay. Property values went up accordingly. But the untimely failure of the great railroad speculator Jay Cook on "Black Friday," September 18, 1873, caused the end of Texas & Pacific plans. Ten miles of graded road were abandoned, and San Diego was left with a number of jobless—and soon to be homeless—railroad workers.

During this time, a few developments occurred in the large City Park. A fair-sized Indian *ranchería* remained in the south part near

Eighth and Date under the leadership of El Capitan, a Kumeyaay who claimed ownership of the entire pueblo. The San Diego Water Company, organized in 1872, had obtained permission from the city to drill a well in Pound (Cabrillo) Canyon named for an animal pound set up by the city for stray cattle and horses. Two reservoirs with 70,000-and 100,000-gallon capacities were built on the mesa flanking the canyon. In 1875 the water company drilled a well at the foot of Sandrock Grade on the river and pumped water up to a reservoir at Fifth and Hawthorne. Unfortunately for San Diego, the lack of water was frequently interrupted by floods that swelled the river over its banks. In 1875 Congress appropriated $80,000 to channel the river back into False Bay (Mission Bay) since silt and sand had washed down until Derby's Dike was no longer functional. Still the park area, high on the mesa, was difficult to supply with water.

The economy had taken a setback in 1873 with the collapse of the railroad, but it seemed to recover year by year. In 1874, Daniel Cleveland and Oliver Sanford, two amateur naturalists living in San Diego, talked about the abundance of plant life and the wide variety of beetles and birds in the area. On the evening of October 1, they were joined by eight business colleagues in forming the San Diego Society of Natural History, which would eventually start a museum. In the backcountry, vineyards and orchards flourished. Pioneer beekeeper J.S. Harbison of Harbison Canyon shipped 33 carloads of honey to the East.

The Southern Pacific railroad finally connected Los Angeles to San Francisco in 1876, and plans continued to be made for a southern connection. A number of Chinese families moved into town after the railroad to Los Angeles was completed. They formed the nucleus of Chinatown around Wo Sung & Co.'s importing house on Third Street. By 1879 a new group of businessmen sent Frank Kimball to Boston to encourage the Santa Fe to build a line to San Diego. The residents of California's most southern city also noted the adoption of the state's new constitution in 1879.

San Diego's first Santa Fe Depot ca. 1880s. *Photo ©San Diego History Center.*

Frank Kimball called upon the president of the Atchison, Topeka & Santa Fe and offered to help form a syndicate to accept subsidies from San Diego and National City. In October 1880, the California Southern Railroad was incorporated. Its route would begin at National City and pass through San Diego, Encinitas, Temecula, and San Jacinto to Colton, where it would cross the Southern Pacific and join the Atlantic & Pacific at Waterman Junction (Barstow). Problems with the Southern Pacific were finally overcome and tracks were laid to San Bernardino.

The Boom of the Eighties

Then, on February 28, 1884, southern California suffered a twenty-inch downpour that washed out the tracks from San Luis Rey to Temecula in an avalanche of mud and water. Repairs began immediately, and on November 9, 1885, the California Southern joined the Atchison, Topeka & Santa Fe, which had bought out the Atlantic & Pacific at Waterman Junction. The first train left the depot at the foot of D Street on November 15 amid praises from both Horton and Kimball. The first train from the East—two coaches, a mail and baggage car—arrived on November 21 in a driving rain but with great excitement. The speculation about things to come set off what would soon be called the "Boom of the Eighties." Passengers could get from coast to coast in a week, and agricultural products such as honey, oranges, lemons, potatoes, salt, fish, butter, and wool could be shipped to new markets.

The decade of the eighties was definitely innovative. The first county fair was held in National City in September 1880, and visitors were impressed by the variety of fruits. Apples, grapes, raisins, peaches, pears, figs, apricots, berries, olives, and citrus fruits were the major crops in fertile valleys south and east of San Diego proper. The El Cajon Valley was blooming with vineyards.

Downtown, five prominent San Diegans met in the parlor of the Consolidated Bank on April 18, 1881, to incorporate the San Diego Gas Company. The company organizers—Ephraim W. Morse, lawyer and businessman; Oliver S. Witherby, judge; Bryant Howard, banker; George Cowles, rancher; James S. Gordon and George W. Hazzard, store owners; and Dr. Robert M. Powers, physician, had met with M.G. Elmore of the San Francisco Petroleum Gas Company early in the year to plan the founding of a company to manufacture gas. All were former easterners who were involved in promoting San Diego, a city with few natural resources that could be turned into energy. Nevertheless, they imported the necessary machinery, shipped in on the steamer *Orizaba*, and began construction of a "gas works" at Tenth and M (Imperial) Streets.

On June 5, 1881, *The San Diego Union* reported that "Fifth Street was thronged last evening by our citizens, old and young, who had turned out to witness the novelty of the inauguration of the new gas works, and the stores and business places presented a brilliant appearance." On June 14, 1881, the board of directors voted that a telephone be placed at "the works." This was the first office phone and joined those of Gordon & Hazzard, the local banks, and about 20 other telephones in use in the city. The San Diego Telephone Company had begun with thirteen subscribers that same month. The Gas Company changed to the production of coal gas in 1883.

Freight and storage wagon belonging to Pioneer Trucking founded by
E.B. Gould and Roscoe Hazard. *Photo courtesy Gary Gould.*

Coal was brought in from Australia, England, and later from Nanaimo
on Vancouver Island.

During 1882, George Marston helped organize the YMCA and
the Public Library, and a year later the Bank of Southern California
was formed with Jacob Gruendike as president. It joined the
Consolidated Bank of San Diego, a merger of the Bank of San Diego
and the Commercial Bank. Gruendike's bank became the First
National Bank in 1885. Dr. Hiram W. Gould, who arrived in mid-
1883, bought some lots at Fifth and C and opened a dental office.

Helen Hunt Jackson's *Ramona*

Helen Hunt Jackson arrived in San Diego in 1883 to gather the
material for *Ramona*, a novel set in California during the Mexican
period. Jackson, author of *A Century of Dishonor*, a book documenting
Indian wrongs during the previous 100 years, hoped to popularize
her information in a novel that would appeal to the reading public.
She was particularly concerned about the treatment of Native
Americans in San Diego and made friends with Father Antonio
Ubach, sponsor of an Indian school.

Father Ubach had moved to New Town and established St.
Joseph's Catholic Church on some lots at Third and Beech Streets

donated by Horton for the church in 1875. Father Ubach became a
model for Jackson's Father Gaspara. In later years, the idea that
Ramona's marriage place was located in Old Town's Estudillo House
was circulated by San Diego promoters. Jackson did spend some time
with Isadora Bandini Couts at Rancho Guajome near San Luis Rey
and studied Indian conditions in the county. Guajome, along with
Rancho Camulos in Ventura County, may also have inspired Jackson's
description of California rancho life.

San Diego High School Founded

On August 8, 1881, the board of trustees set aside 8.48 acres at the
south-central edge of City Park for a grammar school. Joseph Russ,
a lumberman, donated wood to build the school, which was completed
in 1882. It became known as Russ School and later grew into San
Diego High School. Some dedicated citizens cleared the scraggly
ground cover of sagebrush and chaparral to put some plants in the
park's hard dry soil. They irrigated the area from the reservoirs there,
and soon the land began to bloom. In December 1884, eleven persons,
including George Marston, Melville Klauber, and Charles Hamilton,
petitioned the trustees to allow them to plant—at their own expense—
some eucalyptus trees along a rough road in the park and make some
further improvements. New park questions arose as it was officially
surveyed in 1885.

City Park Developments

The US Army offered to trade its downtown San Diego barracks site
for a park location in December 1886, but opponents of the exchange
won out. Supporters pointed out that the cost of improving the land
was far beyond the means of San Diego. Instead, it should be sold in
stages until only a reasonable 640 acres remained. On December 2,
1887, city trustees granted Bryant Howard and Ephraim W. Morse
100 acres on the promontory between 18th Street and Florida canyons
to build an orphan's home, a boys' and girls' home, a kindergarten,
an industrial school, and a school of technology. The money came

Kate Sessions. *Photo courtesy © San Diego Natural History Museum.*

from the J.M. Pierce estate and gifts from Judge Oliver Witherby and others including Howard himself. The trustees also granted five acres for a home for women in adverse circumstances.

Some of the city fathers began to question incursions into the park, and George Marston asked the city not to confirm the grant. It was done nevertheless, and in 1890 Howard planted the grounds of the "Charities Tract" with more than 3,000 trees—mainly blue and sugar gums, acacias, pepper trees, fan palms, and cypresses. Irrigation pipes and roads were laid out to the new Orphan's Home and Women's Home in the park. In 1889 the Ladies Annex of the San Diego Chamber of Commerce had raised $514 and planted trees and bushes on fourteen acres between Juniper and Palm Streets on the west. Under the guidance of pioneer horticulturist Kate Sessions, a graduate of the University of California, Berkeley, the women planted some 700 trees and shrubs. Sessions had tried her hand at teaching biology at Russ School but preferred plants to students.

Irrigation water was a continual problem, so the women began to take water from the fire hydrants near the park. The water company complained but allowed the practice to go on. Residents of the nearby Golden Hill area, led by Leroy Wright and Matt Heller, planted trees, laid out a nine-hole golf course—the city's first—and kept the area as green as possible. When Bryant Howard lost his fortune in the panic of 1893, he could no longer maintain or improve the 100-acre Charities Tract as stipulated in his deed from the city, so the property reverted to the grantor. Soon the Children's Industrial Home burned down.

The Hotel del Coronado

While the "Boom of the Eighties" was in full swing, some key buildings were constructed. Among these were William W. Bowers's beautiful Florence Hotel at Fourth and Fir and the four-story St. James Hotel between Sixth and Seventh on F. But the most exciting hotel of all was that incredible edifice dreamed up by Elisha S. Babcock, a retired railroad executive from Evansville, Indiana, and H.L. Story, a piano manufacturer from Chicago. One of their pastimes had been to row across San Diego Bay and shoot rabbits, so they purchased the entire peninsula in December 1885 for $110,000 and incorporated under the name of Coronado Beach Company. They promised to build the largest hotel in the world—one so elegant that it would be "too gorgeous to be true."

Late in 1886 Babcock brought in brothers James and Merritt Reid, architects originally from New Brunswick, Canada, who attended McGill University and later worked for a prominent firm of architects in Boston. James Reid had moved to Evansville, Indiana, in 1877, where he established the Reid Brothers architectural firm with brother Merritt in 1878. The two brothers met Elisha Babcock, who convinced them to go to San Diego County and build the Hotel del Coronado as a showpiece for his new development.

Babcock and Story auctioned off a million dollars worth of land in a short time and decided that Coronado should be dry except for the hotel, which would have a monopoly on drinks. Babcock and Story built a wharf, organized the Coronado Ferry Company, and built the San Diego Street Car Company that had lines around the city and up to the park. In September 1886 they bought the Jenney

Hotel del Coronado during the 1880s. *Photo courtesy Natural History Museum of Los Angeles County.*

Electric plant in San Diego that had been operating the first street lights—six electric-carbon arc lamps mounted on 110-foot-tall towers. They planned to install water gas manufacturing equipment to supply electricity and gas to their proposed hotel. Their new company, however, was short lived and merged with the new San Diego Gas, Fuel and Electric Light Company that was formed on April 15, 1887, just as construction began on the hotel. The structure would include electric bells throughout, 2,500 incandescent light bulbs, and several arc lights. It also had gas jets for backup lighting, with gas supplied by the hotel's coke oven.

Babcock and Story promoted their magnificent hotel in newspapers and magazines. They boasted 399 rooms, most with a fireplace and wall safe. The breathtaking circular dining room remained unobstructed by a single pillar, and thousands of guests could move freely about the room. The grand ballroom, conveniently terraced, also provided a spectacular open feeling. The workmen were mostly Chinese from San Francisco, and the hotel staff came from Boston. The Hotel del Coronado, landscaped by Kate Sessions, opened on Saint Valentine's Day 1888—just as the land boom began to collapse around it.

A Search for Water

The water seekers had been busy during this time finding new sources for the growing number of residents. John D. Spreckels—a sugar-refining magnate and son of Claus Spreckels of Hawaii and San Francisco—purchased a half interest in the Otay Water Company in 1885. Under the new name of the Southern California Mountain Water Company, they supplied the city with most of its water and built a large dam. The San Diego Flume Company was organized that same year to bring water from the upper reaches of the San Diego River to the heart of the city. The company built the Cuyamaca Dam, and when its wooden flume was completed in February 1889, a number of dignitaries including Governor Robert Waterman rode down the flume at breakneck speed. A giant celebration was staged in San Diego with fountains of water 125 feet high streaming out of nozzles on street corners. No longer would the city be dependent upon exhaustible wells. The actual flume water had been held up— but no matter—they celebrated with water from wells and soon the "real" water arrived.

Spreckels went on to invest in other businesses, primarily a warehouse on the waterfront called Spreckels Brothers Commercial Company. He was an economic survivor. He eventually took over most of the Babcock and Story interests as their fortunes collapsed with falling land prices. In 1903 Spreckels assumed complete ownership of the luxurious Hotel del Coronado, all unsold lots on Coronado, the Silver Strand, and North Island. He also bought up various streetcar lines as they, too, failed.

A Decade of Firsts

There were other firsts of the decade—the San Diego Yacht Club, founded with 55 members on June 8, 1886, in Horton Hall, used the Ballast Point Lighthouse as a clubhouse beginning in 1891. The Cuyamaca Club, established in 1887 for purely social purposes, was immediately popular with the growing business community. In 1888 a group of San Diegans formed the Excelsior Rowing and Swim Club but dropped the name Excelsior in 1891 and became the San Diego Rowing Club. In eight years members raised the $2,000 necessary to build their first boathouse on pilings in San Diego Harbor that would

Owner Jesse Shepard;
Villa Montezuma. *Photos by Steven Schoenherr.*

house the Rowing Club for 79 years. The ZLAC Rowing Club for women was founded in 1892 and presently occupies a boathouse in Pacific Beach. These "wholesome" activities offset somewhat the 71 saloons and alleged 120 houses of prostitution.

The Fourth of July, 1888, brought fireworks, a brass band, and a special celebration featuring an oration by Clara Shortridge Foltz, the first woman admitted to the practice of law in California. In 1888 her residence and office was on Seventh and F Streets. She edited a daily newspaper, the *Bee*, along with her other activities. The *Bee* merged with *The San Diego Union* in 1889, and Foltz became a deputy district attorney in Los Angeles. She ran for governor in 1930. The year 1889 also saw the founding of the San Diego Savings Bank.

The Villa Montezuma

Another famous resident of San Diego was the mysterious Benjamin Henry Jesse Francis Shepard, a slender man with a handlebar mustache. He arrived in town at the age of 38 with the trappings of great wealth. With the help of local developers, he built a beautiful Victorian home at the corner of 20th and K Streets and called it the Villa Montezuma. Shepard was quite a singer with an impressive range—four octaves from low to high C. Concerts and seances were held at the villa, and some said Shepard was in tune with the spirit world. Father Ubach encouraged him to give up spiritualism, and in

1889 he joined the Catholic Church. Just after that, he moved to Los Angeles, but his magnificent villa has been preserved by the city and restored by the San Diego Historical Society. It is a showplace of stained glass windows, hand-carved fireplaces, and other Victorian features such as a gabled roof with cupolas and towers. The interior features Spanish cedar, redwood, and Douglas fir. It would be difficult to exaggerate the beauty of this historic house.

Beach Devlopment

Mission Bay was known as False Bay until Harr Wagner, a San Francisco publisher, came to town and produced a literary journal called the *Golden Era*. He ran a contest to rename the bay since he thought it was a miniature of San Diego Bay. Rose Hartwick Thorpe won the contest with the name "Mission" and *Golden Era* ran a poem that spoke of the "peaceful waters of fair Mission Bay—now blue, now gray." Pacific Beach—hoping to gain settlers for its new subdivision—advertised the establishment of the San Diego College of Letters at Lamont and Garnet Streets.

By 1887, La Jolla was also promoting itself as an ideal beach town with fascinating caves and popular picnic spots along its shores. Frank T. Botsford and George W. Heald, the first subdividers, planted more than 1,000 trees on the barren cliffs above the ocean. Many trees died from lack of water, but those that survived enhance La Jolla today.

Ocean Beach was developed by William (Billy) Carlson and Frank J. Higgins. They changed the name from Mussel Beach, so given by Old Towners who gathered mussels there for Sunday picnics. They called Ocean Beach the greatest seaside resort in southern California and opened the Cliff House Hotel in 1888. The promised rail connection from Old Town through Roseville and over the hill (Point Loma) to Ocean Beach failed because of mudslides, and the hotel burned down in 1894.

Carlson and Higgins also promoted Monument City, near today's San Ysidro, at the southeast corner of the United States. They

The Lakeside Inn ca. 1889; torn down in 1920. *Photo ©San Diego History Center.*

promised a beautiful hotel, but it suffered the same fate as other developments in the area such as Oneanta by the Sea, a health resort in the Tia Juana River Valley; Tia Juana City, five miles inland; and Otay "the Magic City" ten miles southeast of San Diego. When the boom of the '80s ended, these cities were only paper promotions. Santiago Argüello's huge rancho near the border area remained essentially as it was during the Mexican period. A survivor of the boom was the luxurious Lakeside Inn, a three-story hotel with 89 rooms on Lindo Lake. Built in 1887, it was a popular stage stop after a four-hour ride from San Diego. The opening of a railroad in 1889 made the trip much easier. The inn continued to operate until 1916.

City Government

Key developments took place in city government during the final year of the decade. Voters prohibited further sale of the remaining pueblo lands and reserved 369 acres to preserve the Torrey pines. A new charter made San Diego a class four city and provided for the election of a mayor. The state legislature approved the new charter on March 16. Douglas Gunn became the first elected mayor in 37 years, and

La Jolla Cove ca. 1889. *Photo courtesy ©San Diego History Center.*

the new form of government—including a paid fire department under a board of fire commissioners and a board of harbor commissioners— went into operation in May. It came into being just as city and county assessments dropped seriously—from $40 million in 1888 to $25 million in 1890.

The collapse of the boom was disastrous to a number of land speculators and especially to New San Diego's prime mover Alonzo Horton. He was then 75 and living in his white mansion on First Street. In 1889 his wife Sarah was tragically killed in a carriage accident. During the next few years, he lost some of his remaining properties because of delinquent taxes, but kept his hand in San Diego's development. As the 1890s dawned, the population of the city had leveled off to around 16,000. Although it was a large drop from previous years, it seemed stable. Much would happen during the next few decades, but events could hardly equal those of the previous 20 years.

Chapter VII

THE VICTORIAN ERA: 1890–1910

The decade of the 1890s began with a minor recession. San Diego's natural resources could not readily be seen by the casual visitor entering the harbor, since the productive agricultural land lay inland and to the north. The El Cajon Valley, Lemon Grove, the Valle de las Viejas, Julian, Mesa Grande, Escondido, Bear Valley, Fallbrook, and Santa Margarita all produced fair crops of grain even when other southern California areas failed. The possibilities for vineyards and citrus production were great. Some of the new arrivals moved into these areas and became successful farmers.

Financial Failures

The "Boom of the Eighties," however, had not depended upon agricultural productivity in the backcountry. It grew from land speculation involving hundreds of urban lots in the center of town and on the coast. These lots, although in ideal locations, were useful only for permanent homes, vacation cottages, or businesses—all of which depended upon an influx of people. When the dreamed-of thousands of newcomers went home or failed to come at all—the many lots from Carlsbad through Del Mar, La Jolla, and southward to the Mexican border went begging. The sunshine and healthful climate attracted some, but even "immunity from lightning, tornadoes and storms of any kind, from hydrophobia, yellow fever, cholera and other things" could not stop the panic of 1893 from hitting the county. Nevertheless, permanent and positive gains were made.

At the beginning of the 1890s, San Diego was still not on any main railroad line and began to feel the pinch of rivalry with Los Angeles. Passengers bound for San Diego were warned that there was no good drinking water in the southern city and were told to buy jugs of water if they insisted upon going. John D. Spreckels, who purchased *The San Diego Union* in 1890, combated such bad publicity by promoting the city's positive aspects. Nevertheless, Spreckels kept his Coronado interests definitely separate, since he favored Coronado's withdrawal from San Diego by municipal election in 1890. Even though Coronado was incorporated separately in 1891, Spreckels remained tied to San Diego through ownership of the streetcar line and promotion of a railroad to the East.

A little-known failure of the early 1890s was a branch campus of the University of Southern California that gave its name to University Avenue. In June 1886, the College Hill Land Association of San Diego, largely through efforts of the Reverend Edwin S. Chase of the San Diego Methodist Church, donated 450 acres of land north and east of the city for purchase of a building and endowment of a branch of USC. Plans and specifications for the San Diego College of Fine Arts were secured from a New York architect, excavation completed, foundation constructed, and cornerstone laid. Some houses were built in the University Heights tract west of Park Boulevard, but a lack of funds caused work on the college to be stopped.

Classes were held in the San Diego Bank of Commerce building until further financial setbacks forced USC to discontinue its San Diego branch. In 1896 the directors reconveyed the original site and unfinished foundation to the land company with the provision that it be donated to the state for a normal school. An Escondido seminary built by USC at a cost of $40,000 also had to be abandoned and the land was sold to the Escondido School District.

As a result of the financial panic of 1893, five of the eight San

The Family of Ah Quin, 1899. *Photo ©San Diego History Center.*

Diego banks failed, leaving only the First National Bank, Bank of Commerce, and San Diego Savings Bank, which later became the San Diego Trust & Savings Bank. The latter institution, under President Joseph W. Sefton, withstood the panic while the First National Bank, with which it shared premises, closed its doors temporarily on June 21, 1893. When depositors thought San Diego Savings had also closed, Sefton ordered the common doors reopened and, according to *The San Diego Union*, placed a notice in the window that his bank was not closed and would not be. "'We have our own vaults,' said President Sefton, 'and our accounts and our money are kept separate from those of the First National Bank.'" In order to avoid further problems, Sefton moved the bank to new quarters in the Keating Block at Fifth and F Streets in 1894.

New Businesses

Even though times were difficult, some early businesses, such as Marston's, remained solvent, and some new ones began. Joseph Jessop opened a jewelry store in 1890, and Matt Heller started a cash-and-carry grocery store. The Chinese cornered the laundry and produce businesses. Cable cars came to San Diego in 1890 and a powerhouse was built on the southwest corner of Fourth and Spruce. On June 7, 1890, the first cable car, carrying the San Diego Guard Band, ran down Fourth to C, then to Sixth, and down Sixth to the waterfront. The cable cars worked well and the line was extended out Fourth to University Avenue and then out Normal to the bluffs overlooking Mission Valley. John Spreckels soon built Mission Cliff Gardens, a beautiful little park to be seen on the cable car ride.

Exotic Newcomers

Ulysses S. Grant Jr. came to San Diego in 1892, bought the Horton House in 1895, and made plans to build the US Grant Hotel. Grant bought a three-story mansion at Eighth and Ash built in 1888 by Ora S. Hubbell, a local banker and president of the San Diego Gas, Fuel and Electric Light Company. The mansion had a magnificent view and contained 25 rooms, a spiral staircase, stained-glass windows, and marble fireplaces.

The Grant's governess, Miss Anna Held, a German immigrant, began buying land in La Jolla soon after her arrival and in 1894 started building some small cottages above La Jolla Cove. She called them the Green Dragon Colony. She married Max Heinrich, a singer and musician, and together they designated their colony as a cultural center for artists, musicians, and writers. Anna Held Heinrich later sold her La Jolla property and returned to Germany, leaving there for London when Hitler came to power.

The lavishly decorated Fisher Opera House also opened its doors in 1892, but it did not remain self-sustaining for long. John C. Fisher had built it at the cost of $100,000 on money borrowed from the California National Bank. It was built of steel and brick with a seating capacity of 1,400. It was decorated with red Brussels carpeting, red velvet seats, and elegant crystal chandeliers. To the dismay of local opera fans, it was sold to theosophist Katherine Tingley for her dramatic productions.

CABRILLO ENTERING SAN DIEGO BAY.

On Sept. 28 A.D. 1542, Juan Rodriguez Cabrillo in command of two Spanish ships, discovered & entered the Bay of San Diego, which he described as "a land-locked and very good harbor."

1542 SAN DIEGO 1892

The Cabrillo Celebration

One bright light amidst the financial failures of 1892 was the 350th anniversary of Juan Rodríguez Cabrillo's landing on California shores. Mayor Matthew Sherman sent out engraved invitations to the festivities to be held on the wharf at the foot of D Street. Manuel Cabral, a Portuguese fisherman, dressed in a velvet suit and plumed hat, was scheduled to arrive at high tide in a ship representing the *San Salvador.* He missed the high tide mark and the ship stuck in the mud 300 feet from dry land. The awaiting crowd surged to the railing to get a better look, but the rickety wooden structure gave way, and many dignitaries, including Mayor Sherman, fell into the mud. Cabral nevertheless unfurled the Spanish flag and took possession of the area in the name of Spain. Marching military bands, including one from Mexico City, took part in the parade down D Street to Horton Plaza. Father Ubach brought a group of Indians from San Luis Rey to perform their native dances. The three-day celebration cost the city $5,000 but began a tradition continuing to the present.

Other "historic" traditions included a half-day excursion to the "Old Spanish Lighthouse" by "Reuben the Guide." Reuben dressed as a Mexican and told stories about the Point Loma lighthouse, which had actually been built in 1854 by the United States government.

San Diego State Normal School. *Fitch photo courtesy San Diego Gas & Electric Company.*

Robert D. Israel and his family lived on the point and tended the light from 1871 to 1891. The Israels delighted in visits by tourists who made the long trek out to see the lighthouse. Later, in 1913, Spanish, Portuguese, and American traditions were combined in the Cabrillo National Monument.

A State Normal School

The chamber of commerce promoted the idea of a state normal school for San Diego in 1894. In 1895 a bill passed the state legislature authorizing the school but was vetoed by the governor. Finally, in 1897, it passed again and became the law. The first class met in rooms in a new building at Sixth and F built on the site of Horton's Hall that had burned the previous year. The normal schools were established by the state for teacher training, and those attending had to sign an agreement to teach at the completion of their studies. When the school's president, Samuel T. Black, began to look for a new site for the expanding classes, the College Hill Land Association that had promoted the University Heights development offered eleven acres at Normal and El Cajon Boulevard for the state school. A magnificent white building with Doric columns was dedicated on May 1, 1899, with Alonzo Horton as honored guest. University Heights grammar school had opened at University and Vermont during the mid-1890s.

Landscaping City Park

In 1892, Kate Sessions leased 30 acres of City Park land at Sixth and Upas for a plant nursery in exchange for setting out 100 park trees per year and giving the city another 300 trees. She introduced the cork oak from Spain, camphor from Asia, rubber trees from the tropics, and several kinds of eucalyptus from Australia. She cultivated seeds from Baja California, South America, and elsewhere to earn the name "Mother of Balboa Park."

But the greatest impetus to park development came in 1902 when the San Diego Chamber of Commerce formed a Park Improvement Committee to develop a master plan and solicit funds. At the urging of Sessions, horticulturist Mary Coulston, Julius Wangenheim, and others on the chamber committee, George Marston offered to bring in a professional landscape artist to design the park. He hired Samuel Parsons Jr., president of the American Society of Landscape Architects and former superintendent of New York's Central Park. Parsons, who had studied seventeenth and eighteenth century picturesque parks in England and France, arrived in San Diego in 1902. He was not put off by the rocky, barren terrain. To him, it formed a "great natural picture" with its "rugged, picturesque canyons" and "spreading mesas." He staked out all tentative park roads, proposed the main trees, and sketched the overall design. From 1902–1904, Marston paid out more than $20,000, in addition to the original $10,000 paid for the Parsons Plan, and the park began to take shape.

On March 17, 1904, 2,500 school children celebrated Arbor Day by planting 60 pines and cypresses on the west edge of Cabrillo Canyon. President Theodore Roosevelt sent a telegram of congratulations saying, "Your love of trees now will make you as men and women, lovers of forests, both for their natural beauty and economic value." From 1904–1906, some 14,000 more trees and shrubs were planted in an effort to create a "natural" setting. The park was heartily supported by civic leaders, and exemplified the City Beautiful movement begun in Chicago in 1893. E.W. Scripps, owner of the *San Diego Sun* since 1891, thought that a rose garden supplying free roses "would give the plain people of the city the idea that their interest and pleasure was as much considered by the Park Commission as that of the people who rode in carriages and autos."

Planning for the Panama-California Exposition

In 1909 G. Aubrey Davidson, president of the chamber of commerce, suggested that San Diego hold an exposition to celebrate the opening of the Panama Canal in 1915. The Panama-California Exposition Company, formed in September 1909, supported a private subscription and city bond issue that raised $2 million. Park commissioners Thomas O'Halloran, Moses A. Luce, and Leroy Wright adopted the name Balboa Park since Vasco Nuñez de Balboa discovered the Pacific Ocean on September 29, 1513, and claimed the entire west coast for Spain. Other possible names considered were Cabrillo, Silver Gate, Sunset, Sierra, Paradise, Panama, and Grant. Besides tying the park to Panama, the celebration could be combined with Cabrillo's September 28th arrival. The hiring of project architect Bertram G. Goodhue brought rich decoration, exotic architecture, and multiple uses to the park. Goodhue's central complex of stuccoed Spanish colonial buildings forever set aside the Parsons Plan for a natural picturesque park—free of man-made obstructions.

The Nolen Report

In addition to park planning, the chamber of commerce hired John Nolen, a city planner from Cambridge, Massachusetts, to do a master improvement plan for the city in general. The Nolen Report of 1908 recommended the construction of a wide landscaped walkway called the Paseo descending twelve blocks between Date and Elm Streets from the park to the bay. In the best Hispanic tradition, the Paseo would have been a unique and beautiful tree-lined promenade in the heart of the city. San Diegans missed a great opportunity to enhance the downtown area when they failed to implement the plan.

San Diego Union Building. *Photo courtesy Al JaCoby.*

Competition for the News

Newspaper competition was strong during the late nineteenth century. *The San Diego Union* saw its greatest growth under John Spreckels' ownership. The installation of a Linotype in 1895 enhanced the eight-page daily, and in 1896 the *Union* outbid four rival newspapers—*Sun*, *Vidette*, *Record*, and *Tribune*—for the county tax list. James D. MacMullen, managing editor of Spreckels's San Francisco *Call*, joined the staff in 1899 and served as editor-manager until his death in 1933. Soon after MacMullen's arrival, the competition lessened. The *Union* purchased the plant of the *Morning Call*, formerly the *Vidette*, in 1900, and took over the *Tribune* (started in 1895) in September 1901. The combined papers moved into the Horton Bank Building at Third and Broadway in December 1901, and in fewer than six years built a new six-story structure, complete with a sixteen-page press.

Despite publishing rival newspapers, John Spreckels and E.W. Scripps, owner of Miramar Ranch, had common interests. With A.G. Spalding of sporting goods fame, they had purchased 7,000 acres of the Fanita Ranch in Santee in 1898. Scripps eventually bought the others out and added the Fanita Ranch to his Miramar holdings as a horse-breeding farm. In 1907, Spreckels, Scripps, and Spalding joined George Marston and Charles Kelly to protect and finally purchase the site of the ruined San Diego presidio. After publication of William E. Smythe's *History of San Diego* in 1908, the public began to take an interest in the hill behind Old Town as the "Plymouth Rock" of the Pacific coast. Another twenty years would pass before Presidio Hill would become a public park.

Spreckels and Scripps also joined Spalding on the county road commission created by the board of supervisors in 1909 to provide roads into the backcountry. Auto roads were laid out or graded from San Diego to El Cajon, north to Santee, Lakeside, Ramona, and Julian; from Julian to Cuyamaca, through Green Valley to Descanso and Pine Valley; from Fallbrook to Pala, Rincon, Warner's Hot Springs, Santa Ysabel, and Escondido, which in turn connected Escondido to Vista and Oceanside on the coast. Scripps's sister, Ellen Browning Scripps, also cooperated in city interests by helping to sponsor an institution for marine biological research in La Jolla under Dr. William Ritter in 1905 and by protecting Torrey pines on land adjacent to Torrey Pines Reserve.

The Little Landers

Historian William E. Smythe had come to San Diego from Massachusetts and run unsuccessfully for Congress in 1902. He claimed San Diego was ridden with monopolies and corruption. With George P. Hall, he promoted a cooperative farming community with a campaign of "a little land and a living" south of San Diego. The "Little Landers" purchased 550 acres in the Tia Juana River Valley and sold one-acre plots from $350 to $550 and lots at $250. On opening day January 11, 1909, twelve families bought lots, and the colony began. The "farmers" consisted mostly of professional people who attempted to survive by growing their own food and sharing their profits. Many had to work outside the area to sustain the experiment.

The Point Loma Theosophical Institute

Another cooperative effort on a much larger scale was the theosophical movement promoted by Katherine Tingley on 132 acres of choice Point Loma land. An attractive, thrice-married, childless matron

Point Loma Theosophical Society ca. 1910. Inset, Katherine Tingley. *Photo Point Loma Nazarene.*

from Massachusetts, Madame Tingley had successfully taken over leadership of a group of theosophists whose origins were in the East. Theosophy—a word derived from *theos* (God) and *sophia* (wisdom)— can be defined as speculative thought about God and the universe arising from either mystical insight or from a comparison of the teachings of various religions. Inspiration for the Point Loma community came indirectly through Helena Petrovna Blavatsky (1831–1891), a controversial Russian woman who had a great interest in spiritualism and the teachings of Indian mahatmas.

Upon Blavatsky's death, several successors struggled for leadership in theosophical thinking, but Katherine Tingley had the wisdom and foresight to win control of a major branch of followers. She proposed the founding of the School for the Revival of Lost Mysteries of Antiquity in 1896 after the aged General John Fremont in New York confirmed her dream about a place where she could build a "white city in a golden land by the sundown sea." Fremont told her of Point Loma. Without further investigation, she had her agents purchase the tract in 1896. The cornerstone for the first building was laid on February 24, 1897.

Following Tingley's leadership, theosophists from the Boston Society formed the Universal Brotherhood of Theosophists in 1900 at Point Loma. After the original School of Antiquity was completed, the Isis Conservatory of Music and Drama, the Lotus Home for refugee Cuban children, and the glass-domed Temple of Peace appeared on the landscape. A Greek theater overlooked the Pacific Ocean, and eventually there were 50 buildings on the grounds. The personal magnetism of Katherine Tingley inspired converts from all walks of life and included A.G. Spalding. Visitors frequently commented on the orderly, almost military atmosphere where uniforms were common and children sat rigidly at dining tables, observing a rule of silence. Formal classroom instruction at the Raja Yoga School was never more than three hours a day, but the students excelled in spelling, arithmetic, music, and other subjects. They also learned gardening and various useful crafts.

In October 1901, the *Los Angeles Times* published a scathing article entitled "Outrages at Point Loma exposed by an 'Escapee' from Tingley. Startling Tales told in this City. Women and Children starved and treated like Convicts. Thrilling Rescue." Katherine Tingley sued the Times Mirror Company owned by Harrison Gray Otis for libel. In 1907 the California Supreme Court upheld an award of $7,500 in favor of Mrs. Tingley. (*Tingley v. Time Mirror* 1907 151 Cal. 1.) Later, in 1923, the California Supreme Court upheld an award of damages for $100,000 against Mrs. Tingley in favor of Mrs. Irene Mohn, who had sued for alienation of affection of her husband, Dr. George Mohn. Tingley's fortunes rose and fell, but she was able during her lifetime to maintain the utopian community as a prosperous experiment.

Katherine Tingley, who died in 1929 at age 82, was succeeded by Gottfried de Purucker, a supporter as early as 1896. When de Purucker died in 1942, the theosophists left Point Loma. The site became the home of California Western University after World War II. Today it is Point Loma Nazarene College. Several of the original buildings grace the campus of this institution of higher learning.

City Builders

The turn of the century had seen San Diego embark upon a new era. In addition to already active businessmen, a group of newcomers

The US Grant Hotel ca. 1910. *Photo ©San Diego History Center.*

with equal vision took the lead. Louis J. Wilde, who arrived in 1903, organized four new banks—the Citizens Savings Bank, the American National Bank, the United States National Bank, and the First National Bank of Escondido. He built the Pickwick Theatre in 1904, the Louis J. Wilde Building, and the ten-story American National Bank building at Fifth and D Streets soon after. In 1908, when the US Grant Hotel suffered financial setbacks and looked as if it would not open, Wilde raised enough money to complete it and joined U.S. Grant Jr. as a partner. The luxury hotel, opened in 1910, cost more than $1 million and featured an exotic fountain designed by noted architect Irving Gill. The fountain—illuminated by electric lights with fifteen color effects—fittingly contained the portraits of Juan Rodríguez Cabrillo, Junípero Serra, and Alonzo Horton. Louis Wilde urged changing D Street to Broadway in 1914.

Other city builders were D.C. Collier, a promoter of Ocean Beach, and O.W. Cotton, developer of Pacific Beach and East San Diego. Ed Fletcher, a young produce merchant from Littleton, Massachusetts, thought that water to develop coastal regions could be obtained from the San Luis Rey River and other sources in the backcountry. He and his partner Frank Salmons worked for the South Coast Land

Company, which bought up lands and existing water rights along the San Luis Rey River. It obtained all of the original settlement of Del Mar, more than 800 acres in Leucadia, 1,400 acres of Agua Hedionda, nearly all of Carlsbad, and large holdings in Oceanside. Salmons meanwhile discovered a gemstone (kunzite) mine in Pala while Ed Fletcher worked on water development.

San Diego & Arizona Eastern Railway

John D. Spreckels, whose successes and power were feared by some, had retained his home in San Francisco until failing health and the great earthquake and fire of 1906 drove him to San Diego. Since his health took an immediate turn for the better, he built a mansion, complete with pipe organ, in Coronado across from his hotel. After his permanent move to San Diego, Spreckels began to promote the railroad to Yuma in earnest. After solving a series of problems involving the Southern Pacific Railroad, he and his partners surveyed the proposed route that would go through National City, the Carrizo Gorge, and 44 miles of territory in Baja California to avoid the rugged Laguna Mountains and across newly created Imperial County.

Spreckels personally obtained the right-of-way from Mexico, and Mayor John F. Forward Jr. turned the first sod on ground-breaking day, September 9, 1907. Honored guests were Alonzo Horton and Frank Kimball who must have imagined their dreams finally coming true. Because of problems of the Mexican Revolution after 1910, flooding of the Imperial Valley, World War I, and the need for 21 tunnels, the line was not completed until 1919. It cost $18 million and was an important link with Arizona. The line was partly destroyed by flash flooding from Hurricane Kathleen in 1976 but was repaired in 1980. Several tunnel fires hampered repairs during the 1980s and 1990s, and the bridge over Carrizo Gorge has needed heavy reinforcement. Today, the Carrizo Gorge Railway, an independent company contracting with the San Diego Metropolitan Transit Board, operates a freight line over the tracks from Plaster City to Tijuana. The Union Pacific Railroad operates the line from Plaster City into

San Diego & Arizona Eastern Railway trestle. *Photo ©San Diego History Center.*

Yuma, Arizona, and the San Diego Railroad Museum runs a tourist line from Campo to Miller Creek.

Irrigation Projects in the Imperial Valley

During this period, other changes were taking place to the east of San Diego. The California Development Company had made an unnatural cut in the Colorado River for an irrigation project in the Imperial Valley. Beginning in late 1905, flood waters had poured through the Colorado River bank for 16 months causing considerable damage to the New River channel and finally to creating the Salton Sea in the depressed Salton Sink area. In 1907, Imperial County was formed from 4,089 square miles of San Diego County on petition of residents there who felt that the high Laguna Mountain range divided them naturally and it was a hardship to conduct county business in San Diego. In 1908 the cities of El Centro, as county seat, and Calexico, on the Mexican border across from Mexicali, were incorporated.

The United States Navy in San Diego

San Diego made national headlines as a result of the USS *Bennington* disaster on July 21, 1905. The navy gunboat was anchored in the harbor when observers heard a deafening noise. Boilers had exploded below decks, killing 60 men and injuring 46. Dr. W.L. Kneedler, army surgeon at Fort Rosecrans, helped in rescue operations, and all San Diego physicians were called for assistance. Open wagons carried injured men to hospitals. Funeral services and a mass burial were held on July 23 at the post cemetery at Fort Rosecrans. The last rites were conducted by the Reverend J.A.M. Richey, rector of St. Paul's, and by Father Antonio Ubach of St. Joseph's.

On a different note, President Theodore Roosevelt sent the navy's Great White Fleet on a world tour in December 1907, to impress Japan and other potential rivals with America's determination to play a significant role in economic and political affairs. Sixteen battleships, seven destroyers, and four auxiliary ships under the command of Rear Admiral R.D. Evans stayed four days in San Diego harbor. Sixteen thousand sailors visited the city. Curiously, the San Francisco earthquake of 1906, coupled with anti-Japanese legislation in the northern city, had precipitated a move by many Japanese families to San Diego. Several Japanese businessmen, the nucleus of a Japanese business community around Fifth and Market Streets, were on hand to greet the Great White Fleet on April 14, 1908.

Plans for the Future

The idea of an isthmian canal was being widely discussed in San Diego as well as Washington, D.C., especially when it was shown how difficult it had been for the US Pacific Fleet to reach Cuba during the Spanish-American War. The war, which ended in August 1898, fulfilled the expansive ideas of those who wanted the United States to become a world power. The Philippine Islands and Guam, along with Puerto Rico—the remaining Spanish territories from the period of discovery and exploration—were added to the American domain. The San Diego Chamber of Commerce and other Pacific coast organizations favored a canal through Nicaragua rather than the Panama site. No matter where the canal was located, however, it meant potential new business for the port of San Diego.

By the end of the decade, San Diego's progress could easily be measured. The population had nearly reached 40,000, and the influx

The San Diego Flume ca. 1886. *Photo ©San Diego History Center.*

of people had brought business stability. Headway had also been made in solving the problem of an adequate water supply. Since an average rainfall of ten inches per year was insufficient, private companies had developed the mountain reservoirs and were selling water to the city on contract basis. From 1887 to 1897, these companies constructed six major dams in the county. Two large private concerns fought over which one could best serve the city.

The San Diego Flume Company was successful for a few years, but an eleven-year drought between 1895 and 1905 dried up the Flume's reservoir and forced it to pump brackish San Diego River water. The Southern California Mountain Water Company, organized by Elisha Babcock of Coronado and taken over by John Spreckels, had built the Upper and Lower Otay and Morena Dams. In 1906 the company agreed to deliver a maximum of nearly eight million gallons of water daily to the city at a stipulated low price for ten years. Finally, in 1913, the city, which had already purchased the San Diego Water Company in 1901, added the facilities of the Southern California Mountain Water Company and boasted a wholly owned municipal water system.

The Bishop's School 1927. *Photo courtesy of The Bishop's School.*

The Right Reverend Joseph Horsfall Johnson, bishop of the Episcopal Diocese of Los Angeles, founded the Bishop's School in 1909. Designed by Irving Gill, the La Jolla campus was made possible by gifts of land and money from Ellen Browning Scripps and her half-sister Virginia Scripps. A second tower, designed for the chapel by Carleton Winslow, was added in 1930. Originally a girls' school, Bishop's merged with the San Miguel School for Boys in 1971.

Certain key figures of New San Diego had died, but a new generation was taking over the reins of government. Ephraim W. Morse, pioneer in many areas of business, died in 1906; Father Antonio Ubach in 1907; and both William Heath Davis and Alonzo Horton in 1909. Lydia Knapp Horton, an attractive widow whom Alonzo had married in 1890, summed up her husband's feelings at the end of his life. "He had a broad vision and faith in San Diego," she said, and he "was never surprised at any of the great improvements that were made here in his later years." Nor was he sorry when the Horton House was torn down. On the contrary, he was glad to see the fine new building go up. Lydia Horton and others would see even greater changes during the next few decades.

Chapter VIII

World War I and
Postwar Progress: 1910–1930

At the time of the official ground breaking for Balboa Park's Panama-California Exposition in 1911, San Diego was an optimistic, progressive metropolis of almost 40,000 people. By the end of the decade its population would reach 75,000—a number that would nearly double again by 1930. President William Howard Taft brought national attention to the exposition's first ceremony on July 19, 1911, when at exactly 4:00 p.m. he pressed an electric button in the East Room of the White House (7 p.m. EST) and unfurled an American flag at the site. Bishop Thomas J. Conaty from Los Angeles celebrated the first pontifical military mass in San Diego since Father Serra's arrival in 1769.

Casa de Estudillo

A concurrent San Diego project completed with the opening of the Panama Canal and the Panama-California Exposition was the restoration of the Estudillo family home in Old Town. John D. Spreckels, whose streetcar line ran to the area, hired Hazel Wood Waterman, a well-known designer of local homes and colleague of noted architect Irving Gill. Waterman, the widowed daughter-in-law of California governor Robert Waterman, had achieved an excellent reputation in San Diego for her design talent. Beginning in 1910, she tackled the Estudillo house with her customary thoroughness and skill. Sally Bullard Thornton, in her biography of Hazel Waterman, has summarized her contributions. After visiting the long uninhabited site, Hazel Waterman asked herself a number of questions:

"What was here to make the preservation of this pathetic ruin worthwhile? Was there only an incident in a novel, a legend?... Father Ubach, who was like Father Gaspara in the novel [*Ramona*] had lived in a house back of the Estudillo house that was more appealing to the imagination, and so in "Ramona" we read that 'Father Gaspara's room was at the end of a long low adobe building, which...was now fallen into decay.'"

According to Thornton, Waterman arduously pursued the task of restoration by studying original manuscripts, old photographs, and the precise method of preparing adobe bricks. Only Mexican laborers were to be hired who would prepare the bricks by hand. The original floor plan was faithfully followed with each room opening to the long, low veranda. The U-shaped building had thick adobe walls with niches for religious objects. Every bedroom had a single barred window facing the street side. The Estudillo project was instantly successful and John Spreckels was pleased to promote tours to the house on his electric railway from his Hotel del Coronado.

Transportation Development

Transportation and communication by sea and land were seen as keys to the future when the Pacific Navigation Company's steamship *Yale* arrived with 400 excursionists on March 4, 1911. The ship's officers and passengers were driven around the city in automobiles decked with Yale and Harvard pennants representing the company's two new steamships. San Diegans had received 325 new cars in 1910, and road building commanded great priority. When the *Yale* departed, the pilot of an airplane from the Curtiss Flying School bombarded it with oranges to symbolize California agriculture and a new hope for the future—aviation.

John J. Montgomery had made the first controlled wing flight south of San Diego in 1883, but the Wright Brothers with their

Curtiss Flying School, North Island. *Photo courtesy Teledyne Ryan.*

immortal powered flight at Kittyhawk, North Carolina, in 1903 had made flying a national pastime for many and a commercial venture for an enterprising few. Californians soon held aviation meets, formed aero clubs, and watched barnstorming spectaculars. In 1908, Glenn Hammond Curtiss from Hammondsport, New York, built his first airplane. A year later he won the Gordon Bennett Cup race in the *Golden Flyer*. In 1911, the Spreckels-owned Coronado Beach Company offered Curtiss the use of North Island for three years to run a flying school. This was the beginning of San Diego's national reputation as a pioneering center of flight.

On January 26, 1911, Curtiss made aviation history in the world's first successful seaplane as he took off from the mile-long waters of Spanish Bight (now filled in) between Coronado and North Island. Curtiss invited the military to provide the first students for his flying school, and Lieutenant Theodore G. Ellyson became the first pupil and Navy Pilot Number One. Three army lieutenants—Paul W. Beck, G.E.M. Kelly, and John C. Walker—and three civilians—Charles Witmer, Robert St. Henry, and Lincoln Beachey, also joined the class of 1911. Curtiss and his two associates, Hugh Robinson and Eugene B. Ely, performed numerous aerial stunts at a meet sponsored by D.C. Collier's San Diego Aero Club on January 26 and 27, 1911.

Congressman William Kettner and the United States Military

William Kettner, a charter member of the Aero Club and longtime city promoter, was elected to Congress in 1912 and began to promote San Diego's ideal location for the military. The US Army Signal Corps Training School temporarily moved to North Island in 1913. It became known as Rockwell Field in 1914. Since the Coronado Beach Company had allowed Curtiss and the army to use the land free, while they paid $50,000 in taxes, they wanted the premises vacated. Kettner framed a bill for federal takeover of the property, and in 1917 sponsored an act authorizing the United States to take possession of North Island as a permanent army and navy aviation school. The act also appropriated the necessary money to compensate the landowners.

Camp Kearny

The US Army established Camp Kearny on the mesa north of Mission Valley in May 1917, based upon the ability of the San Diego Consolidated Gas and Electric Company to furnish utilities. The task of extending electric lines and gas mains 15 miles north of the city, across the San Diego River bed and over rough terrain beyond the bluffs of Mission Valley, gave the company a tough assignment. Since no gas mains lay within 10 miles of the camp, the gas-line extension had to begin from Tenth and University in Hillcrest. Construction began on June 30 and was completed on schedule August 5. Gas was used for cooking and baking in 238 mess halls, for heating water throughout the camp, and for heating in the hospital units and general offices. Even though the war ended on November 11, 1918, Camp Kearny continued in existence until 1920. A portion of the land was set aside for a marine corps installation in 1937, but the navy took over the site and built Camp Elliott during World War II.

Eleventh Naval District Headquarters

Despite the Bennington disaster of 1905, San Diego, with the help of the chamber of commerce and persons like William Kettner, was

World War I Naval Formation in Balboa Park 1917. *Photo ©San Diego History Center.*

destined to become a major base for naval operations. In 1918, the chamber raised $280,000 to purchase tidelands at the foot of 32nd Street for the Navy's first principal facility in the city, later to become a large destroyer base. In 1922 the navy completed its hospital in Balboa Park, and San Diego was named headquarters for the Eleventh Naval District. In 1923, with the beginning of the Naval Training Station, there were ten navy or marine corps bases being built or authorized, and nearly $4 million were being spent on the Naval Air Station at North Island and Ream Field in the South Bay area. With Fort Rosecrans and the marine base established in 1919, the military had become a significant factor in the city's growth. On March 12, 1925, a total of 120 ships, including scout cruisers, battleships, destroyers, submarines, and auxiliaries entered the harbor and headed for moorings in the channel. The fifteen commanding admirals and their subordinates were entertained throughout the city, beginning a tradition for San Diego as a "navy town."

Commercial Aviation in San Diego

San Diego had also readily taken to the air. The first airmail service was inaugurated in 1918 and in 1922 North Island Army Air Service Lieutenants Oakley Kelly and John Macready set a sustained flight record of 35 hours and 18 minutes. Lieutenant James H. Doolittle then set a coast-to-coast record of 21 hours and 19 minutes from Jacksonville, Florida, to San Diego. Kelly and Macready made the first nonstop transcontinental flight from New York to San Diego in May 1923 and were greeted upon their arrival by T. Claude Ryan, a young army reserve pilot from Parsons, Kansas.

Ryan, a graduate of the cadet schools at March Field in Riverside and Mather Field in Sacramento, had come to San Diego in 1922 and decided there was a future in commercial aviation. He convinced San Diego's harbormaster to let him use a small dirt landing strip on the tidelands at the foot of Broadway and bought a war surplus biplane for $400. By 1925 he had purchased more planes and moved to Dutch Flats opposite the marine base. With partner B. Franklin Mahoney, the two organized Ryan Airlines and began an air service between San Diego and Los Angeles, the first regularly scheduled year-round passenger airline in the United States. Ryan soon became dissatisfied with available airplanes and designed a high-wing monoplane—the M-l. It was produced in 90 days and tested on February 1, 1926. Later it flew more than 1,100 miles from Vancouver Field, Washington, to Los Angeles in just under ten hours.

The *Spirit of St. Louis*

Meanwhile, across the country on a night flight between St. Louis and Chicago in the fall of 1926, a young airmail pilot was thinking of the $25,000 offered as a prize for the first nonstop transatlantic flight. Charles A. Lindbergh had obtained the financial backing of his employers and other businessmen in St. Louis but could not find the proper airplane. When he read about Ryan's M-l, he felt that, with modifications, it would be right. The company was then working on a larger plane for speed flyer Frank Hawks. Ryan, who had sold his interest in Ryan Airlines but was still manager of the company, responded to Lindbergh's request for a plane by offering in 60 days a plane that could cross from New York to Paris nonstop.

Lindbergh came to San Diego to inspect the M-l. He signed a contract on February 28, 1927, for a plane to meet his requirements.

Charles Lindbergh and the *Spirit of St. Louis 1927*. *Photos courtesy Teledyne Ryan.*

When all tests were completed, the *Spirit of St. Louis*—costing just over $10,000—exceeded expectations. Lindbergh left Rockwell Field for St. Louis and completed his historic 33¹/₂ -hour flight from New York to Paris on May 21. His success brought honor and prestige to the Ryan organization and presaged the aviation industry's move into the space age. That same year, the harbor was dredged to provide a turning basin for the USS *Lexington* and *Saratoga*, the nation's first major aircraft carriers. The dredged material became the fill for Lindbergh Field, dedicated on August 16, 1928.

The Magonistas and the Mexican Revolution

San Diego's otherwise peaceful existence was interrupted by the outbreak of the Mexican Revolution in 1910. A number of conspirators, led by Ricardo Flores Magón, began slipping arms across the border into Baja California. They were members of the Marxist Liberal Party, not the mainstream revolutionaries that had overthrown Mexico's longtime dictator Porfírio Díaz. In Los Angeles they received help from members of the Industrial Workers of the World (IWW) who had come to California to organize agricultural workers. Magón had dispatched a tiny army to the Imperial Valley. These men met at the IWW headquarters in Holtville and then joined Mexicans across the border. The rebels captured Mexicali and Tecate, pressing on toward Tijuana. In San Diego, support for the rebel cause was urged by anarchist Emma Goldman who felt that American troops patrolling the border should be removed. Other IWW members arrived in San Diego and began openly recruiting rebels. When the Magonistas captured Tijuana on May 9, 1911, they hoisted a red flag with the slogan *"tierra y libertad"* meaning "land and liberty." Once the battle was over, however, no substantive changes were made and San Diego tourists began crossing the border to drink, gamble, witness a few "battles," and take home a souvenir.

The IWW in San Diego

Many IWW members remained in San Diego and began calling for the overthrow of capitalism. A confrontation with local merchants led to the passing of a city ordinance banning street-corner speaking in certain downtown areas. On February 9, 1912, police arrested 41 men for violating the anti-speech ordinance and gave impetus to the free speech movement. In March a mob of some 5,000 people gathered near the city jail but were dispersed by fire hoses. A vigilante committee of local citizens succeeded in running most IWW members out of town in April. On May 8, European-born socialist Joseph Mikolasek was shot during an encounter with police, and riots exploded in the downtown area. When Emma Goldman tried to speak in the city a week later, she too was taken by the vigilantes and placed on a train heading out of the city. This ended the IWW movement in San Diego, but the Mexican Revolution continued throughout the decade. The effects north of the California border were thereafter minor. Mexican problems began to take second place as San Diego responded to the news of Archduke Franz Ferdinand's assassination on June 28, 1914, and threats of an impending global conflict.

Opening the Panama-California Exposition in Balboa Park

The opening of the Panama-California Exposition in Balboa Park at midnight, January 1, 1915, overshadowed the spark that set off World War I. Bertram Goodhue's completed buildings represented the Spanish colonial style that he had studied and enjoyed on a visit to Mexico. Since his first assistant, architect Irving Gill, had a simpler

The Cathedral
Over the Treetops
of the Plaza

Sketch by Bertram Goodhue (inset) made during travels in Mexico in 1892.

style in mind, Goodhue hired Carleton M. Winslow of New York to help carry out the Hispanic theme. Frank P. Allen, a veteran of Seattle's World's Fair, became chief engineer and John P. Morley left a position in Los Angeles to become superintendent of parks.

Since San Francisco was planning a world's fair at the same time, San Diego decided to keep its exposition regional in character. The Santa Fe Railroad built an Indian village similar to the Pueblo of Taos, although the plan as a whole—with its baroque buildings, tree-shaded promenade (*el prado*) and open plazas—suggested a typical Spanish city of the seventeenth century. The magnificent approach via Cabrillo Canyon Bridge presented such a breathtaking view that, years later, visitors would still be impressed by Goodhue's feeling of Spain with its Mediterranean and Moorish counterparts.

At the White House, President Woodrow Wilson touched an electric button that turned on a light suspended by a balloon to open the exposition. The guns at Fort Rosecrans and those on the ships in the harbor fired in unison to signal the event. A fireworks display at the Spreckels Organ Pavilion portrayed a replica of the Panama Canal from which the prow of a ship labeled "1915" emerged. The phrase "The land divided—the world united—San Diego the first port of call" was outlined in flame.

Mayor Charles O'Neall commented with pride that the future of San Diego—metropolis of the West—seemed assured. Governor Hiram Johnson presented the California Building and California Tower to G. Aubrey Davidson, president of the exposition, for the people of San Diego. Secretary of the Treasury William Gibbs McAdoo represented President Wilson, and the Conde del Valle de Salazar appeared for King Alfonso XII of Spain at the opening. Balboa Stadium in the park was hailed as the world's largest municipal structure. Other famous visitors were Vice President Thomas R. Marshall; Theodore Roosevelt, who complimented himself for making completion of the canal possible; William Jennings Bryan; and Undersecretary of the Navy Franklin D. Roosevelt. Because of its success, the exposition was held open through 1916.

Driving Mr. Fletcher

To stimulate interest in driving to the fair, Ed Fletcher, William Gross, the actor for whom Grossmont was named, and Wilbur Hall, a magazine writer, left for Washington, D.C., on November 2, 1915, with driver Harry Taylor. They traveled the plank road to Yuma and over the new bridge spanning the Colorado River. The car—minus a few passengers—reached the Capitol after 23½ days without difficulty. San Diego had a direct automobile link with the East, but the drive presented quite a challenge to the casual visitor. The fair officially closed on December 31, 1916. At 11:59 p.m., taps sounded an emotional ending to the celebration from the Plaza de Panama, and, at the stroke of midnight, Madame Ernestine Schumann-Heink sang a tearful "Auld Lang Syne" at the Organ Pavilion. A fireworks display spelled out "World's Peace, 1917."

Smokestacks vs. Geraniums

With the closing of the fair, opinions were divided about San Diego's future course. Banker Louis Wilde promoted industrial development,

Spreckels Organ Pavilion—1915 Panama-California Exposition opening in Balboa Park.
Photo ©San Diego History Center.

while George Marston, an early promoter of environmental concerns, preferred city beautification. Indicative of the time, which included a slump in real estate sales, "smokestacks" won out over "geraniums," and Wilde was elected mayor in April 1917. The advent of World War I brought San Diego out of its economic downturn and Marston continued to promote his clean growth values for the next several decades.

The San Diego Zoo

One of the most permanent and significant results of the Panama-California Exposition was the San Diego Zoo formed around the menagerie of creatures brought together for the occasion. Since the animals' future seemed uncertain during the fair's second year, Dr. Harry Wegeforth and his brother Dr. Paul Wegeforth advertised in *The San Diego Union* of September 27, 1916, for interested parties to join with them and Drs. J.C. Thompson and Fred Baker in forming a zoological garden. The four physicians convinced naturalist Frank Stephens of the Natural History Society to join them as director. His wife, Kate Stephens, also a naturalist, was curator of mollusks at the Museum of Natural History. The first meeting of the official board of directors was held at Dr. Baker's home. His hobby was conchology, and he helped found the Marine Biological Institution that became Scripps Institution of Oceanography in 1925. His wife, Dr. Charlotte Baker, also a leading physician, encouraged the zoo's development.

Dr. Thompson, a neurosurgeon assigned to the Navy Hospital, was involved in planning the zoo's educational program but had to leave the board in April 1917 for government duty. Joseph Sefton Jr. replaced him and contributed much of his time and money to the project. Carl H. Heilbron and D.C. Collier helped purchase the first group of animals from nearby Ocean Beach Wonderland. The few bears and other animals were kept in cages along Park Boulevard until 1922 when the zoo moved to its present location. Dr. Harry Wegeforth worked hard from 1916 to 1922 to attract interest and money in the zoo and received help from Ellen Browning Scripps, John D. Spreckels, George White Marston, John Burnham, Ralph Granger, and Frank C. Spalding. Money, nevertheless, was difficult to raise for zoo projects.

In 1921 the San Diego City Council agreed to appropriate $5,000 for maintenance and improvements and approved the zoo's current site by city ordinance. The zoo slowly grew from a meager exhibit of wild animals to an institution, but its future was never secure until the mid-1930s when the city took over support. Mrs. Belle Jennings Benchley, who became bookkeeper at the zoo in 1925, gradually assumed more responsibilities until, after only a year and seven months, she became the first full-time director. She ran the zoo successfully through a combination of studied competence, patient determination, a love of animals, and what she liked to call "animal instinct." Belle Benchley—then the only woman zoo director in the United States—remained at the helm until her retirement in 1953.

William Templeton Johnson

Other park developments included the building in 1926 of the Fine Arts Gallery, today's San Diego Museum of Art, designed by architect William Templeton Johnson. A native of New York, Johnson had spent considerable time in Mexico absorbing the influence of Spanish

San Diego Museum of Art (formerly Fine Arts Gallery), Balboa Park.

colonial art forms. He patterned the entrance to the gallery after that of the University of Salamanca in Spanish Renaissance style. His later Natural History Museum building emphasized the classical revival mode with Mediterranean features. In 1926 Johnson was chosen from a group of six architectural contestants to design the three American buildings of the Iberian-American Exposition in Seville, Spain.

Because of his excellent reputation, Johnson was selected by Joseph W. Sefton Jr., son of the founder of the San Diego Trust and Savings Bank, to design a new bank building at Sixth and Broadway. Sefton had served as director of publicity for the Panama-California Exposition and had a deep interest in construction and design. The bank had purchased the 100-by-500-foot lot in 1924 for $600,000 and demolished the Hotel Beacon. The new building, completed in April 1928, remains today as a prime example of early Renaissance Revival style. Its arcaded tower and penthouse are a prominent feature of San Diego's modern skyline. When the bank closed in 1996, the Marriot Courtyard Hotel chain took over the historic building and gave it a new life. Other buildings designed by Johnson included the Serra Museum, Lion Clothing Store, Francis W. Parker School founded in San Diego in 1913, and numerous landmark homes.

Hatfield the Rainmaker

The problem of water continued to occupy the minds of San Diego's civic leaders. Each crisis was met with equanimity until the city fathers began to talk about a possible shortage toward the end of 1915. Rainfall that year had been reasonably good—13.62 inches compared with an annual average of 9.25 during the previous five years. Nevertheless, Morena Reservoir had not been filled since its construction in 1897 and was holding only five billion of its fifteen-billion-gallon capacity. Other reservoirs had not been filled, and the city's demands were increasing monthly.

Water rights were much discussed since City Attorney Terence B. Cosgrove, an expert in water matters, had decided that a grant from the king of Spain allowed San Diego to proceed against ranch owners upstream on the San Diego River who had appropriated much of the water. Los Angeles had made good a similar claim on the Los Angeles River and, although there was never such a grant, the courts had held that somehow a Spanish "pueblo" had a right to all the waters it needed from the river on which it was founded. This gave city inhabitants rights over upstream farmers who conceivably could obstruct the city's supply. Los Angeles had added to its local water rights by building the Los Angeles aqueduct to import water more than 200 miles from the Owens River. San Diego would also need to make plans to bring in water from distant places.

Into this atmosphere of impending drought stepped a rainmaker of some repute—Charles Mallory Hatfield. The Hatfields had moved to San Diego from Fort Scott, Kansas, in 1886 and worked in the sewing machine business while trading property throughout southern California. In 1902 they lived on a ranch in Gopher Canyon in Bonsall where Charley began experimenting in rainmaking operations. With the help of brother Paul, he set up a number of towers and apparently induced some rain in dry areas. Hatfield enjoyed several "successes" between 1903 and 1912 in the Southwest and as far north as Alaska.

Old Town Bridge over the San Diego River in the 1916 Flood. Inset: Charles Hatfield.
Photo ©San Diego History Center.

San Diego realtor Fred Binney suggested Hatfield to the city council as early as 1912, but the time was not right. In December 1915, Charley offered his services to the city on a "no rain—no pay" basis. He agreed to fill Morena Reservoir free to four-fifths capacity and charge only for the 40th to 50th inch at $1,000 per inch. Cosgrove said the contract would be legal, and his assistant Shelley Higgins began to prepare the draft. Hatfield started operations at Morena Dam on the first of January, and by the fifth it began to rain. A heavier rain fell on January 10 and on the 14th it reached torrential proportions. The San Diego River overflowed its banks on the 17th, and the Tia Juana River destroyed the "Little Landers" homes and gardens on the 18th. *The San Diego Union* headlined: "Is Rainmaker at Work?" "Hatfield's scheme was on almost every tongue yesterday," the paper reported. "Many were inclined to jest, but all agreed that things were going his way."

But the rain did not stop. During the next few days, it washed away roads and bridges. The backcountry was isolated, and a veritable river rushed out of the canyons of Balboa Park. Lower Otay Dam gave way on January 27, causing untold damage and injuring a large number of Japanese farmers living in Otay Valley. Hatfield appeared at city hall to collect his $10,000 but was blamed for the flood damage. He finally sued the city but gave up any hope of payment when Cosgrove insisted upon his being liable for all flood claims against the city. The city decided to plan for future water resources in a more realistic manner.

The Boulder Canyon Project

As early as 1917, San Diego led the formation of the League of the Southwest to promote the Boulder Canyon project on the Colorado River. This water supply could ensure San Diego's dreams of becoming a major port and industrial center. The city went ahead with other plans and in 1922 completed Barrett Dam on Cottonwood Creek; in 1924 voters approved a bond issue for construction of El Capitan Dam. San Diego also purchased the San Dieguito Water System and won its case against upstream Cuyamaca Water Company, asserting its right as a "pueblo" to all San Diego River water. Because of its early interest in the Colorado River, the city applied to the California Division of Water Resources in 1926 for the right to 112,000-acre-feet (100 million gallons) of water a day from that source. The right was granted and later extended to include the county.

By 1928, the fight for Boulder Dam and the All-American Canal in the Imperial Valley was ending. Despite protests from Arizona, Congressman Phil Swing finally maneuvered the Swing-Johnson Bill to the floor of the House, where it passed on May 25, and Hiram Johnson, California's former progressive governor, fought it through the Senate. When Johnson agreed to limit California's share, the bill passed on December 14. San Diego, hoping to construct its own facilities through the mountains, did not at this time join the Metropolitan Water District formed by Los Angeles and other cities for distribution of Colorado River water to southern California.

San Diego Promoters

San Diegans continued to promote their area as one of the most ideal places to live in the United States. The San Diego-California Club,

A.G. Spalding driving his new automobile. *Photo ©San Diego History Center.*

formed in 1919 with Oscar W. Cotton as secretary, carried on a program of advertising in the Midwest and East to market San Diego's delightful year-round climate, scenic beauty, clean air, orange groves, and seaside resorts. Slowly people responded and by 1923, the city's population, with the adjoining communities of East San Diego, Coronado, and National City, had grown remarkably. A rapid increase in automobiles brought improved backcountry roads and paved streets within the city. An early "flight to the suburbs" began, and San Diego's prosperity seemed assured.

Both city builders John D. Spreckels and E.W. Scripps died in 1926, but their activities were carried forward. The Spreckels's interests in *The San Diego Union* and *Evening Tribune* were purchased in early 1928 by Colonel Ira C. Copley of Aurora, Illinois. The colonel's parents had established residence in San Diego in 1890, and Ira had joined the Cuyamaca Club in 1907. A rival newspaper, the *Independent*—founded by George Marston, Ed Fletcher, and others to oppose Spreckels—went out of business. Copley also bought Spreckels's 20-room mansion in Coronado and appointed William Wheeler president of the Union-Tribune Publishing Company.

The San Diego Historical Society

San Diegans organized their first historical society on January 24, 1880, "for the diffusion of a general knowledge of natural and civil history" and for the collection of a cabinet of curiosities. When interest in the society waned in the late 1880s, other organizations such as the Native Sons and Native Daughters of the Golden West took its place. Finally, the Pioneer Society of San Diego, incorporated in 1911, began collecting documents, books, and a few artifacts to form the nucleus of a small museum and library. On December 13, 1928, George W. Marston, as founder and first president, incorporated the San Diego Historical Society as a nonprofit cultural and educational institution. He was assisted by his close friends Julius Wangenheim and Society vice president Leroy Wright. Marston had begun to acquire land on Presidio Hill overlooking Old Town as early as 1907, and by 1928 he had twenty acres.

The San Diego Chamber of Commerce, which observed its 50th anniversary in 1920, hired city planner John Nolen to develop and landscape a park. Marston employed architect William Templeton Johnson to design a building appropriate for the Pioneer Society collections and to honor Father Junípero Serra. Johnson chose the simple yet imposing Mission Revival style with its stark, clean lines and graceful arches. The dedication ceremonies were held on July 16, 1929, the mission's 160th birthday. The city accepted Marston's gift reluctantly and agreed to provide only water for the park. Marston paid expenses for maintenance and improvement for nearly a decade.

The Serra Museum, with its commanding view of the city and bay, today stands atop Presidio Hill as a monument to both Native Americans and the Hispanic heritage of San Diego, along with the generosity of George Marston. A number of Indian burials attest to the fact that the native village of Cosoy also stood near this historic spot. Its grassy slopes and rolling mounds protect the archeological evidence of an earlier time while future plans include investigation into what is considered the birthplace of our present state of California.

The Serra Museum designed by William Templeton Johnson on land donated by George Marston. *Photo ©San Diego History Center.*

Kensington—San Diego Moves East

A few miles farther to the east, the area of Kensington, first developed in 1910, was experiencing a boom. The Kensington Land Company had installed curbs, sidewalks, and ornamental streetlights. Richard Requa, known for his Spanish colonial-style homes, headed its architectural board. Requa, originally from Rock Island, Illinois, had been an apprentice in the office of Irving Gill and had developed a unique design that he called Southern California Style. The minimum requirement for most Kensington homes was 1,500 square feet, and by 1926, a number of homes built in a Spanish or Mission style overlooked Mission Valley. Farther east the communities of East San Diego (City Heights), La Mesa, Grossmont, El Cajon, Spring Valley, and Lemon Grove were also experiencing growth.

Rancho Santa Fe

Richard Requa had entered into a partnership with Herbert Jackson in 1920 and the firm received a commission from the Santa Fe Land and Improvement Company, a division of the Santa Fe Railroad, to design a community based on the California-Spanish style. Located on the site of the former Rancho San Dieguito land grant, Rancho Santa Fe's rolling terrain provided the perfect setting for a planned community. The town plan and layout of all streets and roads was done in 1922 by L.G. Sinnard, an agricultural community development specialist. He began with a wide, landscaped avenue as the focal point for the community. The Requa firm sent their young associate, Lilian Jenette Rice, to plan and supervise the initial development. This capable young woman worked tirelessly on the entire project. The use of adobe wall construction, tiled roofs, inner courtyards, and grillwork around windows and doorways, a Requa concept, gave the impression of a transplanted Spanish village. By 1927, the community in Rancho Santa Fe consisted of 230 separate estates. Nearby, the estate of Douglas Fairbanks and Mary Pickford provided the setting for a large man-made lake and dam.

Tourists Come to the Californias

By the end of the 1920s, San Diego and its nearby suburbs had taken on a modern look. Neon tube lighting had become popular and was available for outdoor use in a variety of colors. Because it could stand out even in the daytime, neon was fast becoming the element of choice in all types of advertising. With the advent of "talking pictures," the number of movie theaters increased and the new lighting effects brightened the streets of downtown and suburban areas from Chula Vista to Carlsbad.

Just below the border, the town of Tijuana was growing as a result of a heavy tourist trade. The magnificent Agua Caliente Hotel attracted those crossing into Mexico to avoid the prohibition of the sale of alcoholic beverages in the United States. It offered gambling, in the hotel's giant, beautifully decorated casino. Racing was another popular attraction for California residents. On the San Diego side, the downtown area had also kept up with modern building trends. All seemed to be going well as the decade of the 1920s came to a close.

Chapter IX

From Depression through World War II: 1930–1950

It took several months for the effects of the stock-market crash of October 29, 1929, to be felt in San Diego. By the early 1930s, however, land promotions had collapsed, the number of building permits dropped, and bankruptcies ran high. Fortunately, federal and state projects for water development, harbor improvement, and highway construction eased unemployment in the county. San Diego, like much of the rest of the nation, had been riding the crest of prosperity during the late 1920s. Lindbergh's successful flight, completion of the "Broadway of America" coast-to-coast automobile route, assurance of water from the Colorado River, and the opening of Mexico's multi-million dollar Agua Caliente gambling resort all had given residents throughout the county a sense of lasting well being. They were ill prepared for the Great Depression felt throughout the country.

San Diego County Development

The city of Carlsbad had become the "Avocado Capital of the World" while Encinitas was known as the "Home of the Mid-Winter Flower Show." La Mesa, calling itself "Jewel of the Hills," competed with Chula Vista, which was "Truly California at its Best," and National City "Where Rail and Water Meet." Escondido became the "Sunkist Vale" with its flourishing citrus industry while Ramona was called the "Turkey Capital." In downtown San Diego, the Gildred Brothers, Philip and Theodore, covered a full block bounded by A, B, Seventh, and Eighth Streets with a ten-floor garage, a four-story department store, and the magnificent Fox Theater, third largest theater on the Pacific coast. San Diego was variously called "the playground of America" and "the capital of the Southland's empire of amusement." The city's population reached nearly 150,000.

Progress in San Diego

Some gains were made during the early 1930s in air-related industries. Pacific Air Transport, soon a part of United Air Lines, extended its Seattle–Los Angeles service to San Diego. American Airways, predecessor of American Air Lines, added San Diego to its Phoenix connection. Edmund Price of Solar Aircraft took his wife and three children on a cross-country flight from San Diego to New Bedford, Massachusetts, to attract business in 1931. They received great publicity but sold no airplanes.

The mild climate in San Diego made standing in breadlines at least more comfortable. A city bond issue provided $300,000 for recreational projects including a golf course and tennis courts in Balboa Park. A new city charter approved in April 1931 initiated a clear-cut city manager plan. Appointed by the council, the city manager would have authority over fire, police, health, and other city departments, but not over the harbor, city attorney, city clerk, auditor and controller, or civil service. The six-member city council would be nominated by districts and elected at large. The mayor, nominated and elected at large as a seventh and presiding member of the city council, would be ceremonial chief of the city. The charter also provided for a hydraulic engineer, a water department, and an accounting system to determine water costs. The sum of $150,000 a year was allocated for harbor work. Bond money of $3.6 million to construct El Capitan Dam was approved by voters in December 1931, and the La Mesa, Lemon Grove, and Spring Valley (later Helix) Irrigation District received the right to appropriate two million gallons of water daily.

San Diego State College in 1931. *Photo courtesy San Diego Gas & Electric Co.*

San Diego State College

The new San Diego State College campus ten miles east of downtown was dedicated in a three-day ceremony beginning on May 1, 1931. The Mission Revival-style buildings, in keeping with the city's heritage and its recent architectural emphasis, accommodated 2,000 students enrolled and a curriculum of 200 courses. The United States Commissioner of Education, William John Cooper, spent most of his dedication speech justifying the construction of a new campus so far from the center of town. George W. Marston, a former trustee of the college, laid the cornerstone. Marston had also promoted restoration of the Spanish Mission San Diego de Alcalá across the valley, which had served to inspire the college's bell tower, white stucco walls, and red tile roofs. It was completed in the fall of that year.

From Manufactured Gas to Natural Gas

In October 1932 a minor technological change took place in San Diego that had a widespread impact on local residents. The San Diego Consolidated Gas and Electric Company changed from the manufacture and distribution of gas made from coal to the importation of natural gas from near Bakersfield, California. Since natural gas contained nearly twice as much heat per cubic foot as manufactured gas, the same amount would cook nearly twice as many meals or keep the home warm for nearly twice as long. The changeover, however, made it necessary for every gas appliance in San Diego county to be adjusted so that the openings through which the gas flowed were reduced to allow only about 60 percent as much gas to enter. Approximately 400 men were trained for two to four weeks in appliance work by the gas company to make the changeover, which took about six weeks to complete. An artificial odorant had to be added to give the new odorless gas a distinctive aroma. The changeover brought an unexpected boost to the economy with an increased demand for gas appliances.

The Anza-Borrego Desert State Park

Because of the increased interest in developing the Imperial Valley, certain persons in San Diego wanted to ensure preservation of a portion of the Anza-Borrego Desert as a park. Frederick Law Olmstead, a well-known landscape architect, had surveyed park possibilities in California in 1928 and emphasized the fragile nature of the deserts. Clinton G. Abbott, director of San Diego's Museum of Natural History and Guy L. Fleming of La Jolla, guardian of the rare Torrey pines, submitted plans for a park in the Anza-Borrego area. Since voters rejected a bond to match state funds, George Marston personally purchased 2,320 acres in or near Borrego's Palm Canyon, deeded them to the state, and induced others to sell 5,500 more acres for state acquisition. With the backing of Marston and the State Park Commission, a second Swing-Johnson Act transferred 200,000 acres of federal land to Anza-Borrego Desert State Park in March 1933.

Depression Measures

In the presidential election, Franklin D. Roosevelt led Herbert Hoover by 10,000 votes in San Diego County, although at the local level Republican George Burnham defeated Phil Swing for the House seat. Swing, an attorney, continued his work with water by representing the Imperial Valley Irrigation District in Washington, D.C., to gain approval for the All-American Canal. It was approved as an emergency

San Diego High School in the 1930s. *Photo courtesy San Diego Gas & Electric Co.*

project of the Public Works Administration in October. At the end of 1933, four national and six state banks were operating successfully in San Diego.

By 1934, the Depression seemed to have reached its full effect in San Diego, but a number of government measures encouraged recovery. Prohibition of liquor—the eighteenth amendment—was repealed in 1933 and legal sales resumed. The navy spent $1.4 million and the army $1.8 million on construction projects. Price's Solar Aircraft stayed alive with Fred Rohr, formerly with Ryan Airlines, as plant manager.

Major Reuben H. Fleet, president of Consolidated Aircraft Corporation in Buffalo, New York, made a most far-reaching decision when he decided to move his plant with 800 employees and $9 million in orders to San Diego. Fleet had learned to fly at Rockwell Field with the army signal corps during World War I. He had examined a number of locations and found San Diego to have everything he needed—a good airport, a publicly-owned waterfront, an excellent harbor, a city large enough to furnish labor and materials, and a proper climate for test flying and deliveries. Consolidated began operating in San Diego in October 1935. This move almost single-handedly assured San Diego's future as an industrial center. In retail sales, another significant move was made when R.M. Walker joined George A. Scott in signing a 20-year lease on a downtown building to begin the San Diego-based Walker Scott department store chain.

The 1935 California Pacific International Exposition

The highlight of the mid-1930s was the planning of a second major exposition—San Diego's first World's Fair. Promoter Frank Drugan returned from Chicago with pictures of that city's Century of Progress and promised that exhibits would be available to San Diego. The chamber of commerce directors discussed the pros and cons of such an ambitious undertaking amidst the financial crisis of the time. With characteristic optimism, they approved the concept, called it the California Pacific International Exposition and appointed attorney Walter Ames to organize a nonprofit corporation.

Unlike other times, few corporations had any profits to make "tax deductible gift giving" attractive, so some contributions were in the form of loans. G. Aubrey Davidson, president of the 1915–1916 exposition, became chairman of the board of directors, and young Frank G. Belcher of the Spreckels Companies, president. Oscar W. Cotton agreed to chair the campaign to raise $500,000—a tough assignment. Cotton and his committee convinced the people of San Diego that they could certainly better the record of 40,000 people who had pledged $1 million in 1915. After all, the benefits of the exposition would far outweigh the cost, and San Diego could celebrate completion of the Metropolitan Aqueduct from Boulder Dam and other federal projects.

By the end of September, the fund drive topped its goal at $700,000, and Richard S. Requa became director of architecture. In his book, *Inside Lights on the Building of San Diego's Exposition: 1935*, Requa explained that he wanted to provide examples of all styles used during the Spanish period in America, including the prehistoric and Indian architecture of the American Southwest, central Mexico, and Yucatan. The new area would be laid out around a spacious plaza southwest of the Spreckels Organ Pavilion. Just four months before the scheduled

Natural History Museum design sketch by William Templeton Johnson.

opening, Edsel Ford, who had visited the 1915–1916 fair on his honeymoon, decided to participate and brought other industries in at the last minute. Congress passed a bill appropriating funds for a permanent federal building copied from the Mayan Palace of Governors in Uxmal, Yucatan.

Three internationally famous gardens were selected for reappearance in Balboa Park—one from the Moorish section of Ronda, Spain; another from a patio garden in Guadalajara, Mexico; and the third duplicating that adjoining the Alcazar in Seville, Spain. The original 1915–1916 buildings—as well as the newer Fine Arts Gallery (1927) and Natural History Museum (1933)—were incorporated into the grand plan. Other new structures included the Old Globe Shakespearean Theater, a Spanish village, and a series of small cottages housing representatives of Latin American countries. New outdoor lighting enhanced the nighttime view.

The changeover to natural gas in San Diego was of immense benefit to the fair. The San Diego Gas & Electric Company's crews installed nearly two miles of gas mains to ensure ample service to the new buildings. All restaurants utilized gas for cooking, including the large Cafe of the World seating 900 people. Gas also fired the glass-melting furnace for the Venetian glassblowers' exhibit and provided fuel utilized in the Ford exhibit and the Coca-Cola bottling display.

Balboa Park in 1935. *Photo courtesy San Diego Gas & Electric Co.*

Opening Days of the 1935 Balboa Park Fair

The exposition officially opened on May 29, 1935, at 11 a.m. with a United States Marine color guard leading a parade across Cabrillo Bridge into the Plaza del Pacifico. That night at eight, President Franklin Roosevelt telephoned a signal for the lights to go on and congratulated the people of San Diego for their courage and confidence in putting on the fair. The first day's attendance was 60,000. Operating expenses were higher than anticipated, but managing director Philip Gildred kept it going successfully. President Roosevelt stayed at the Hotel del Coronado and personally visited the park in October. He saw the exposition as a sign that the country's economic future was indeed brighter.

There were a number of special days during the first year at the fair. July 21 was to honor the great contralto Madame Ernestine Schumann-Heink, then 74. She sang the national anthem before a San Diego audience for the last time. September 24 honored Kate Sessions, the "Mother of Balboa Park," and October 30 was dedicated to the memory of John D. Spreckels, donor of the organ pavilion.

The Old Globe Theater, located to the north of the California Building (today's Museum of Man) drew a large audience and, at that time, was in the open air with only a canopy to keep out inclement weather. Five or six of Shakespeare's plays were presented daily with tickets selling for 40 cents for adults and 15 cents for children under twelve. Weekday matinees were 25 cents.

Alpha, a 2,000 lb. chrome-plated robot, was the main attraction in the Palace of Science. He stood up, sat down, blinked his eyes, and even answered questions, although some of his movements were controlled by an unseen operator. Probably the most controversial exhibit was the nudist colony in the Zoro gardens. Even though certain local residents protested the show, the fair's directors were not going to close down a major attraction. The second year featured an entire Amusement Zone, complete with an Enchanted Land for children.

Changing Times

The closing of Mexico's $10 million gambling and racetrack resort at Agua Caliente came as a shock to many when Mexican President Lázaro Cárdenas banned games of chance on July 21, 1935. Economic repercussions were felt on both sides of the border. Fortunately, President Roosevelt had inaugurated the Works Progress Administration in the summer of 1935 with a number of massive projects earmarked for San Diego. The year closed with the ground breaking for the new civic center made possible through federal relief financing. City builders George Marston, G. Aubrey Davidson, Julius Wangenheim, and others—including Ralph E. Jenney, a San Diegan directing the California Relief Commission—had obtained $300,000 for a combined city and county building on the tidelands. Several sketches were submitted for the waterfront edifice. President Roosevelt dedicated the completed $2 million structure on July 16, 1938. Other WPA projects included $5 million for construction of a racetrack and county fairgrounds at Del Mar, additions to the San Diego Zoo, enlargement of Lindbergh Field, and the building of a stadium at San Diego State College.

By the end of the decade, the nation's economy had responded to the threat of war in Europe. Germany's invasion of Poland in September 1939 brought increased contracts for aircraft industries and naval facilities. Fred H. Rohr set up his own company to provide special airplane components. He started in a garage, moved to a warehouse, and then built a new plant in Chula Vista. Consolidated

Aircraft increased its employees to 9,000 during 1940, while eight navy and marine establishments occupied nearly 4,000 acres with 634 buildings—an investment of $51 million.

With the purchase of Scripps's *San Diego Sun* by the Copley interests in 1939, San Diego's news was reported by its two main daily papers— *The San Diego Union* and *Evening Tribune*—and several smaller publications such as the *Southwestern Jewish Review* (later *Heritage*) published for a sizable Jewish community; the *Southern Cross*, official journal of the San Diego Roman Catholic Diocese; the *Sud-California Deutsche Zeitung*, a German weekly; and the monthly *Zoonooz*. Two radio stations—KGB and KFSD—were based in San Diego while seven Tijuana stations broadcast throughout the area. A young Art Linkletter talked on the radio about various displays in Balboa Park on December 3, 1935.

Ethnic Communities of San Diego

San Diego's African American community numbered about 4,500 during the mid-1930s and had settled mainly in the region between K Street and Logan Avenue with a business center at 30th and Imperial Avenue. By 1937 they had built nine churches and were active in local community affairs. The area known as today's Gaslamp Quarter featured a number of establishments owned by African Americans. The Douglas Hotel built in 1924 at 206 Market Street by businessman George Ramsey had some of the best entertainment that could be found in the city during the 1930s.

The Asian population remained relatively small—about 5 percent—with Chinese merchants still active in the area from Fourth Avenue and Market Street to the waterfront. About 1,000 Japanese residents divided their efforts among the fishing industry, landscaping, and vegetable growing south and east of the city. Wives of fishermen worked in the canneries. Long subjected to discriminatory laws along with the Chinese, a final blow came to the Japanese community with the outbreak of World War II. All persons of Japanese ancestry were removed by federal order in April 1942 to relocation centers in the

Left to right: Skippy Smith, CEO of the Pacific Parachute Company, Mayor Harley Knox, and heavyweight boxing champion Joe Louis, July 1943. *Photo courtesy of Donna Sefton.*

desert. After the war ended, most returned to their native San Diego to pick up the pieces of their lives. Their success in doing so is a story of courage, dedication, and hard work.

The native-born residents of Mexican descent continued to live in or near Old Town, many working in the restaurant business. Mexican immigrants arriving between 1910 and 1930 settled principally in the Logan Heights area and found work on the railroads, in building activities, or in agriculture. As the Depression hit California during the early 1930s, a number of families returned or were forced to return to Mexico. By the early 1940s, however, the demands of war provided employment for a new group of immigrants who crossed the border to work in war-related industries. The areas of San Ysidro, Chula Vista, and National City could boast a large Mexican population with cultural ties on both sides of the border. The Church of the Immaculate Conception in Old Town and Our Lady of Guadalupe Church near Crosby Street (now Cesar Chavez Parkway) served as popular religious centers for the Mexican community. Logan Heights (Barrio Logan), home to many Spanish-speaking families, was cut through and divided by Interstate 5 during the 1950s.

San Diego's Fishing Industry

San Diego's fishing industry contributed a large share to the city's growing economy. The 1939 tuna catch was for the first time over 100 million pounds. The fleet of tuna clippers had increased in value to $10 million, and the harbor had become the leading tuna port of the Pacific. During World War II, many of the clippers were pressed into wartime service and served in a number of capacities overseas. Sometimes known as "the Pork-Chop Express," the fleet transported food to naval ships in the Pacific.

The bulk of fishing was divided between the Portuguese residents of Point Loma and the Italians of the Middletown area near India and Columbia streets. The Portuguese colony of San Diego—many originally from the Azores and Madeira Islands—operated a large fleet of boats as early as the 1920s. St. Agnes Church, so significant in the annual blessing of the fleet, became a noted religious and cultural center. Portuguese women and children formed a close-knit group in the absence of their husbands at sea.

The Italians, almost as numerous as the Portuguese, came mainly from Sicily or northern Italy in the Genoa area. Our Lady of the Rosary Church, built in 1925, with its beautiful stained-glass windows and magnificent murals by Venetian painter Fausto Tasca, formed the nucleus of their community. The area of Little Italy just north of downtown and centered around India Street was a charming residential area. It was also cut through by Interstate 5 in the 1950s. Prominent Italians of the early decades included the DeFalcos in the grocery business, the Ghios of Anthony's restaurant fame, and the Crivellos in the tuna industry.

Population Growth

The federal census of 1940 showed that San Diego's population had grown to more than 200,000 and that of the county was nearing 300,000. With the outbreak of World War II, the rate of San Diego's growth increased tremendously. Local aircraft plants attracted workers

Linda Vista housing project World War II. *Photo ©San Diego History Center.*

from other states. All existing military establishments were expanded and new facilities were acquired as San Diego became a center for pilot training. As a major West Coast port, San Diego experienced a rapid increase of all branches of military personnel. San Diego's climate was ideal for the year-round training of army, navy, and marine corps recruits. With 22 miles of landlocked harbor, San Diego had long been recognized as a major naval center and, by 1940, $42 million had already been invested by the US Navy. The navy represented more than $2.5 million to the San Diego community in monthly payrolls and expenditures.

Because of the demand for skilled labor during World War II, thousands of families poured into the metropolitan area. From 1940 to 1942 the population rose by 20 percent, bringing the total number of people in the city to 250,000. Major problems facing local governments at this time were needs for adequate housing, expanded water and sewer systems, improved transportation networks, and additional educational facilities. Large-scale housing projects, both military and private, changed the face of the city and county as new areas were developed.

World War II Measures

Linda Vista, known in its early stages as Defense Housing Project No. 4092, was a $14 million project covering an area of 1,459 acres overlooking the bay and Mission Valley. Sponsored by the National Housing Authority, ground was broken on October 31, 1941, and 3,001 houses were constructed in 200 days. All were rented to defense workers and military personnel by April 1942. In May, another contract was let for the building of 1,846 more units. The family homes were built on large lots with paved streets and four schools located in the immediate vicinity.

Defense precautions dictated that thousands of street lamps had to be partially blacked-out with paint, in varying degrees, while at the same time saving as much light as possible for public convenience and safety. The top half of car headlights had to be painted over and speed limits on city streets were substantially lowered. Gas and other commodities such as meat, sugar, butter, and nylon hose were rationed. The planting of "victory gardens" featuring home-grown vegetables were encouraged throughout the city. Consumers found it almost impossible to purchase new appliances because appliance factories had been converted to the manufacture of war materials. The purchase of new automobiles had to wait until the war was over.

Camp Callan for US Army artillerymen occupied a five-mile stretch of land along Torrey Pines mesa. An amphibious base was developed by the navy on Coronado Strand along with Brown Field on Otay Mesa, Ream Field in Imperial Beach, and Miramar Naval Air Station. The marines acquired more than 123,000 acres of historic Rancho Santa Margarita to build Camp Pendleton, the world's largest military base. They also set up Camp Elliott on Kearny Mesa. Since the added population needed an assured water supply, the federal government worked with the city and county to determine the most feasible method for obtaining additional sources.

San Diego County Water Authority

In 1926 San Diego received rights to the Colorado River for 112,000 acre feet per annum. In 1934, the city contracted with the federal government to receive its share of this water through the All-American Canal in Imperial Valley. By 1941, wartime demands made it

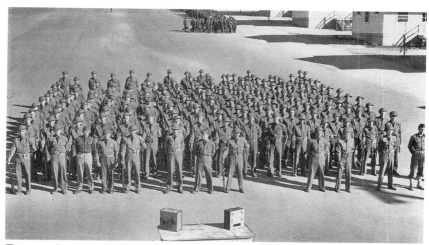

Troops in formation at Camp Callan ca. 1941. *Photo ©San Diego History Center.*

necessary to bring in Colorado River water immediately. San Vicente Dam was completed in 1943 and San Diego studied the feasibility of connecting to the Colorado River Aqueduct of the Metropolitan Water District (MWD) or a conduit to Imperial County. The San Diego County Water Authority, with nine member agencies, was organized on June 9, 1944, for the express purpose of importing this water.

On November 29, 1944, before the feasibility studies were completed, President Franklin Roosevelt directed the departments concerned to commence construction of an acqueduct from MWD's acqueduct to San Vicente Reservoir. The authority's annexation to MWD occurred in April 1946. The 71.1 mile-long San Diego aqueduct, completed in November 1947, delivered 41,000 acre-feet of water by June 30, 1948. Without it, San Diego could not have met the water needs of its nearly 432,000 people in 1948. Because of prevailing drought conditions and population increases, San Diego exceeded its original right within ten years. By 1980 it would be using four times its original right.

Not Always Sunny San Diego

San Diegans exerienced one of the coldest winters on record in early 1949. A wave of freezing temperatures occurred during the first week

Ventura Bridge, Mission Bay. *Photo ©San Diego History Center.*

of January, when temperatures dropped to 29 degrees in the city. The demand for gas for heating was so great that the San Diego Gas & Electric Company put its old gas manufacturing plant into top production to avoid a major crisis. On January 12, the streets of San Diego were covered with snow. Many schools were closed since San Diego had seldom coped with transporting students over snow-covered roads. Even the libraries were forced to close for the day because of inadequate heating. La Jolla librarians wore gloves to serve patrons while others struggled to keep libraries open with small oil burners.

Mission Bay Development

World War II brought San Diego a new prosperity. Many members of the military decided to bring their families from the Midwest and East and live permanently by the blue Pacific. In 1945, San Diego voters approved a bond issue of $2 million to begin development of a magnificent aquatic playground in Mission Bay. John Spreckels's $4 million Belmont Park, built in the 1920s, had passed into city ownership, and many thought the region comparable to Newport Beach.

Glenn C. Rick, San Diego's planning director, first suggested the Mission Bay concept in 1935. His original idea did not include hotel accomodations. After the war, Rick, Mayor Harley Knox, and others continued the planning with recreation as a major goal. Roscoe E. Hazard and Elwyn B. Gould sold 500 acres they had purchased in the early 1920s to the city for $300 per acre—the same price they had paid. Dredging operations were proposed to divert the San Diego River directly into the ocean through a series of rock jetties at Mission Bay to prevent further silting. The fill would be used to create small islands. The city's work, well underway by the end of the decade, allowed the first phase of Mission Bay Park to be dedicated in 1949. San Diego's climate and natural advantages dictated that recreation would be a major trend in the city's future growth. There already were 200 baseball teams on local fields, and the San Diego Padres, a popular Pacific Coast League baseball club, commanded a steady attendance at Lane Field on the downtown waterfront.

Planning for Higher Education

Also in 1949, the Most Reverend Charles Buddy, bishop of the Catholic diocese of San Diego, saw the realization of a dream he had conceived upon his arrival in 1937. He and the Reverend Mother Rosalie Hill of the Society of the Sacred Heart in San Francisco had planned an institution of higher learning to be built in the architectural style of the Spanish Renaissance. A contract was entered into with the architectural firm of Frank L. Hope in May 1948. Hope personally took charge of Mother Hill's blueprints and Bishop Buddy's dream. The final plans were approved by the Mother House of the Society of the Sacred Heart in Rome on March 31, 1949. A charter was granted, and construction began on the campus that would eventually reach 180 acres on the Linda Vista mesa overlooking Mission Valley.

At the same time, a private Methodist-related university was being planned for the grounds of Katherine Tingley's theosophical institute. California Western University, an outgrowth of Balboa College in downtown, received permission to relocate on Point Loma. The next few decades would witness a phenomenal growth of Cal Western and other of San Diego's institutions of higher education.

Marston House, now a museum administered by the San Diego History Center. Inset: George White Marson. *Photo ©San Diego History Center.*

Problems of Growth

New leaders of San Diego's future would emerge in the postwar years. San Diegans mourned the deaths of city fathers Julius Wangenheim in 1942 and George White Marston in 1946. A younger generation, with new goals and interests, would take the lead. Solutions to problems of growth would not come easily and the ideal way between dreams and reality would sometimes be impossible to reach. No longer would San Diego be held together in its aims by promotion of New Town, planning a world's fair, fighting the Depression or stepping up production for wartime needs. The next decades would witness a strain between developing a civic and business center downtown and the desirability of moving to the suburbs. Voters had rejected the grouping of public buildings on Cedar Street Mall in 1947 and looked outward to areas east, south, and north. Shopping centers and freeways—the wave of the 1950s—would cause public and private interests to clash on numerous occasions. One of the major areas of controversy would be the development of Mission Valley.

Chapter X

THE CHANGING PATTERN OF CITY GROWTH: 1950–1970

The Automobile Age

The decades between 1950 and 1970 witnessed the increasing popularity of the automobile and its contribution to the geographical expansion of the area. The automobile affected almost every major decision regarding the direction taken by San Diego planners during the post-World War II decades. Not the least among its effects was the changing pattern of retail shopping—self-contained business centers in regions remote from downtown. San Diego did not face this phenomenon alone. The rise of the automobile and expansion of highways led to a flight from the center of American cities.

The result was the collapse of all but a few mass transportation systems in the United States. It was a circular process—increasing reliance on automobiles made less money available for public transportation, which therefore became less efficient and less desirable. On the other hand, greater mobility encouraged cities everywhere to consolidate a larger geographical area and more people under a single autonomous government. Large city departments run by experts were favored over neighborhood agencies.

This policy, which also widened the city's tax base, led to annexation of surrounding areas. San Diego grew from 99 square miles in 1950 to some 307 square miles in 1970. The idea that "bigger is better" prevailed until well into the 1960s, when citizens began to feel detached and voiced concern over their lack of effective control of local issues. On the one hand, many wanted government to remain small and close to the people; but on the other, county or even regional planning seemed to be the answer to contemporary issues, such as water distribution, freeway expansion, or air pollution—problems that needed solutions aimed at the overall benefit of a area.

Promoting Growth

From the time of their city's founding, San Diegans had looked for ways to promote growth because people meant prosperity. These were the days before the third member of the trio—pollution— appeared. Because there was available land to accommodate more people, those in city government sought to achieve a balance between downtown control and neighborhood integrity. Not only did San Diego face decisions about growth, nearly every incorporated area in the county experienced this same postwar expansion.

From 1950 to 1970, El Cajon grew from 5,600 to 52,273; Escondido from 6,544 to 36,792; Chula Vista from 15,927 to 67,901; and Oceanside from 12,881 to 40,494. San Diego's population doubled from 334,387 to 696,769. An alternative to central city annexation that still allowed for efficiency in certain areas of government was the creation of special service districts. This type of legal institution—first used as early as 1790 by Philadelphia to administer schools, prisons, public health, and the port—gave an agency limited powers to meet specific educational, medical, water, sewer, or other regional needs.

One advantage of San Diego's downtown area was its relatively young age. Its original commitment to wide streets prevented the crowding and decay that had occurred in older Eastern cities. But the preference for single-family dwellings in outlying areas, the lack of a scenic promenade along the waterfront, and the absence of high-rise residential units precluded the development of a large core of permanent residents in the city's center.

Shelter Island prior to development in the 1950s. *Photo courtesy San Diego Yacht Club.*

The failure of the Nolen Plan and the Cedar Street Mall temporarily delayed further downtown projects. Even though the San Diego Symphony had been founded in 1927 and San Diegans supported other musical and theatrical performances, construction of a decent auditorium and civic center did not follow easily. The Harbor Department did make one concession to Nolen by assigning the lee side of Point Loma to recreation. Creation of Shelter Island through dredging operations provided the city with a valuable and scenic piece of real estate. Anderson Borthwick, Harbor Commission chairman, met the opposition of Point Loma residents by assuring them that the island would be devoted to fine hotels, private marinas, and a public park. A second recreational island would be created off Harbor Drive during the 1960s.

Although cutbacks had been made in military spending, the outbreak of the Korean War in 1950 brought new life to San Diego's aircraft industries. Convair received new contracts and began work on the Atlas missile. Ryan Aeronautical, which had been producing the high-performance Navion, returned to manufacturing components. Since the city failed to act upon its right to use the Miramar air field, the navy—which had used it before and during World War II—kept possession of the area for use as a naval air station. Miramar absorbed Camp Elliott's 7,532 acres in 1961 and added NASA's Sycamore Canyon missile testing annex in 1972.

A Freeway through Balboa Park

A controversial highway was planned through Balboa Park connecting Mission Valley with downtown. Park defenders opposed the move. But others said that so large a park had been a mistake—smaller parks more strategically located would have served a greater number of people. Those who did not want to abandon downtown saw the park as an obstacle choking off the life-support system to the city's heart. The compromise was a seven-mile divided state highway through Cabrillo Canyon with a large green belt in the middle zone. The State Division of Highways set out 500,000 plants and trees—28 varieties—to beautify the parkway. Further attempts to remove the trees or widen the highway were blocked, giving downtown commuters (many unable to spend time in the park) an opportunity to view one of the most luxuriant freeway settings in California.

Controversy also arose over developments inside Balboa Park. During World War II, virtually all park facilities except the zoo had been turned over to the navy as a giant hospital complex. Museum collections were moved out and beds moved in—960 in the Museum of Natural History, 759 in the Museum of Man, and 423 in the Fine Arts Gallery. The House of Hospitality became the nurses' dormitory and the Ford Building an aircraft training school. The park was temporarily named Camp Kidd after Admiral Isaac Kidd. The navy returned the buildings after the war and paid out nearly $1 million for damages.

The Balboa Park Protective Association, formed in 1950, opposed further encroachments in the park, including the proposed Switzer and Maple Canyon freeways. The Balboa Park Citizens Committee in 1956 led by Dr. Douglas McElfresh worked hard to develop satisfactory park guidelines. The city council followed up the committees' report by hiring Harland Bartholomew & Associates, a firm of landscape architects and city planners to prepare a master

Route of the freeway under Cabrillo Bridge. *Photo ©San Diego History Center.*

plan. The Bartholomew Report adopted in 1961 is today's basic document for park development. Much of it has been implemented especially in the museum area. A major problem has been the traffic pattern—competition between pedestrians and automobiles and open spaces versus parking spaces.

Changes in City Government

Mayor Harley Knox had guided the city through several trials, but failing health prompted his decision not to run again in 1951. Attorney John D. Butler, a former San Diego State football star, won the election to become the first native son to serve in the city s highest office. The 1950s witnessed a setback in the grouping of public buildings around a central mall when the historic Andrew Carnegie Public Library and the county courthouse were torn down. In 1956 when only three cities over 250,000 in population were without a public auditorium (San Diego numbered more than 500,000), an $8.5 million general obligation bond issue was placed on the ballot. Because of location problems the Civic Theater and Convention Hall failed to receive the required two-thirds majority.

In the late 1950s, Mayor Charles C. Dail still had little success in promoting the center. The El Cortez Hotel with its outside elevator sparked interest in downtown but not enough. George A. Scott continued his plans for a major shopping center at the junction of Federal Boulevard and College Avenue but he had no plans for Walker-Scott to abandon downtown. He was only following the successful experience of other cities. A Fiesta del Pacifico was promoted during four summers (1956 to 1959) to advertise San Diego. It presented an elaborate state pageant entitled the California Story, but even though the pageant was well done, it did not receive the overall support originally expected.

Mission Valley Changes Forever

One of the turning points in the pattern of San Diego's growth was the decision by the May Company of Los Angeles in 1957 to build a shopping center in Mission Valley near the junction of US Highways 80 and 395 (now Interstate 8 and State 163). This meant rezoning agricultural and residential land to commercial use. Some large shopping centers—groups of stores with a ample areas for parking—had already been built in Linda Vista and at South Bay Plaza. In Mission Valley, rezoning had permitted a new baseball park for the minor league Padres, and some hotels were under construction. Charles H. Brown's Atlas Hotels helped bring tourists into the area with the Town & Country Hotel built in 1953. Its convention center was added in 1970. Brown envisioned ranch-type facilities with swimming pools and tennis courts. He later expanded Hotel Circle with the Hanalei Hotel and others.

Although flooding of the valley did not occur during the 1950s, the May Company and others were warned of the potential danger. The May Company executives assured the city council that all structures in the shopping center would rest on nine-foot fill—higher than any flooding ever recorded. The city's planning department, however, had been working on a master plan for the valley that provided for flood control and envisioned recreational development. They argued: "Mission Valley is the gateway to potentially the finest recreational area in the world. It will develop into an area complementing

Looking east over development of the shopping mall in Mission Valley. *Photo ©San Diego History Center.*

Mission Bay, offering accommodations and entertainment to visitors and residents. It would be possible for some future generation to tie Mission Valley, Old San Diego, and Mission Bay Park together by a motor-boat canal, scenic roadway, bridle trails, and a scenic railway—further enhancing our position as a tourist center."

Harry Haelsig, city planning director, felt that the May Company's proposal was not in keeping with the city's long-range planning. City staff members feared that once Mission Valley was paved with commercial enterprises, it would be lost forever as an open area. The planning commission overruled its staff, three to two, and a formal hearing was set by the city council in June 1958. The May Company threatened to go elsewhere if it could not build on the proposed site. Downtown merchants who opposed the center were accused of not wanting competition, but George Scott insisted their concern was future flooding and the cost of appropriate protection.

Opposition to Mission Valley Development

Hamilton Marston, grandson of George White Marston and his successor in retail merchandising, pleaded with the council to consider the consequences of opening the door to rezoning. He agreed that shopping centers were "a fact of mid-twentieth century American life" but asked that the city analyze how they fit into the pattern of residential, recreational, commercial, industrial, and administrative land use. Arthur Jessop asked that the council consider all future possibilities for the valley because if it did not, it might "as well tatoo on the Council walls: 'Thus died planning in San Diego.'"

Guilford Whitney feared a new central city just four minutes from downtown would cause a slum business district in the original area. Others supported the concept of a conveniently-located shopping center and were afraid the May Company might change its mind. But the May Company pledged cooperation and friendship and agreed to pay its fair share of community services. The council adopted the zone change unanimously. Opponents felt the city had lost an opportunity to make Mission Valley a unique area with a proper blending of hotels, recreational facilities, and shopping. Flood control was still a part of the city's overall plan.

Soon other shopping centers became a reality. Broadway-Hale department stores acquired a site in Chula Vista while the Marston Company joined in the planning of Grossmont Center, built by Del Webb of Phoenix. George Scott's College Grove opened in July 1960 and Mission Valley Center in February 1961. Broadway-Hale bought out Marston's, the oldest name in San Diego merchandising, to open in Grossmont Center in the fall of 1961. El Cajon's Parkway Plaza opened in 1973. Other shopping clusters throughout the county were not far behind. New suburban strip malls also grew with the birth of such communities as Clairemont, Kearny Mesa, University City, Del Cerro, and Allied Gardens, filling in the gaps between San Diego and neighboring cities.

Mission Bay Development

In the meantime, Mission Bay planners were experiencing problems. A basic question arose over who was to enjoy the facilities—local residents who could come for the day or tourists wanting to stay in large convention-like hotels and take advantage of the sun and beach. There were also major environmental concerns. Glenn Rick resisted a too-rigid master plan to allow for greater flexibility. Commitments

Mission Bay Development. *Photo courtesy San Diego Yacht Club.*

had already been made to the state for a wildlife preserve on the northern half of the eastern bay area. Seventy-seven acres of sanctuary were made a part of the master plan in 1958 although scientists warned that the ecological balance would never be the same.

The slowness in reaching any agreement created numerous problems. The federal government contributed $10 million, the city $19 million, and the state $3.5 million for initial dredging, development, and flood control. No plan could be totally successful, but the bay began to unfold as a tremendous aquatic playground with almost 2,000 acres of navigable water, more than 2,000 acres of parkland, and almost 32 miles of shoreline. Areas were designated for boat launchings, picnicking, playgrounds, hotels, motels, and beaches. Of the available land, 25 percent was for commercial purposes to make the park self-supporting.

The master plan was opposed by some members of the Mission Bay Commission, but it passed the city council unanimously in 1958. In early 1960, the Department of Parks and Recreation took over direction of Mission Bay development. All hotels and facilities had to meet certain standards. The year 1964 witnessed the opening of Sea World, one of the most successful marine-life parks in the United States. Not only did it give Mission Bay a popular focal point with its outdoor exhibits and marine life, it provided an exotic fish collection and educational displays depicting man's relationship with the sea. It also included a 300-foot observation tower with a revolving elevator.

Problems of San Diego Bay

San Diego Bay's problems were very different from those of Mission Bay. Because the bay was used primarily for commercial and military purposes and not for swimming or waterskiing, there was less concern about its quality. Prior to 1943, the city let raw sewage flow into the bay through twenty outfalls. By 1948, waste from National City, Lemon Grove, La Mesa, and North Island poured into the bay. Voters refused to approve a sewer bond issue of $16 million in 1954 to correct the problem. A more elaborate plan for a treatment plant and ocean outfall at Point Loma was estimated at $26 million, with all metropolitan area users sharing costs. Finally approved by the city and built in 1963 at an eventual cost of $51 million, it contained 27 miles of drains. The federal government added a connection with the sewer system of Tijuana for emergency conditions to prevent emptying of sewage through the Tia Juana (later called Tijuana) River bed and resulting pollution of beaches.

Residents of Imperial Beach, Chula Vista, National City, and Coronado have also had a large stake with San Diego in port development. In 1953 the chamber of commerce sponsored a study to create a San Diego Unified Port District. Later, state Senator Hugo Fisher and Assemblyman James Mills sponsored an act creating the district. It was approved in 1962 by city officials of all but Coronado. Many South Bay residents favored a second entrance into the bay at Imperial Beach, but it has been set aside for environmental purposes.

San Diego Water Issues

In July 1948, the San Diego County Water Authority studied the need for a second barrel to the first San Diego aqueduct. Negotiations led to an Act of Congress in October 1951 that authorized the navy to complete the San Diego Aqueduct by constructing the second barrel. Construction commenced in October 1952 and was completed in

San Vicente Dam. *Photo courtesy San Diego County Water Authority.*

October 1954. The Authority continued its constant and systematic planning under the leadership of chairman Fred Heilbron and guidance of General Counsel William H. Jennings, also a member of the State Water Commission. Population growth, increased agricultural needs, and expansion of its area required additional delivery capacity. By 1960 the authority's boundaries had grown from 94,706 acres in 1948 to 732,028 acres, and its population from 432,000 to 956,400.

The 22 member agencies of the San Diego County Water Authority were the Fallbrook Public Utility District; the five cities of Del Mar, Escondido, National City, Oceanside, and San Diego; the irrigation districts of Helix, San Dieguito, Santa Fe, and South Bay; and the municipal water districts of Bueno Colorado, Carlsbad, De Luz Heights, Olivenhain, Otay, Poway, Rainbow, Ramona, Rincon del Diablo, Padre Dam, Valley Center, and Yuima.

On July 9, 1959 the state passed the Burns-Porter Act, which called for an election to approve a bond issue of $1,758,000,000 for construction of Oroville Dam on the Feather River and an aqueduct to deliver water into southern California. The Metropolitan Water District (MWD) and the state agreed on November 4, 1960, for payment and delivery of 1.5 million acre-feet annually of state project water. On November 8, 1960, voters barely approved the bond issue 1.06 to 1. San Diego County's vote was critical because it carried 4.1 to 1.

On June 7, 1966, voters in the San Diego County Water Authority District approved a $30 million bond issue to fund construction of Pipeline 4—the second pipeline of the second San Diego aqueduct. Again MWD agreed to build the north part from Skinner Reservoir in Riverside County to the authority's delivery point 6 miles south of the San Diego County line, which was completed in 1971. When the authority's part from the delivery point to Miramar Reservoir was completed in 1973, they were capable of delivering about one million acre-feet per year. Financing for an additional pipeline (5) did not require a bond issue, but was made under section 8 of the act, by issuance of certificates of indebtedness.

Higher Education in San Diego

Higher education expanded significantly in San Diego during the 1950s. Early in the decade, the board of regents of the University of California system considered a move to San Diego. John Jay Hopkins, chairman of Convair and General Dynamics Corporation, urged the location of a scientific and technical campus in the La Jolla area. If this were done, he would provide a grant of $1 million and build his own research center estimated at $10 million. The new campus would be highly specialized and tie into Scripps Institution of Oceanography. On July 10, 1956, Hopkins dedicated a site for the new university on Torrey Pines mesa, former pueblo lands that had been voted by the people for a new atomic research center.

Robert H. Biron chaired a San Diego Chamber of Commerce committee to gain the state legislature's approval for a University of California San Diego (UCSD) campus. The committee then led a successful city ballot campaign. Dr. Roger Revelle, director of Scripps Institution, emphasized the graduate nature of the new campus, although the board of regents believed undergraduate training to be essential. The university as proposed would be built on 1,000 acres and serve 10,000 students by 1970. Actual figures showed UCSD with 4,400 students and 1,900 acres for its three colleges in 1970.

From its inception, UCSD attracted scholars from throughout the United States. Dr. Herbert York, former US director of defense research and engineering, became the university's first chancellor.

Founders Hall looking at the Immaculata at the University of San Diego.

Revelle left San Diego to head Harvard's Center for Population Studies but returned to UCSD in 1975. Within a short time, the distinguished reputation of UCSD, in conjunction with Scripps Institution of Oceanography, became known worldwide.

The plans of San Diego Bishop Charles F. Buddy and Mother Rosalie Clifton Hill, RSCJ, reached completion when the Society of the Sacred Heart's College for Women opened in 1952. The College for Men and the School of Law, sponsored by the diocese of San Diego, began classes in 1954. California Western University also opened in 1952 in Point Loma on the site formerly occupied by Katherine Tingley's theosophical community. San Diego State College had an enrollment of 4,134 students that year. Community colleges included San Diego Junior (now City) College and Vocational School.

The Salk Institute for Biological Research was founded in 1963 in La Jolla by Dr. Jonas Salk, developer of the polio vaccine. The institute has provided research facilities for scientists from throughout the nation. La Jolla, long known for its scenic beauty, emerged in the 1960s as a burgeoning center of education and research. The La Jolla Museum of Contemporary Art emphasized the modern era in its excellent collection of paintings, sculptures, and graphic arts. The outstanding writer of children's books, Theodor Geisel, better known as "Dr. Suess," became an often-honored La Jolla resident.

Revitalizing Downtown

The revitalization of the downtown area began in the 1960s with a wave of high-rise construction. Fortunately, downtown had never actually been neglected, even with construction of outlying shopping centers. The San Diego Chamber of Commerce and the Convention & Visitors Bureau had been attracting businesses and promoting tourism; in the 1960s the Economic Development Corporation was launched to spur industrial growth. The first new skyscraper housed the offices of Home Federal Savings & Loan Association, headed by Charles K. Fletcher, son of pioneer developer Ed Fletcher. The younger Fletchers would all play active roles in San Diego's business community.

A second skyscraper was completed at Second and Broadway to house C. Arnholt Smith's United States National Bank. Irvin Kahn's 24-story First and C Building also enhanced the skyline. A new organization called San Diegans, Inc. headed by Joseph Jessop Sr. grew out of the Downtown Association and began to work with the city planning department. The city council finally authorized a master plan for downtown and came up with a proposal for a new city hall, convention center and auditorium, a civic theater and parking garage at a total cost of $15 million. Financing would come from the county's purchase of the city's half of the civic center for $3.5 million, $8.5 million borrowed from the city employees retirement fund and $2 million from capital outlay.

The remainder would be raised by private contributions. Guilford Whitney led the fund-raising campaign and received tremendous backing from many including James S. Copley, publisher of *The San Diego Union* and the *Evening Tribune*; Morley H. Golden, a general contractor active with San Diegans, Inc.; First National Bank of San Diego (now California First); Bank of America; Home Federal Savings; San Diego Federal Savings (later Great American Savings

Charles Dail Community Concourse and Civic Theater. *Photo ©San Diego History Center.*

and then Wells Fargo Bank); US Grant Hotel; San Diego Gas & Electric Company; and others.

The new and modern Charles Dail Community Concourse was dedicated on September 16, 1964, and the magnificent 3,000-seat Civic Theater, designed by Lloyd Ruocco, opened in January 1965. This first grouping of public buildings achieved by San Diego won the city a designation as an All-American City by the National Municipal League. Even though an economic recession during the 1960s threatened the future of some institutions, more high-rise buildings continued to appear against the horizon.

Television Development

The advent of television in the late 1940s brought about a change in the social pattern of American life perhaps as great as the invention of the automobile. Its overall effects, however, would be more difficult to assess. Cities everywhere in the United States competed for FCC licensing. San Diego was no exception. KFMB, on the radio since 1943, beamed its first television broadcast from the Continental Room of the Hotel San Diego at 8:01 p.m. on Monday, May 16, 1949. Its transmitter was located on Mount Soledad. San Diego became the 36th American city (63rd license issued) with its own channel. The station cost owner Jack Gross $300,000 to build. As early as 1950, there were 25,000 television sets in San Diego County, although many families were still gathering in front of appliance stores to catch a glimpse of a nine-inch black-and-white screen.

KFMB-TV, Channel 8, under new ownership, moved briefly to 1375 Pacific Highway. Such local programs as *Smokey Rogers* and *People in the News* attracted a large audience. Channel 8 was purchased by John A. Kennedy of West Virginia, owner of the short-lived *San Diego Daily Journal.* He moved that station into the former newspaper headquarters at Fifth and Ash. Howard Chernoff, general manager of the *Journal,* took over management of the television and radio stations. Channel 8 broadcast all three major network programs until NBC went with the new Channel 10 in 1953 and ABC affiliated with Channel 6 in 1955. Channel 8, which remained with CBS, featured such local personalities as Harold Keen and Ray Wilson in news broadcasting and Bob Dale with the Payday Movie. Helen Alvarez (Smith) and Jack Wrather, owners of a Tulsa, Oklahoma, channel, purchased KFMB in 1953. Channel 8 became a part of Trans-Continent Broadcasting in 1959 and was sold in 1964 to Midwest Television with August C. Meyer, president. Under General Manager Robert L. Myers, Channel 8 moved into modern new studios in Kearny Mesa in 1977 and with its affiliates KFMB-AM and FM, remained highly competitive.

San Diego's second television station, XETV Channel 6, was conceived in 1950 by Al Flanagan of Channel 8. Because of a freeze on new television licenses begun in late 1948, Flanagan met with Mexican television executives George Rivera and Emilio Azcarraga, with whom he purchased television equipment in New York for a transmitter and studios in Tijuana atop Mount San Antonio. The television station was licensed in Mexico and began broadcasting on January 29, 1953. Julian Kaufman, a young executive working in Phoenix television, joined XETV as general manager after its first seven months. He successfully overcame some of the prejudices against the Mexican station.

Channel 7/39 NBC moved to downtown San Diego headquarters in 2004.

Channel 6 carried both English and Spanish programs until the mid-1950s when Channel 12, XEWT, began operating entirely in Spanish. Fear that a lack of FCC restrictions would allow Channel 6 to recklessly beam unwanted programs into San Diego proved unfounded. XETV affiliated with ABC from 1955 until 1973 when it again became independent. The first offices were on Park Boulevard, but Channel 6 built a modern facility with a Mexican architectural theme in Kearny Mesa and moved there in 1976. The station featured mainly movies and reruns. With production facilities in Tijuana, XEWT Channel 12 served the Spanish-speaking community on both sides of the border. The free-trade negotiations then being conducted between the United States and Mexico increased the value of programming directed at populations in these two countries.

KGTV, Channel 10, like Channel 8, grew out of radio. Licensed in 1925, its call letters became KFSD in 1926. Programs were broadcast from the US Grant Hotel with a flattop antenna from 1933 to 1948 when its transmitter was moved to Emerald Hills. The station could not get a television license during the freeze, but owner-applicant Thomas E. Sharp received one of the earliest licenses allotted after the freeze was lifted. Channel 10's first program as KFSD-TV was aired in 1953, with its transmitter located on Mount Soledad.

The station—an NBC affiliate—was sold by Sharp's Airfan Radio Corporation in 1954 to Fox, Wells & Rogers, who built the new TV-AM-FM studios at 47th Street and Highway 94 in 1958. The 43,000-square-foot building housed the most modern equipment available at the time. William E. Goetze served as general manager from 1954 to 1963, during which time the station call letters were changed from KFSD to KOGO and it was sold to Time-Life Broadcast, Inc. When McGraw-Hill bought the station in June 1971, Channel 10 was forced to give up its radio affiliation with KOGO-AM and KFSD-FM. The call letters were changed from KOGO-TV to KGTV, and in 1977 Channel 10 joined ABC.

The youngest commercial television station in San Diego is KNSD, formerly KCST, UHF Channel 39. It got off to a shaky start as KAAR-TV in 1966 under the ownership of Atlas Hotel magnate Charles H. Brown. During the first year of broadcasting, Brown was heavily involved in problems with the Hanalei Hotel and could not devote attention to the station. His sudden death in 1967 left son Terry Brown with multiple responsibilities, and the station went off the air. It was purchased by Bass Brothers Broadcasting and returned to the air on January 28, 1968, with an emphasis on sports.

San Diego Sports

The minor league Pacific Coast San Diego Padres were a popular and pennant-winning baseball team playing in Mission Valley's Westgate Park. When the National League expanded in 1969, San Diego received a major league franchise. The name Padres was retained, and Emil J. "Buzzie" Bavasi, long associated with the Los Angeles Dodgers, became part owner with C. Arnholt Smith. They would share San Diego's new stadium with professional and college football.

As early as 1958, Barron Hilton, owner of the newly formed American Football League's Los Angeles Chargers, indicated his desire to move to San Diego. The city council agreed to renovate Balboa Stadium and increase its seating capacity from 23,000 to 34,500, but the Chargers were definitely a part of the planning for a

Jack Murphy Stadium (renamed Qualcomm in 1997). *Photo ©San Diego History Center.*

new municipal stadium in Mission Valley. The architectural and engineering firm of Frank L. Hope & Associates selected the site and designed the $27.6 million ultra-modern structure seating more than 50,000 spectators. Voters enthusiastically approved the stadium bonds in November 1965. It was opened and ready for use in August 1967 and renamed in 1981 Jack Murphy Stadium to honor local sportswriter Murphy who died in 1982. The name was changed to Qualcomm Stadium in 1997 in exchange for an $18 million gift to the city.

The San Diego Chargers won four division championships during the 1960s. Under head coach Sid Gillman, formerly of the Rams, the team boasted such popular and effective players as John Hadl, Lance Alworth, Ron Mix, Paul Lowe, Keith Lincoln, Speedy Duncan, Gary Garrison, Walt Sweeney, Ernie Ladd, and Earl Faison. In August 1966 Barron Hilton sold the Chargers to a group headed by Eugene Klein and Samuel Shulman for $10 million. The Hiltons retained a minor interest. After 1969, the AFL merged with the NFL, and the Chargers suffered some rough times. Old-time fans looked back longingly to 1961 and the very first game in Balboa Stadium when the Chargers defeated the Oakland Raiders, 44–0.

The Sports Arena

The city also promoted construction of the International Sports Arena in November 1966. Costing $6.5 million, it was designed to seat 13,000 spectators for hockey and 13,700 for basketball and other public events. The Sports Arena was built on city-owned land through private investors led by Robert Breitbard. In 1966, Breitbard obtained a franchise in the Western Hockey League, the Gulls, and in 1967 obtained a franchise for a National Basketball Association expansion team he called the Rockets. Both teams were popular but short lived. On October 12, 2010, the arena's name was changed to the "Valley View Casino Center" under a $1.5 million, 5-year agreement between the arena operator AEG, the San Pasqual Band of Diegueño Mission Indians and the city of San Diego.

Old Town San Diego State Historic Park

In 1964, State Assemblyman James Mills, because of his long-abiding interest in local history, introduced a resolution to determine the feasibility of creating a state historic park at Old Town. Some building restoration for San Diego's Bicentennial celebration was also proposed. The study, completed in 1966, recommended that Old Town, an area architecturally and historically significant to California as well as to the nation, be made a state park. Even before that time, however, other efforts to preserve the history of Old Town had taken place. *The San Diego Union* had restored its first home near the plaza and built a small museum. Outside the park, the Historic Shrine Foundation had saved the Whaley House, the George Pendleton Home, and the Mason Street School while the city had restored the Adobe Chapel. The Casa de Lopez, located in the path of Interstate 5, was faithfully rebuilt on a new location with private funds and became a candle shop.

Community members who opposed park control by the state believed that local city and county governments could better direct

The Coronado Bridge completed in 1969 brought change to Coronado.

the project. Nevertheless, Mills was successful, and in 1965 the State Board of Park Commissioners designated nineteen structures for restoration. Initial property acquisition began in 1967. As the master plan for the park developed, it was decided that the interpretive period would be from 1821 to 1872, allowing a blend of both Mexican and American structures and cultures. The University of San Diego and the state of California carried out archeological investigations of the sites.

While the state began work on the Estudillo and Machado-Stewart houses, San Diego planned its 1969 bicentennial program. Although much of Old Town's land was purchased by the state by the beginning of the year, little restoration was actually completed. A number of temporary buildings and booths were put up to capture an atmosphere of the Spanish and Mexican periods. City residents decorated their houses with gold lights, and Mayor Frank Curran officiated at the opening ceremonies. Special activities were held at Old Town, and even though visitors were fewer than hoped for during 1969, it brought new interest to San Diego's historic center.

The Coronado Bridge

The decade of the 1960s also brought a significant change to the city of Coronado. Local residents had known for several years that the delay in crossing the bay by ferry was beginning to outweigh the advantages of insularity. The Coronado City Council asked as early as 1952 for a feasibility study of a bridge. John Alessio, who purchased the Hotel del Coronado in 1960, spent more than $2 million refurbishing the hotel's interior. He approached the Coronado council for immediate approval of a bridge to speed access to the hotel. The council voted it down, three to two, but the San Diego Unified Port District gave the necessary approval.

As the bridge came closer to reality, a number of residents who wanted to protect Coronado from excessive traffic opposed it. Alessio sold the "Hotel del" in 1963 to Larry Lawrence, who continued to work for the bridge in political circles. Lawrence enlarged the hotel with a seven-story addition and made a number of improvements. Other areas earmarked for development at that time included Coronado Shores, ten high-rise condominium units on 22 acres of land southwest of the hotel, and the bayshore community of Coronado Cays further south on the Silver Strand.

The navy did not object to the bridge as long as it stood 200 feet above the water to permit ship and aircraft operations in the bay. The army corps of engineers approved the design and location. The California Toll-Bridge Authority, of which Governor Edmund G. "Pat" Brown was a member, voted to build it with revenue bonds. Sadly, the historic Coronado Ferry Company was purchased and, like similar ferry companies throughout California, went out of business. A smaller ferry service would finally be reestablished in 1990.

Appropriate points of entry and exit and new traffic patterns were finally decided by the state. The San Diego-Coronado Bay Bridge, a magnificent structure designed by Robert Mosher of La Jolla, presented a graceful curve across the water on the day of its opening August 3, 1969. Dr. W. Paul Vetter, mayor of Coronado and long-time member of the planning commission, officiated at the ceremony with the state's new governor, Ronald Reagan. Coincidentally, the towering Interstate 805 bridge that spans Mission Valley was also completed that year.

Chapter XI

BIRTH OF THE MODERN ERA: 1970–1990

A New San Diego

When Alonzo Horton began his New Town by the bay, he envisioned a future city with a vibrant downtown, an active multipurpose harbor, and a supportive surrounding population. As the San Diego Chamber of Commerce celebrated its 100th birthday in January 1970, city leaders were still working toward that goal. Those most concerned with the city's economic and cultural well-being pointed with pride to many areas of progress. Experts predicted that even though a slight recession was probable for the decade of the 1970s, San Diego would be only slightly affected. They were right. The region's growth was steady and permanent. By 1980, San Diego had passed San Francisco to become the second largest city in California and by 1990, San Diego's population had passed the 1 million mark with the county reaching nearly 2.5 million; the city by then had become the 7th largest in the nation.

Pete Wilson and the Political Arena

San Diego politics during the 1970s witnessed the forceful enthusiasm of its hardworking mayor Pete Wilson, a former state assemblyman who decided to direct his energies toward the local scene. Elected in 1971, Mayor Wilson emerged as a vital, dominant factor in controlling economic policy and determining patterns of growth. In 1972, when the Republican National Convention pulled out of San Diego for Miami, Wilson quipped that San Diego was an "unconventional city" and decided to use the convention week to promote San Diego as "America's Finest City." Among Wilson's top priorities for improving the quality of life was revitalizing the downtown area. Wilson also created a municipal environmental protection agency to monitor the effects of proposed growth and encouraged light rail transit to lessen freeway congestion.

After a disappointing bid for governor in 1980, Republican Party leaders persuaded Wilson to run for the United States Senate in 1982. Wilson captured the nomination and won the seat after a hard-fought campaign against former California governor Jerry Brown. Wilson was literally pushed into the national spotlight in 1985 when, while recovering from an emergency appendectomy, he reached the Senate floor in a wheelchair to cast the tie vote on the budget, thus enabling Vice President George Bush to break the tie in favor of the Reagan administration. Wilson's star rose quickly and he became a major contributor in a nationwide crackdown on crime, especially drugs. He also kept his San Diego constituents in mind and supported programs to benefit San Diego's aerospace and defense-electronics industries and supported the Equal Rights Amendment. In 1988 Wilson fought off a challenge by Lieutenant Governor Leo McCarthy to win reelection to the United States Senate by the largest margin of any candidate in the country.

Then, a mere three weeks after his election, Wilson announced his intention to run for the governorship of California. He opposed San Francisco mayor Dianne Feinstein and promised a disciplined government—especially in view of an estimated $7 billion state budget deficit. Wilson won the California election by a slim margin of 49%–46% in November 1990 and took office amidst the worst budget crisis in the state's history. Feinstein then won a special election to gain Wilson's US Senate seat, while Wilson was forced to oppose the conservative wing of the Republican Party in his own

Pete Wilson and Clair Burgener share a walk in Sacramento. *Photo courtesy of Clair Burgener.*

state. He pushed through new taxes and severe budget cuts in programs affecting education and welfare. Despite stepping on many toes statewide, Governor Wilson was praised for his willingness to face the facts squarely.

Key Politicians

One of the persons most responsible for the success of Pete Wilson, directing his Senate strategy committee, was former Republican congressman Clair W. Burgener—the first San Diegan to hold office at all three levels of government. Burgener, a member of the San Diego City Council from 1953 to 1957, a California assemblyman from 1963 to 1966, and a state senator from 1967 to 1972, went to Congress that year, representing San Diego and part of Orange County. Burgener became a member of the powerful House Committee on Appropriations and its Subcommittee on Energy and Water Development in 1975. He decided to retire from public office in June 1983.

Another key San Diego politician during that period was Lionel Van Deerlin. He started his career in the news business before World War II as a reporter for the old *San Diego Sun.* During the 1950s, he switched from newspapers to TV news as commentator and news director for Channels 6 and 10. And then, in 1962, he took another career turn. He ran for the US Congress in the 40th District and won—no small feat for a Democrat in San Diego. He was once described as "San Diego Republicans' favorite Democrat and the Democrats' favorite Republican" serving in Congress until 1980.

Mayors Hedgcock and O'Connor

The election of Pete Wilson to the US Senate left a vacancy in San Diego's top office. Two major candidates sought election—Roger Hedgcock, a lawyer and six-year veteran of the San Diego County Board of Supervisors and Maureen O'Connor, a former member of the city council, endorsed by San Diego's Copley Press. Although local elections are technically nonpartisan, voters knew that Hedgcock was a Republican and O'Connor a Democrat. In a tight race with many crossover votes, Hedgcock edged out O'Connor with a 4 percent margin in a 51 percent turnout on May 3, 1983, becoming at age 37 the second youngest mayor in San Diego's history. A graduate of St. Augustine High School and the University of California, Santa Barbara, Hedgcock was a forceful and creative leader.

Shortly after the election, in a seemingly unrelated incident, the financial empire of J. David Dominelli, a local stock promoter and philanthropist, collapsed. Dominelli liquidated his company for bankruptcy officials but was convicted and jailed for defrauding his investors. Ironically caught in the web of Dominelli's manipulations, Mayor Hedgcock, facing trial on charges of not properly reporting campaign contributions from the company, was forced to resign as mayor on December 10, 1985. The following February, Dominelli pleaded guilty to charges of illegally funneling J. David and Co. funds into Hedgcock's campaign. Hedgcock, who soon after became a popular and successful radio talk-show host, was acquitted of all charges by a Supreme Court ruling in 1991.

The 1986 mayor's race featured Maureen O'Connor, a favorite of the post-World War II baby boomers, running against popular council member and Deputy Mayor Bill Cleator, also a Republican.

O'Connor, a native San Diegan and the eighth of 13 children, was a graduate of Rosary High School and San Diego State University. She had served two terms on the city council beginning in 1971, the youngest person to hold that position at age 25, served on the Metropolitan Transit Development Board from 1976 through 1981, and as a port commissioner from 1980 to 1985.

O'Connor was elected San Diego's first woman mayor in June 1986 and reelected in June 1988 for a four-year term. O'Connor took a tight hold on the reins of city government and increased San Diego's fair share of federal and state funding by over 60% to almost $100 million in 1988. Among her priorities were management of the city's growth, raising money for local arts groups, and the creation of a triennial City Arts Festival.

Problems of Growth Countywide

The population boom in southern California brought with it new problems of growth. Fortunately, long-range water planning carried the region through a major drought in the mid-1970s, but it could not prevent the damage caused by flooding during periods of intense rainfall from 1978 through 1980. The water supply was barely adequate to carry San Diego through even more serious drought conditions from 1986 through 1991. The San Diego County Water Authority, the agency responsible for delivering water to all member agencies in the county, embarked upon a campaign for water conservation designed to prevent water shortages during drought years.

Pressures of urbanization drove land and housings costs up from 1970 to 1990 and greatly lessened the amount of acreage in agricultural production, often erasing boundaries between urban and rural areas. As farmers looked at increased labor costs and the ordinary expenses of growing crops, they were lured by the extraordinary profits of converting land into housing developments. The rolling hills and pastures of Rancho Bernardo and Rancho Los Peñasquitos became multimillion-dollar urbanized centers. To the south and east, remote areas like Rancho Jamacha became the planned community of Rancho

The home of sporting goods magnate A.G. Spalding, member of Theosophical Society, was converted into the administration building of Point Loma Nazarene University in 1973.

San Diego, and Viejas Valley Ranch (now Palo Verde) in Alpine was transformed into two-and three-acre estates commanding top prices.

Closer to the heart of the city, houses in Mira Mesa and Tierrasanta stretched across the landscape at a rate hardly imagined in San Diego's history. Light to dark brown condominiums filled up hills and canyons throughout the county as alternatives to expensive single-family dwellings. During the decade of the 1980s, only the colors had changed to pink, light blue, and gray. Property along the beachfronts skyrocketed in value. The price of an average house in the county increased from $26,900 in 1970 to $102,400 in 1979. By 1990, the average house was selling for more than $200,000.

The area of North County, which collectively refers to the communities north of Torrey Pines along the coast and north of San Diego's neighborhood of Mira Mesa inland, extends to the county's northern border with Orange and Riverside Counties. It experienced the most rapid growth during the 1980s when the populations of San Marcos and Vista doubled while Carlsbad grew by 78% and Escondido and Oceanside by more than 65%. In 1988 Escondido received an influx of 30,000 new residents, and spent $15.7 million on a handsome, architecturally significant city hall.

Mayan Hall at Southwestern College in Chula Vista.

Point Loma Nazarene University took over the former site of Katherine Tingley's Theosophical Society in 1973. A new branch of the state educational system, California State University, San Marcos, began as a satellite campus of San Diego State University in the fall of 1979. It developed into an independent campus beginning classes in 1990. The new campus provided a center for major events and helped unify the communities of North County. Residents of Ranchos Peñasquitos and Bernardo, which are included within the city of San Diego, could also take advantage of the less-crowded state campus.

To the south of San Diego, Chula Vista became the second-largest city in San Diego County with a population of 135,000 in 1990. The community redesigned its waterfront with a park and marina, while residential areas developed rapidly in the eastern portions of the city. The new freeway route SR 125 served the new planned communities of Eastlake and Otay Ranch. Southwestern Community College, with its high percentage of Latino students, provided classes for the South Bay area from Bonita to San Ysidro and to the neighborhoods of Harborside, Castle Park, and Otay. National City, the second-oldest city in San Diego County, had only a slight population increase since its potential for growth was limited by the lack of available land within the city's boundaries. National City's economy, depending to a large extent upon the navy or civilian employees of the 32nd Street Naval Station, was affected by cutbacks in military spending.

Downtown Redevelopment

The downtown area was at the center of revitalization plans of Mayors Wilson and O'Connor. The city council, with chamber of commerce backing, established the Centre City Development Corporation (CCDC) in 1975 as the agency to administer redevelopment of 1,200 acres encompassing the Horton Plaza, Marina, and Columbia redevelopment projects. The mayor worked closely with planners to create a complex that would be a "dynamic renaissance" of the city's heartland, giving it an entirely new lifestyle as envisioned by Alonzo Horton and John Nolen. Some controversy developed over selecting which buildings should or should not be preserved and restored as historic sites. But all agreed that downtown was a viable part of the community and a key to future city growth.

Horton Plaza, a 41.5-acre downtown project, incorporated fifteen city blocks from Broadway to G Street between Union and Fourth. The focal point, a 11.5-acre shopping center with 155 stores and restaurants, movie theaters, and Lyceum stage, plus $1 million in fine artwork, was developed by Ernest Hahn Inc. beginning in 1974. The genius behind the center was architect Jon Jerde, who designed the $140 million structure as a combination of California casual, Renaissance England, and Palazzo Italiano in 49 different colors. The unusual multilevel center has won numerous awards and the *New York Times* called it "One of the most ambitious retail structures ever built in a single stroke in an American city...architecturally stunning." It opened on August 9, 1985, and provided an exciting combination of commercial, retail, hotel, recreational, and entertainment facilities with sufficient parking areas.

The Horton Plaza project area also incorporated the historic landmarks of the Spreckels Building, Balboa Theatre, and Horton Plaza Park along with the Meridian, a 27-story 172-unit luxury high-rise condominium tower. The US Grant Hotel, which underwent

Horton Plaza Shopping Mall in downtown San Diego. Inset: Ernest Hahn.

complete renovation at a cost of nearly $80 million between August 1983 and December 1985, faces the historic Horton Plaza fountain and commercial center.

The Marina Project was San Diego's first truly urban residential development planned since the turn of the century. It included Horton House, a fourteen-story tower providing 150 apartments for senior citizens, some of whom were residents of other downtown hotels. The San Diego Marriott Hotel and Marina built between 1982 and 1987, the Embassy Suites completed in 1988, and the 39-story Hyatt Regency Hotel completed in 1992 provided a significant number of new hotel rooms to complement the Convention Center complex. Included in the Marina Project was One Harbor Drive, twin 41-story 202-unit condominium high-rise towers completed in 1992. A 500-slip marina and ocean-oriented park were also developed by the San Diego Port District to fully utilize the waterfront acreage.

The Columbia Redevelopment Project was the connecting link between the central business district and the Embarcadero, Marina Park, and Park Row, low-rise condominiums in a medium-priced bracket, were completed in 1984 and 1985. The 56-acre project located between Pacific Highway and Union Street, bounded by Ash and Broadway, also accommodates office and residential areas surrounding the restored Santa Fe Railway Depot. High-rise office buildings completed on Broadway included the Koll Center in 1989, the Emerald-Shapery Center in 1990, and One America Plaza, containing a 50-foot galleria housing the main transfer station for the Bayside Trolley Line, in 1991. Altogether the plans included 2,000 housing units—garden apartments, townhouses, and condominiums—with a waterfront theme.

The San Diego Convention Center

The story of San Diego's Convention Center was not one that unfolded easily. Powerful opponents of downtown development were able to deal the city an occasional blow along the way. When funding for an early attempt to build the center was placed on the city's first mail-in ballot in 1981, opponents questioned the city's competence to run the center, the need for such a large investment, and the high costs, stressing facilities already in place in Mission Valley. The measure lost 174,083 to 112,848. Four years later, the San Diego Port District funded the project and construction began in 1985. The Convention Center, costing $165 million, became one of the largest of the 139 major projects initiated by CCDC that have involved $150 million in public investment and $3.9 billion in private investment. The massive waterfront structure, which occupies 11 acres of land at the foot of Fifth Avenue, is truly spectacular.

Arthur Erikson of Los Angeles, who based his ideas on the center's location on the water, was the primary designer. He was responsible for the vaulted glass ceilings to allow natural sunlight into the interior and the fabric tents on top to give the appearance of sails and allow protection from rain. The center, which has three levels, contains 254,000 square feet of exhibit space, 32 meeting rooms, a 40,000 square-foot ballroom, a 100,000 square-foot lobby and registration area, a 400-seat bayside amphitheater, and 90,000 square feet of

Louis Bank of Commerce and Nesmith-Greeley Building in the Gaslamp Quarter, 1888.

waterfront terraces. There are six rooftop lighted championship tennis courts, a pro shop, and an exercise facility. In 1992, plans were made for the center's expansion on a 15-acre parcel to the south.

The Gaslamp Quarter

The Convention Center is located next to the historic Gaslamp Quarter, a 38-acre project covering sixteen blocks from Broadway to Market Street between Fourth and Sixth Streets. The owners in the Gaslamp District who sponsored this privately financed and culturally rewarding project were aided in 1977 by the State Historic Building Code that allowed greater latitude for those restoring old buildings rather than building new ones. Supported by the San Diego City Council in the form of a Planned District Ordinance adopted in 1976, the concept differed from redevelopment because its primary objective was the preservation of landmarks of historic, architectural, and cultural value that provided continuity with the past.

By 1980 the major restored buildings in the Gaslamp Quarter included the Jewelers Exchange Building, constructed by Nathan Watts in 1912; the post-Victorian Lester Hotel; a two-story Victorian-era storefront hotel at Fifth and Market Streets, restored by Drs. Antonia Pantoja and Wilhelmina Perry; and the 1880s Grand Pacific Hotel, restored by Shirley Bernard. The successful Old Spaghetti

Factory restaurant chain chose the Gaslamp Quarter as the site of its San Diego branch (re-created as an upscale restaurant in 2005). The Francis Family Antique Warehouse was one of the earliest rehabilitation projects and other antique shops have since opened in the district. By 1983 the city had spent $3 million on widened brick sidewalks, period street lamps, benches and landscaping. By 1987, $6 million in public improvements had been made.

The Gaslamp Quarter during the 1990s emerged as a major attraction for San Diego, an "international restaurant row." Charles Tyson bought San Diego's oldest city hall, later known as the Crystal Theater, at Fifth and G, and turned the historic building into commercial and restaurant space. The Gaslamp continues to struggle against inadequate parking, traffic congestion, and limited public funds, but its gains have been spectacular. As residential developments in the downtown area have increased, more people are taking advantage of services in the Gaslamp Quarter. Those who restored buildings have brought the district into the modern era, while preserving its historical identity and the atmosphere of an earlier time.

Another private development adjoining the city's redevelopment project was Seaport Village—a series of shops, walkways, open plazas, and restaurants fronting on the harbor. The 22-acre site, formerly the old Coronado Ferry Station, was leased from the San Diego Port District. Featuring an antique carousel, it complements both the Gaslamp Quarter and Horton Plaza with a marine atmosphere. From Seaport Village it is a short walk along the bay to the ships making up San Diego's Maritime Museum. With a number of seafood specialty stores and restaurants, San Diego's waterfront, with its paved walkway along Harbor Drive all the way to Spanish Landing near the airport, provides an area of scenic interest.

Minority Gains

The Chicano Federation, long active in local affairs affecting Hispanic groups, encouraged the participation of persons of Mexican descent in San Diego's political life. State Assemblyman Pete Chacon promoted

University of San Diego students march on Martin Luther King Day, 1989.

bilingual education for Spanish-speaking individuals. After a long struggle by residents of Barrio Logan and other members of the Chicano community, the area underneath the Coronado Bridge was set aside for a park featuring murals painted by a local artist and representing Mexican themes. While San Diego's Spanish-speaking population increased yearly, the city of Tijuana grew to 709,340 by 1980 and, in 1990, topped the 1 million mark.

The residents and recent migrants to the Tijuana area were soon to take advantage of the employment opportunities there, especially in the *maquiladoras*—tax-exempt export manufacturing and assembly plants—and the highest federally established minimum wage rates in Mexico. By the end of the 1980s there were 638 *maquiladora* plants with over 67,000 workers. Many Tijuana residents were able to shop in the San Diego area and became an important factor in the stability of the city and county's economy. Nevertheless, border issues, illegal immigration, and drug smugglers made crossing the border on a regular basis difficult and time consuming. By the end of the decade San Diego County Hispanic residents accounted for about 20 percent of the total population.

San Diego's African American community made considerable gains between 1970 and 1990 through the activities of business, educational, and religious leaders. The Reverend George Walker Smith served four terms on the San Diego Board of Education from 1963 through 1979. He was a prime mover in upgrading educational facilities for all students in predominantly minority areas. Leon L. Williams became San Diego's first African American councilman in 1969 and was reelected in 1971, 1975, and 1979. Williams, active in the Economic Opportunity Commission, the Neighborhood House Association, and numerous youth groups, was elected to the County Board of Supervisors in 1982. Other successful members of the African American community include Judges Joe Littlejohn and Napoleon Jones; City Councilmen William Jones, Wes Pratt, and George Stevens; and a number of professional athletes.

In 1979 Judge Louis Welsh approved a voluntary plan for integration of the San Diego school system without mandatory busing in *Carlin v. San Diego Board of Education*, a lawsuit commenced in December 1967. San Diego in 1980 had the eighth-largest school district in the nation with a student population of 110,000. A citizens' task force headed by San Diego police chief William Kolender was established by Judge Welsh to monitor the school's voluntary integration efforts. Progress was made in programs of voluntary ethnic transfers, magnet schools, and part-time learning center exchanges.

A Light-Rail Transit System

A person of significant influence in many areas of San Diego life has been James Mills, president of San Diego's Metropolitan Transit Development Board (MTDB). Mills was responsible for legislation creating the port district and Old Town State Historic Park while in the state assembly, and served as president pro tempore of the state senate in 1970. Called "a quiet powerhouse" on the political scene, Mills, a writer of local history, strongly supported measures that benefited San Diego. His bill providing for the use of state gasoline tax revenues to finance light-rail transit systems has had far-reaching effects.

San Diego Trolley.

The purchase in 1979 of the historic San Diego & Arizona Eastern Railway by the San Diego MTDB provided 108 miles of fixed-rail right-of-way and cleared the way for a light-rail transit system. The first leg, which opened on July 26, 1981, operated 15.9 miles from the Santa Fe Depot to San Ysidro, making eleven intermediate stops. The second leg, the "East Line," involved the conversion of a freight branch line from downtown to Lemon Grove, La Mesa, and El Cajon. The extension, which opened in June 1980, runs 18.8 miles from the Santa Fe Depot to the El Cajon transit center. A third segment, added in June 1990, extended southward parallel to San Diego Bay, passing Seaport Village and the Convention Center before rejoining the main line. Additional trolley lines completed in later decades run northward to Old Town, carrying passengers eastward from Old Town to Mission Valley, and finally to Qualcomm Stadium and San Diego State University.

Balboa Park Disaster and Recovery

Balboa Park's history during the 1970s was one of success and sadness. In 1967, Bea Evenson and the Committee of 100 began a successful drive to preserve the Spanish Colonial architecture of the 1915 exposition buildings. When the old Food and Beverage Building was demolished, the committee spearheaded a campaign to raise funds and pass a bond issue to allow authentic reconstruction. The ornamental facade was exactly reproduced. Completed in 1971 and renamed the Casa del Prado, the building meets many community needs. Funds were requested for restoration of other exposition buildings, but the public turned down a second bond proposal in 1972. The San Diego Department of Parks and Recreation then planned a phased remodeling effort. New additions included the Reuben H. Fleet Space Theater and Science Center completed in 1973.

In July 1974, Mary G. Marston, eldest daughter of George White and Anna Gunn Marston, retaining a life estate, gave her house and grounds at 3525 Seventh Avenue, approximately 4 1/2 acres adjoining the north end of Balboa Park, to the city for public park purposes. Ownership of the home actually passed to the city of San Diego when Mary Marston died in 1987 just a few weeks before her 108th birthday. The Marston family home was originally designed in 1904 by architects William Sterling Hebbard and Irving Gill. Both Hebbard and Gill had spent time in Chicago and were influenced by the American Arts and Crafts movement. Gill, especially, influenced by Frank Lloyd Wright, was known for his simplicity and efficiency in design. The Marstons moved into their home in the fall of 1905, and it was continuously occupied and improved by the family until Mary Marston's death. Presently under the care of the city and the Save Our Heritage Organization (SOHO), the house is an interpretive museum depicting the role of the Marston family in San Diego and illustrating the architecture, furnishings, and decorative arts of the craftsman period. A number of other Gill residences can be seen along Seventh Avenue and in the neighborhood known as Banker's Hill.

Rebuilding the Aerospace Museum

A grant from the federal Economic Development Agency provided $5 million for reconstruction of the Electric Building that housed San Diego's Aerospace Museum and Hall of Fame. By mid-February 1978, workers from Ninteman Construction Company had finished

San Diego Air and Space Museum in the 1935 Ford Building in Balboa Park. *Photo by Joe Allen.*

removing the last of 200 unique molds on the building from which the entire new facade, originally inspired by the Casa Consistorial in Palma, Mallorca, was to be duplicated. Just ten days later, on the night of February 22, the building went up in flames. All the treasures of the museum, including the only flyable replica of the *Spirit of St. Louis*, the Ryan M-l, the Consolidated PT-3, the Luscombe Phantom, and many others were destroyed. In addition to irreplaceable Lindbergh memorabilia and other priceless items, aviation researchers lost an important library and archives. Out of the charred remains, some things were saved—three wrought-iron balcony railings, a moon rock, and contents of the Hall of Fame office.

Under the leadership of the San Diego Chamber of Commerce, the organization promptly raised $110,000 to rebuild the *Spirit of St. Louis* replica. Other funds began pouring in to replace the rest of the collection and the aerospace exhibits formally moved into the renovated 1935 Ford Building early in 1980. The San Diego Air and Space Museum exhibits more than 65 vintage aircrafts displayed in chronological order. The museum also features a full-scale restoration shop and sponsors various educational programs.

Casa de Balboa

The rebuilt Electric Building, known variously as the Canadian Building and Palace of Electricity, was then approved to house the headquarters of the San Diego Historical Society (today's San Diego History Center), the Model Railroad Club, the Hall of Champions, and the Museum of Photographic Arts. It was renamed the Casa de Balboa. The historical society, formerly housed at the Serra Museum in Presidio Park, moved its curatorial and research collection, plus its photographic archives, into the first floor of the reconstructed building in 1983. During the mid-1980s, the historical society carried on a capital campaign to raise funds to design, furnish, carpet, and paint its nearly 50,000 square feet of the Casa de Balboa's hollow interior. Its research library, which houses extensive archival collections, including thousands of photographs from the Title Insurance and Trust Company and *The San Diego Union-Tribune*, occupies the ground floor. The History Center also directs the Serra Museum on Presidio Hill that features Native American and Spanish colonial exhibits.

Next door to the San Diego History Center on the main floor facing the Prado is the Museum of Photographic Arts, one of the first and most renowned museums in the country devoted solely to this medium. The exhibits span the history of photography, motion pictures, and video, displaying everything from nineteenth century daguerreotypes to the latest in computer-controlled imagery, video art, and laser scan. Founding director Arthur Ollman is an exhibiting photographer in his own right and came to San Diego with experience in New York and San Francisco. Downstairs, the Model Railroad Museum is a gem for enthusiasts of all ages. It features intricate displays and miniature replicas of local railroads such as the San Diego, Arizona & Eastern tracks through Carrizo Gorge on its way to Yuma.

Rebuilding the Old Globe Theatre

Just two weeks after the Aerospace Museum disaster, another Balboa Park fire sent shock waves through San Diego. The incomparable

Old Globe Theatre rebuilt after 1978 fire. Inset: Original Old Globe Theatre built in 1935. *Photo ©San Diego History Center.*

Old Globe Theatre—the revered reproduction of Shakespeare's original built for the 1935 California-Pacific Exposition—was totally gutted. Director Craig Noel's first thoughts turned toward the upcoming productions, especially the Shakespeare Summer Festival, one of San Diego's most popular attractions. With more than 600 performances annually on its two stages and on tour, the Old Globe had one of the heaviest annual production schedules of any theater in the United States. The emotional support of the beloved theater was so great that $6 million equally divided between private and public sectors was raised in a little over one year. The new theater, faithfully reconstructed with only slight modifications to seat some 525 to 550 people, was dedicated on January 5, 1982.

In the meantime, the city approved construction of the Festival Stage, a 750-seat outdoor theater set in the canyon to the east of the Carter Center Stage. Architect Robert Mosher had planned the outdoor facility in 1974, but it failed to become a reality. With completion of the "new" Old Globe, the complex, which is the Donald and Darlene Shiley Stage and Conrad Prebys Theatre Center, includes the historic Old Globe Theatre; the Sheryl and Harvey White Theatre, and the outdoor Lowell Davies Festival Theatre.

Other Balboa Park improvements have involved restoration and repair of other exposition buildings and appropriate use of all areas within the park. The San Diego Automotive Museum opened in 1986. Located in the original 35,000 square-foot conference building originally constructed for the 1935 exposition, the museum has a comprehensive program that involves automotive enthusiasts from all over the world. Its rotating displays include vintage racers, town cars, and a research library of publications, photographs, and vintage films. There is also a restoration workshop that demonstrates authentic restoration techniques.

PSA Crash

In September 1978, somber headlines rivaling those of the 1905 *Bennington* disaster emanated from San Diego when PSA Flight 182 from Sacramento collided at 9 a.m. with a private airplane over North Park and crashed, claiming 144 lives. It was the United States' worst air disaster up to that time. The *Evening Tribune*'s extensive coverage of the crash earned the newspaper a Pulitzer Prize. As a result, the whole issue of air traffic control came under heavy scrutiny in San Diego and a TCA (terminal control area) Class 2 was finally established at Lindbergh Field in 1980. A new west terminal was added to Lindbergh Field in 1979 to ease passenger congestion, but some felt the airport needed to be moved to an outlying area. Several new sites, including Otay Mesa, have been suggested but no alternatives have yet been agreed upon. (See pages 234–236.)

Financial Crises

The United States National Bank of San Diego, one of the oldest and largest financial institutions in the city, was declared insolvent by the comptroller of the currency on October 8, 1973. Founded in 1913 and purchased by C. Arnholt Smith in 1933, the bank had grown to the 26th largest in the nation with 62 branches in southern California and deposits in excess of $1 billion. A lawsuit commenced by the Securities Exchange Commission in May 1973 precipitated the collapse of USNB and Westgate Corporation, a Smith-controlled conglomerate of tuna boats and canneries, airlines, taxicabs, insurance companies, real estate holdings, hotels, and other businesses. The failure of the US National Bank presaged problems within banking institutions that would plague the decade of the 1980s.

In 1981, another of San Diego's oldest financial institutions, San Diego Federal Savings, acquired eight other savings and loans and changed its name to Great American Savings to reflect a wider geographic base. It merged in 1986 with Home Federal Savings and Loan in Tucson, adding 41 offices in Arizona and five in California. Great American continued to acquire other institutions from 1986 to 1989, began to own and develop real estate, and changed its name to Great American Bank on July 1, 1989. It was listed in *Fortune* in 1989 as one of the six most admired savings institutions in the nation. Because of financial difficulties shortly afterwards, Great American suffered serious losses. By August 1991, after providing San Diego with 106 years of service, its California branches were sold to Wells Fargo, California's oldest banking institution with headquarters in San Francisco.

Changing Financial Institutions

By the end of the 1980s, economic times had changed. Congress had passed tough new regulations that radically altered thrift accounting rules and penalized savings and loans for owning and developing real estate. Great American's entry into nontraditional businesses combined with the opening of out-of-state branches without sufficient capital contributed to its downfall. Other old-time banking operations such as First Federal and Central Federal Savings also lost their identity during the 1980s. Home Federal Savings of San Diego, founded by Charles K. Fletcher in 1934, became in 1983 one of the first savings and loans to become a well-capitalized public corporation. During the late 1980s, however, Home Federal began making out-of-state real estate loans to companies that became insolvent. By 1992, Home Federal was reorganized. Of the leading financial institutions in the county, only San Diego Trust & Savings, founded in 1889 by Joseph

Sefton, kept its local control for more than 100 years, but it would not survive the 1990s. San Diego banking became a global operation.

New Industries in San Diego

Kazuo Inamori, founder of San Diego-based Kyocera Telecomunications Research Corp., established the nonprofit Inamori Foundation in 1984. The San Diego Supercomputer Center (SDSC), founded in 1985 as an organized research unit of the University of California San Diego, led the way in developing a national cyber-infrastructure. It provided the technological foundation for the next generation of science and engineering advances. With a staff of scientists, software developers, and support personnel, SDSC soon became an international leader in data management, biosciences, geosciences, grid computing, and visualization. The biotech industry established a number of companies in La Jolla and Sorrento Valley.

San Diego Padres

The world of sports in San Diego also became a part of big business. C. Arnholt Smith sold the San Diego Padres baseball team to Ray Kroc, owner of the McDonald's fast food chain, in 1974. After a shakeup in management, the Padres picked up momentum and developed a loyal following with such stars as Cy Young award winners Randy Jones (1976) and Gaylord Perry (1978). With All-Star outfielder Dave Winfield, the Padres finally had a winning season in 1978.

The 1980 season began with high hopes under manager Jerry Coleman and returning veterans Winfield, Ozzie Smith, Rollie Fingers, and Gene Richards. The season did not go well and Jack McKeon, the new general manager, did his best to give Ray Kroc a winning team. The next three seasons proved to be building years and a number of new players such as Tony Gwynn, Garry Templeton, and Kevin McReynolds joined the team. First-baseman Steve Garvey was acquired from the Dodgers in a trade in 1983.

The 1984 season started off on a sad note since owner Ray Kroc had died from heart failure on January 14, 1984. His widow, Joan

San Diego Padres Steve Garvey and Tony Gwynn appear at the Old Globe Theatre in a fundraiser for San Diego charities in 1984. *Photo by Ken Jacques.*

Kroc, took over the helm and the players wore Kroc's initials on their uniforms as extra motivation for the season. With new players, reliever Rich "Goose" Gossage and Graig Nettles, the Padres finally put it all together under Manager Dick Williams. No one emerged as the superstar—it was a team effort that brought the Padres into first place with 92 wins and 70 losses. The Padres lost the first two playoff games against the Chicago Cubs for the National League Pennant. The next three games were in San Diego and the Padres managed to win each one. The final game-winning home run by Steve Garvey before an ecstatic crowd of 58,000 fans was probably the most dramatic moment in Padre history. They lost to the Detroit Tigers in the World Series, but the excitement of the Cubs game lasted well into the next season. Unfortunately, the Padres did not soon repeat their winning performance of 1984.

San Diego Chargers

San Diego's NFL Chargers also took steps to ensure future victories. Owner Eugene Klein selected Tommy Prothro to be head coach from 1974 through 1978. His major rebuilding effort reached fruition under Don Coryell, former head coach of the San Diego State University

The first Chargers Blood Drive was held in 1979 when popular kicker Rolf
Benirschke, pictured here with Louie Kelcher, was diagnosed with ulcerative colitis.
Photo by Teri Cluck.

Aztecs. Coryell had brought the state team through 12 winning seasons
including a 31-game winning streak. Coryell returned to San Diego
after five years with the St. Louis Cardinals. Guided by quarterback
Dan Fouts and backed up by such top-quality pass receivers as Charles
Joiner and John Jefferson, the Chargers won the American Football
Conference's Western Division in 1979 and made the playoffs for the
first time in club history. With other top players such as Kellen
Winslow, Russ Washington, Doug Wilkerson, Louie Kelcher, Gary
Johnson, Fred Dean, and Woodrow Lowe, the Chargers were one of
the NFL's top teams from 1980 to 1983.

After the 1983 season, Klein sold the team to Alex G. Spanos and
the team did not finish higher than third place. Don Coryell retired
in 1986 and was replaced by an inexperienced Al Saunders. Dan
Henning took over as head coach in 1988. Both Dan Fouts and Kellen
Winslow retired after the 1987 season and new stars included All-Pros
Lee Williams, Leslie O'Neal, Gil Byrd, Billy Ray Smith, and Burt
Grossman. Following the 1989 season, Spanos hired former Washington
Redskin Bobby Beathard as general manager.

San Diego Sockers

The San Diego Sockers, representing one of southern California's most popular and fastest-growing sports among young and old, took their place among the other professional teams at the San Diego Stadium in 1978. The Sockers gained steadily in support and, in both 1979 and 1980, came within one playoff game of reaching the championship Soccer Bowl. In 1981 the Sockers became an indoor soccer team and have achieved the winningest record in San Diego. They were champions of the MISL (Major Indoor Socker League) every year but one during ten seasons.

Television Gains

In the world of television, local network channels began to expand their coverages. During the 1980s, KGTV's Channel 10 remained high in the network ratings with such well-known figures as Jack White, Kimberly Hunt, and Carol LeBeau broadcasting the news. In 1988, local sports and newscaster Bill Griffith teamed up with Laura Buxton to present an hour-long show called *Inside San Diego*. With an interview format, the show's hosts discussed events of interest about or affecting San Diego. Outpacing the soap operas on rival channels, *Inside San Diego* kept the public informed about local, national, and world issues, but could not survive as a live broadcast.

In order to capture a young audience, Channel 39 covered every sporting event possible from Little League baseball to major league basketball. Bill Fox, formerly with Channel 8, joined the station as general manager in 1971. Channel 39 affiliated with ABC in April 1973. Storer Broadcasting bought the station in 1974, built a new transmitter on Mount San Miguel, and expanded news coverage. In 1977, Channel 39 affiliated with NBC and began an active competition for audience ratings with the three VHF channels.

By September 16, 1988, the day the NBC affiliate changed its name to KNSD, the station had succeeded in producing imaginative, creative, and even controversial programs to inform San Diegans.

Newscenter 39 with Marty Levin won an Emmy in 1988. During 1989 KNSD profiled the lives of 15 Hispanic men and women who exemplified the spirit of community service. Two other San Diego UHF stations, KUSI Channel 51 and KTTY Channel 69, began during the 1980s. KUSI, starting in 1982 as a syndicated station, added its programming to San Diego Channel 9.

Public Television—KPBS

Public television grew dramatically from its origin in May 1953 as the Public Broadcasting System (PBS). By 1985 it was maintaining over 300 stations nationwide and the Nielsen Rating System concluded that 90 million Americans were watching public television during an average week. San Diego's public broadcasting station KPBS (UHF Channel 15) opened studios on the campus of San Diego State University in 1967 with its transmitter on Mount San Miguel. As a public channel, its programs are funded by San Diego State University, the Corporation for Public Broadcasting, and individual grants. They are also privately funded by viewer membership (about 45% of income), underwriting, and special events.

Offering an alternative to commercial shows, KPBS programs include educational workshops, cultural affairs, sporting events, and public information programs. Some programs are geared to the special concerns and interests of the San Diego community and its minority constituents, while others are geared to senior citizens, teens, or other special groups. Especially popular are children's shows such as *Sesame Street*. KPBS also provided national favorites such as *The MacNeil/Lehrer News Hour* and *Masterpiece Theatre*.

Changes in Radio Broadcasting

According to radio surveys, 99 percent of San Diegans during the 1980s listened to the radio, with the majority being between 18 and 49. After 1980, FM radio broadcasting developed tremendously because of the emergence of MTV, the popular music videos on the cable stations. Listeners wanted to hear on radio the music that was being featured on television. Radio also became more market driven with audience research becoming an important component. People responded to contests, games, information, and personalities.

Marketing research led to the promotion of call-in talk radio shows on the major AM stations such as 760 KFMB, 1130 KSDO, 600 KOGO, and 690 XTRA covering subjects from politics, sports, and economic trends to personal likes and dislikes. All-sports stations including ESPN 800 and 1090 would emerge by 2003. KPBS FM public radio began in 1960 and adopted a format that featured in-depth analysis of current and past events. Trends in music change frequently and stations make adjustments in response to ongoing market research.

San Diego Newspaper Issues

The San Diego Union continued to grow in circulation during the 1970s, and became the area's strongest daily newspaper. Longtime publisher James S. Copley died in October 1973, just as the press moved into new headquarters in Mission Valley. His widow, Helen, took charge of the Copley newspaper chain. She made a number of policy changes to modernize the *Union* and *Evening Tribune* and broaden their scope of news coverage. In 1975 Helen Copley hired as *Union* editor Gerald L. Warren, a former assistant managing editor who had been deputy press secretary in the White House. In 1980, she brought back to San Diego Herb Klein who had served as the nation's first White House director of communications from 1969 to 1973. He became vice president and editor-in-chief of Copley Newspapers. Neil Morgan, a popular columnist since 1948, became editor of the *Evening Tribune* in 1981 and remained as associate editor and senior columnist when the two Copley newspapers merged in February 1992 to become a single enlarged daily paper known as *The San Diego Union-Tribune*.

The *San Diego Daily Transcript* continued to expand as a daily business paper, and in 1978 the *Los Angeles Times* launched a San Diego County edition, providing new competition for the local dailies. The

Times, whose circulation had reached approximately 65,000 by 1992, continued to expand its coverage of San Diego but failed at the end of the year as local interest waned. An alternative news weekly, the *Reader*, founded in October 1972, became the largest of its kind in the country. This free paper is supported by advertising and features a wide range of in-depth reporting. The popular *San Diego Magazine* celebrated its 40th anniversary with special pictorial issues in November and December 1988. A newer publication, *San Diego Home/Garden Lifestyles*, appeared in 1980, as did the weekly *San Diego Business Journal.* Both have continued as successful publications.

The San Diego Wild Animal Park—Today's Safari Park

By the 1970s, the San Diego Zoo had achieved fame throughout the country for the world's largest wild animal collection—more than 5,000 specimens of 1,664 species and subspecies. Dr. Charles Schroeder, zoo director since 1953, was innovative and successful. He realized that more space would be needed if the zoo were to continue to expand. Clayburn LaForce, farm manager for the city, suggested that land in the San Pasqual Valley that had been contemplated for a reservoir be used as an annex to house additional zoo animals. Norman Roberts, chairman of the San Pasqual Study Committee, and Anderson Borthwick, president of the Zoological Society, promoted the concept of a large, open wild animal park of 1,800 acres—larger than all of Balboa Park. It was completed in 1972 and duplicated wildlife areas throughout the world. Its 45-minute electric monorail tour allowed visitors to view a wide variety of animals at close but safe range. Removed in early 2005, the monorail was replaced by buses that tour the Nairobi Village. The park features animal and bird shows, exhibits, and an animal nursery.

Old Town Development

By the mid-1970s several Old Town buildings were completed. These included reconstruction of the Seeley Stables to house the Roscoe Hazard collection of Western Americana and a new Mission Playhouse.

Popular restaurant Casa de Bandini in Old Town San Diego State Historic Park. Today it has been rebuilt as the Cosmopolitan Hotel popular in the late 1860s.

Concessionaire Geoff Mogilner turned the house originally built by Juan Rodríguez during the 1830s into the Tobacco Shop of Racine and Laramie, popular during the 1860s for its various wares. The Machado Silvas adobe was faithfully rebuilt and the interiors of the Casa de Estudillo and Machado Stewart adobe were enhanced, especially with the help of the Colonial Dames of America.

Diane Powers, of Design Center Interiors, created the popular Bazaar del Mundo out of the historic Pico Motor Hotel. The attractive complex of shops and restaurants surrounding a small plaza greatly increased the number of people coming to the area. Powers also converted the Bandini house, which had become the Cosmopolitan Hotel in 1869, into the Casa de Bandini, a picturesque Mexican restaurant. But, in 2005 the state's overall concept for Old Town San Diego State Historic Park was to reconstruct the houses standing during the interpretive period (1821–1872) in phases over the next 25 years. Although the plan has proceeded more slowly than projected because of state funding difficulties, some buildings have been remodeled.

The decade of the 1980s nevertheless witnessed a phenomenal increase in the number of persons touring Old Town, giving the state encouragement to continue its program. The houses restored on the west side of the plaza included the Casa de Machado-Wrightington, a single-story, L-shaped adobe built in 1840; the Light-Freeman House, featuring a segment of African American history; the U.S. House; the Colorado House; and the San Diego Courthouse. Other buildings rebuilt or restored included the Johnson Building, Casa de Alvarado, Robinson-Rose Building, and Little Plaza School. The state of California also developed the San Pasqual Battlefield site near the Wild Animal Park in memory of the battle fought there on December 6, 1846, during the US-Mexican War.

The Save Our Heritage Organization

The Save Our Heritage Organization (SOHO) became a significant force in historic preservation during the 1970s. From inauspicious beginnings—a sign pinned to the Sherman Gilbert House in 1968 by Robert Miles Parker saying "Save This House" and giving his telephone number—it grew by 1980 to a membership of 500 civic-minded citizens. Its first project, saving of the Victorian house built by John Sherman in 1887 and later occupied by the Gilbert sisters, mushroomed into the larger concept of a seven-acre site in Old Town to become known as Heritage Park. The Sherman-Gilbert House was moved to the site at the end of April 1971, and restoration began.

Guided by SOHO recommendations and the Cultural Heritage Committee, the Heritage Park package became San Diego County's Bicentennial project to celebrate the nation's 200th birthday. The project was funded in 1976 by the county, matching grants, and private donations. Dr. William Winter, owner of the Christian House and Burton House originally located on Third Avenue, offered them to the county for the park. These joined the Bushyhead House from Cedar Street, already saved from demolition. The three houses arrived at the site during the last week in August 1976 to make the bicentennial project a reality. Two more structures—the Senlis Cottage donated by Will Hippen and the original home of Temple Beth Israel—took their places alongside the others in 1978 to form the nucleus of a

Star of India under full sail. *Photo courtesy Maritime Museum of San Diego.*

nineteenth-century "town." The Senlis Cottage served as headquarters for SOHO and housed its research library. The Temple building was moved to the park with the support of the Beth Israel congregation and is used by all faiths. The broad green lawn and general landscaping give the houses an attractive setting.

The *Star of India*

Another bicentennial project was the sailing of the 205-foot bark *Star of India* on July 4, 1976. A familiar sight along Harbor Drive on San Diego's waterfront, it is the oldest iron merchant ship afloat. She was first launched at Ramsey, Isle of Man, on November 14, 1863, as the *Euterpe.* The full-rigged ship was intended for cargo and limited passenger service between England and India. Her early sailing years out of Liverpool were fraught with disaster—a collision with a Spanish brig, the loss of all three masts in a hurricane off Madras, and the death of her captain from a tropical fever. In 1871 she was acquired by Shaw Savill & Albion and put on the run from Liverpool to New Zealand and Australia.

The *Euterpe* made the around-the-world voyage by way of the Cape of Good Hope and across the Indian Ocean to Auckland or Wellington. She then caught the prevailing winds across the Pacific, headed around Cape Horn and into the Atlantic for home. The opening of the Suez Canal in 1869 gave steamers a place in world trade so the *Euterpe* was sold to the Pacific Colonial Ship Company of San Francisco and placed under Hawaiian registry. When Hawaii became a US territory, she too became American.

As an American, the *Euterpe* carried timber out of Puget Sound to Australia, coal from Australian ports to Honolulu, and sugar from the islands back to the West Coast. She was sold in 1902 to the Alaska Packers Association of San Francisco. They changed her name in 1906 to *Star of India* to match her stepsisters known around the world as Corry's Irish Stars—the Belfast-built ships *Star of Bengal*, *Star of Italy*, *Star of France*, and *Star of Russia*. From then on it was up to Alaska in the spring and back to San Francisco in late summer with fishermen (mostly Sicilian) and Chinese cannery workers. The packers reduced her from a full-rigged ship to a bark. She made her last voyage to Alaska in 1923 and was headed for the scrappers when she was rescued by James Wood Coffroth, representing a group of San Diegans. She was donated to the San Diego Zoological Society as a floating aquarium and museum.

Unfortunately the onset of the Great Depression prevented plans for restoration. During World War II she sat neglected, her paint cracking and her decks rotting. Her once heavy cordage burned away in the bright sun. The US Navy declared her a menace to aerial navigation and sent a work-party aboard to send down her yards and upper masts. In the late 1940s the Zoological Society gave her to the newly organized Maritime Museum Association of San Diego. With the help of local sail enthusiasts, writer Jerry MacMullen and maritime historian Captain Alan Villiers, restoration efforts were begun.

Giant Dipper in Belmont Park, South Mission Beach, San Diego.

The *Star of India*'s finest hour came on July 4, 1976, when she sailed out of San Diego Bay and into the Pacific Ocean. By then she had been joined by two other historic vessels—the *Berkeley*, an 1898 ferry boat and the *Medea*, a Scottish steam yacht. They are all moored along North Harbor Drive near Ash Street. The *Star* sailed again on November 11, 1984, with new sails, and on Memorial Day, May 28, 1989, with former news correspondent Walter Cronkite on board as honorary sailing master. Mayor O'Connor declared May 28 as "*Star of India* Day." In 2004 the historic PC *Wings* was added to the fleet.

Belmont Park in South Mission Beach

Another San Diego saga in outdoor recreation was the Save the Coaster movement. The Giant Dipper, the roller coaster that had served Mission Beach since its grand opening on July 1, 1925, was doomed to destruction. The amusement center known as Belmont Park, opened by the Spreckels Company in 1925, was donated to the city in 1934 via the State Park Commission. After years of changing ownership, Belmont Park in 1967 came into the hands of Bill Evans, owner of the Bahia and Catamaran Hotels. He planned to tear the coaster down and build a hotel but faced too much opposition. By 1973, the festive carnival atmosphere of the park had degenerated. In December 1976, Belmont Park was closed to the public and became the home of vagrants and vandals. In March 1979, the San Diego

City Council approved a permit for demolition of the coaster, even though it was listed on the National Register of Historic Places. Reprieves were granted and opposition strengthened in the community to save the Giant Dipper. Two fires in March 1981 started by transients set the coaster project back even further. Bill Evans then donated the coaster to the Save the Coaster Committee, formed officially in 1984 under the leadership of Carol Lindenmulder.

Costs of restoration, estimated at $450,000, received a boost in 1985 from the Historic Bond Fund of $150,000 and the donated work of the California Conservation Corps. Many fund-raising activities were held. At the same time, the controversial Belmont Park shopping center project began, and although the city tried to buy back the property, ownership of Belmont Park and the coaster remained in private hands. Despite all of the setbacks, the work progressed. Under hazy sunshine on Saturday, August 11, 1990, coaster lovers lined up to once again ride 2,600 feet of 13 hills at 43 miles per hour. The Giant Dipper, with its sparkly night lights, once again roared to life, giving back to San Diegans a significant piece of their early history as the end of the twentieth century approached.

Economic Forecast

The economic forecast for the San Diego region for the 1990s was more optimistic than for the nation as a whole. As in previous years, the county's trends were expected to follow state rather than national patterns, but high housing costs, the drought, and state budget deficits slowed population gains significantly. Declines in government payrolls because of cuts in defense budgets and other measures limiting public spending added a degree of uncertainty to the region's employment opportunities. Nevertheless, the San Diego Chamber of Commerce and the Economic Development Corporation attracted new industries and corporate headquarters to San Diego. The downtown area continued to grow with the addition during the 1990s of new hotels, residential units, shopping areas, bicycle paths, and neighborhood parks.

Chapter XII

Into the Third Millennium: 1991–2005

San Diego, no longer isolated but still blessed with a highly desirable climate and location, faced a multitude of challenges as the final decade of the twentieth century began. It emerged as a city with a new face and a new skyline—more cosmopolitan and sophisticated than ever before. As California's second-largest city, San Diego evolved into a complex region no longer easy to define. The challenges that came with the area's phenomenal growth involved principally energy, pollution, traffic congestion, border issues, and San Diego's relationship with nations of the Pacific Rim. Downtown city planners, boasting a completed Horton Plaza, a revitalized Gaslamp Quarter, theaters, and high-rise condominiums, set their sights on an expanded convention center, a new ballpark, and plans for a new harbor front.

By March 1992, a five-year drought had come to an end, but future water problems needed to be addressed. A slight economic downturn slowed growth in some areas, but telecommunications and the biotech industry surged ahead. Along with continued development in University Town Center, other areas throughout the county showed increasing activity. Housing trends in Poway and Escondido, as well as in the southern part of the county, especially in the Eastlake area of Chula Vista, outpaced the national average. Downtown businesses, along with residences, were once again in the city's center.

The successful Japan Festival, held in January 1992, indicated San Diego's expanded direction. The international celebration was designed to enhance the mutual understanding and respect between San Diego, Japan, and Mexico by providing a week of in-depth seminars, music, dance, and art. This kind of activity led to selection of San Diego as the site of the 1992 Pacific Rim Forum. The forum, organized for the corporate and political leaders of the Asia/Pacific region, focused on regional economic issues during 25 intensive sessions held during the latter part of May. Other signs of a new ethnic diversity included El Cajon's annual Friendship Festival begun in 1991 to celebrate cultural harmony in the region. International restaurants opened to feature such diverse foods as Iraqi, Russian, Ethiopian, Afghan, Thai, and Brazilian.

Mayor Susan Golding and San Diego Politics

From December 1992 through December 2000, Republican Susan Golding served two terms as mayor of the city of San Diego. Before becoming mayor, she chaired the San Diego County Board of Supervisors, was appointed by the governor to serve as deputy secretary of Business, Transportation and Housing for the state of California, and was a member of the San Diego City Council. When first elected mayor, Golding's priorities were public safety, economic development, international trade, and education. She was successful in decreasing the percentage of violent crime overall for the first time in a decade and in launching the Safe School Initiative. She led the city council to cut the business license tax for small businesses, to cut water and sewer capacity fees, and to establish a one-stop city, county, and state permitting center. As mayor, she encouraged international commerce, established the San Diego World Trade Center, led numerous international trade missions to Asia and Europe, and opened the San Diego Business Development Office-Asia in Hong Kong.

Critics, however, complained that Golding was unfair to minorities and that minority districts were the most polluted in the state. Logan Heights continued to lack necessary police protection and minority employment in the city was down. There was considerable opposition to the $78 million Jack Murphy stadium expansion package, which, in 1995, broke down into a $60 million agreement and an $18 million amendment, money later picked up by telecom giant Qualcomm for naming rights at the stadium. The money was spent in order to make it possible for San Diego to host the Super Bowl in 1998 and 2003.

Despite criticism at the end of her first term, Susan Golding was overwhelmingly reelected by 78 percent of the voters, setting a record for all elections in California. Unfortunately, her ambition to run for the US Senate was perceived as neglecting San Diego, although she dropped out of the Senate race for lack of financial support in competition with Darrell Issa. She was also criticized for not following through on a new downtown library and for cutting an unpopular deal with the San Diego Chargers. In her defense, Golding argued that she was not the one who made the contract for paying the Chargers for unsold tickets when attendance did not reach 60,000—she just received the blame. She contended that because city staff originally negotiated the contract, elected officials were left holding a bag they did not deserve. "Compared to other contracts for other big-city teams, it is still considered one of the better contracts in the country," she declared, "but no one here will ever believe that."

High-Tech Industries in San Diego

The decade of the 1990s brought a new wave of biotechnology development into San Diego. Many companies owed their heritage to Hybritech, founded in 1978 by UCSD assistant professor Dr. Ivor Royston and his research assistant, Howard Birndorf, to explore the use of monoclonal antibodies. Its sale in 1986 to Eli Lilly encouraged other academic scientists to form companies and scores of biotechs were created from UCSD, the Salk Institute, Scripps Research, and other local institutions. In 1992, Royston cofounded Forward Ventures, a venture capital firm that funded biotech start-ups, while

Computer lab at UCSD Supercomputer Center. *Photo courtesy Supercomputer Center.*

Birndorf continued a successful career in various biotech companies. In 2003, according to *The San Diego Union-Tribune*, (Penni Crabtree, Sept. 14) San Diego could count some 500 biomedical companies employing about 24,000 people. Some have called the area of Sorrento Valley/UCSD a mini Silicon Valley.

In another scientific breakthrough, UCSD researchers working in the San Diego Supercomputer Center (SDSC), primarily funded by the National Science Foundation (NSF), conducted research that enabled scientists to shorten the time needed to develop new drug treatments. It also created realistic animation that showed the birth of the solar system. The Supercomputer Center helps to forecast the effects of global climate change on natural ecosystems, and tracks computer viruses in order to protect the Internet.

In a different area of computer technology, UCSD graduate Michael Robertson founded MP3.com and became chairman of its board. He developed software to distribute MPEG Level 3 audio files, which are normally very big, and compress them to about one-tenth the size. Because of this compression, they are then much easier to move around the Internet, but still sound as good as a compact disk (CD). According to Robertson, the MP in the term MP3 came from the International Standards Committee that specified this

Dr. Irwin Mark Jacobs, founder and CEO of Qualcomm.

format, the "moving pictures expert group." MP3 has been of enormous benefit to new artists and music fans. Robertson, CEO of Lindows.com in 2004, was concerned with the preservation of the site's archive of a million or so songs after he sold the company to Vivendi Universal, who in turn sold MP3.com to CNET. The fast-paced world of the Internet speeds on.

Qualcomm

For more than 40 years, Dr. Irwin Mark Jacobs, a former faculty member at UCSD, has been a pioneer in developing innovative applications that have revolutionized digital communications technology. Dr. Jacobs cofounded LINKABIT, a San Diego-based telecommunications company that he guided from several employees in 1969 to over 1,400 in 1985. In 1985, he founded Qualcomm, and served as chairman and CEO at the company's inception. Qualcomm expanded through a period of technical innovation and rapid growth to more than 9,000 employees worldwide, with international activities in digital wireless telephony, mobile satellite communications, and internet software. Dr. Paul E. Jacobs, son of the founder, became CEO, and Steven R. Altman, a Qualcomm executive since 1992, became president of the company in July 2005.

Code Division Multiple Access (CDMA) is a digital wireless technology that was pioneered and commercially developed by Qualcomm. CDMA works by converting speech into digital information, which is then transmitted as a radio signal over a wireless network. Using a unique code to distinguish each call, CDMA enables many more consumers to share the airwaves at the same time without static, cross talk, or interference. Commercially introduced in 1995, CDMA quickly became one of the world's fastest-growing wireless technologies. In 1999, the International Telecommunications Union selected CDMA as the industry standard for new "third-generation" (3G) wireless systems. Many leading wireless carriers are now building or upgrading to 3G CDMA networks in order to provide more capacity for voice traffic, along with high-speed data capabilities. By 2005, San Diego had become a national leader in this new technology.

Cable Television

Cable television or community antenna television (CATV), often shortened to "cable," refers to television, FM radio programming, and other services that are provided to consumers via fixed coaxial cables, rather than by the older and more widespread radio broadcasting (over-the-air) method. It is most common in the United States, Canada, and Europe, though it is present in many other countries. Technically, both cable TV and CATV involve distributing a number of television channels collected at a central location (called a head end or headend) throughout a community by means of a network of optical fibers and/or coaxial cables and broadband amplifiers. As in the case of radio broadcasting, the use of different frequencies allows many channels to be distributed through the same cable, without separate wires for each. The tuner of the TV, VCR, radio, or TV converter box selects one channel from this mixed signal.

By the 1990s, cable television in San Diego had reached a new level. Beginning in 1948, cable television served consumers in areas where the geography made it difficult to receive quality over-the-air

KPBS headquarters at San Diego State University. Inset shows the computers used for broadcasting public programs.

television signals. Cable first came to San Diego in 1961 as Pacific Video with 33 customers. It eventually became Cox Cable and by 1980 had more than 200,000 customers. By 1991, over 700,000 persons, or about 70 percent of the population, subscribed to cable providing upwards of 30 simultaneous broadcasts. By 1992, not only had the number of cable programs and customers increased dramatically, so had the number of companies, although Cox Cable in 1992 was the second-largest cable company in the United States.

By the end of the decade, coaxial cables enabled bidirectional carriage of signals, and it was possible for cable companies such as Cox and Time Warner to provide Internet access, something that the major television networks could not. Although the same cables are used, providing this access still requires a large infrastructure cost. The major competitor to cable television today is satellite television, which provides worldwide coverage.

UCSD won the right through a federal lottery in 1991 to operate its own low power television station. The UC Board of Regents approved the project since they believed it would "reflect the intellectual foundations of the University." At first, the station reached only viewers within a 15 to 25 mile radius of the campus, but by 2004, the station's three channels (18, 66, and 69) could be seen

Mission Trails Golf Course where left-handed Phil Mickelson (inset) began playing golf.

throughout the county. Programs that were originally broadcast about 12 hours per day now run continuously.

Other local television stations include Channel 24, serving the citizens of San Diego since 1998. CityTV is the city of San Diego's municipal government access cable channel and a service of the city's Department of Information Technology and Communications. CityTV provides live televised coverage of the San Diego City Council and other public meetings and produce a large variety of original programming including public service announcements, special event coverage, and documentaries on important issues. CityTV strives to promote and support local arts and culture through producing a variety of music concerts, artist lectures, and profiles of local talent. Public television (KPBS) continued its commitment to cultural awareness with a wide variety of programming.

San Diego Sports

San Diego's numerous golf courses, numbering some 70, have attracted tourists as well as local residents. The former Andy Williams San Diego Open, which has evolved through various sponsorships to become the Buick Invitational of California, is a major tournament held each year at Torrey Pines. It has received national acclaim and attracts movie and television personalities along with golf professionals.

In April 2004, San Diegan Phil Mickelson, in a come-from-behind victory, won the prestigious Master's tournament in Augusta, Georgia. First practicing at Mission Trails Golf Club in San Carlos, and on the backyard putting green of his family's Del Cerro home, Mickelson participated in junior golf in San Diego and then went on to success in the PGA tour, winning at Pebble Beach in 2005.

Despite successful records of the San Diego Sockers and the San Diego Gulls in the Sports Arena, the two major league franchises— the San Diego Chargers and the San Diego Padres—are the leading San Diego teams attracting big business interests, legal entanglements, loyal crowds, and major news coverage—both favorable and highly critical.

The San Diego Padres

The San Diego Padres, having missed winning their second division title by just three games in 1989, were put up for sale by owner Joan Kroc. The purchase in 1990 by television executive Tom Werner and a group of 15 partners, including 10 San Diegans, took the Padres to an all-time low during the next four years. Despite a burst of interest in July 1992, when the Padres hosted the 63rd All-Star Game at Jack Murphy (later Qualcomm) Stadium, with Ted Williams and President George Bush, Sr. on the mound for the ceremonial first pitch, there was not much to cheer about.

All-time great Tony Gwynn, with his .394 career batting average, kept up the team's spirit. Texas businessman John Moores purchased the franchise on December 21, 1994. Moores hired Kevin Towers as general manager on November 17, 1995, and club president Larry Lucchino began aggressive marketing. On the final day of the 1996 season, pinch hitter Chris Gwynn hit a double to defeat the Los Angeles Dodgers and gain the National League West title. Third baseman Ken Caminiti became the only Padre to win the National League's most valuable player title. Despite losing in the playoffs that year, the Padres once again fielded a winning team in 1998 under manager Bruce Bochy and won their second National League Pennant, only to be swept by the Yankees in the World Series.

The year 1998 marked the most important and far-reaching event in the major league Padres history—the passing of a ballot measure approving construction of a new downtown ballpark with a proposed opening date of 2002. Nevertheless, a series of lawsuits filed mainly by former San Diego city councilman Bruce Henderson delayed construction and the opening date until April 2004.

In the meantime, records were set in Qualcomm that included Tony Gwynn's 3,000th hit in 1999; Trevor Hoffman's 300th save in 2001; and Ricky Henderson's 2,063rd walk to pass Babe Ruth in 2001, his 2,246th run to pass leader Ty Cobb in 2001, and his 3,000th hit on October 7, 2001. On September 28, 2003, the Padres played their last game in Qualcomm Stadium.

The construction of Petco Park, at a total cost of $453.4 million, and the changing nature of a newly named downtown "East Village" area, were not without problems. The San Diego Padres and owner John Moores, in conjunction with the Centre City Development Corporation and the Historical Site Preservation board, did their best to save historic buildings and relocate sensitive businesses. Some, like the original San Diego Gas & Electric building at 11th Avenue and Imperial, did not make the cut, but not before pictures were taken and significant items preserved. Twenty thousand people attended the "implosion event" that was televised on KUSI and other local channels. The century-old Western Metals building on 7th Avenue was preserved and located in the stadium seating area. In probably one of the key preservation events, the 30,000 square-foot Showley Brothers Candy Factory was moved from the corner of Eighth Avenue and K to a new foundation about a block away. The historic building set a record as the largest unreinforced masonry building ever to be moved and perhaps setting another record—a cost of $3 million to move 280 feet.

Opening day at Petco Park on April 9, 2004, brought together a crowd of some 42,000 fans to watch former president Jimmy Carter

Showley Brothers building after move. Inset: original candy factory. *Photo ©San Diego History Center.*

throw the first ceremonial pitch and hometown pitcher David Wells (Point Loma High School) take the Padres to a 5–4 win over the San Francisco Giants. The day was not without its ironies, considering the lawsuits, delays, and all those who were perfectly happy with Qualcomm Stadium. The facility, designed by HOK Sport, features an elevated grass park beyond the center field fence called the "Park at the Park" with lawn seating opportunities. Much of the crowd travels by trolley or finds parking in some new but expensive lots. Some businesses surrounding the park have enjoyed a newfound success while downtown residents can finally take a "walk to the park."

In 2003, despite the outstanding performance of closing pitcher Trevor Hoffman, and the optimism surrounding the future opening of Petco Park, the Padres finished their fifth straight losing season. By 2004, in their first season at Petco, the Padres rebounded with a winning record, finishing just six games out of first place.

The San Diego Chargers

San Diego's National Football League franchise spent nearly a decade on a rough downhill ride from the "Cinderella Chargers" playing in the 1995 Miami Super Bowl to a losing team entangled in a lawsuit with the City of San Diego and a corresponding loss of fan support.

The continuing publicity over the city guarantee of "unsold tickets," made worse by a lack of attendance, did not make the Chargers' bid for a new stadium popular. The Chargers' complaints over an "inadequate Qualcomm stadium" have not been convincing to the general public since some $78 million were spent to enclose and improve the stadium for the 1998 and 2003 Super Bowls. The closure of the southeast end brought the total to 70,000 seats, but made a sold-out game less likely.

Nevertheless, the decade of the 1990s brought the San Diego Chargers their finest hour. Their dream came true under Coach Bobby Ross on a rainy and humid January day in Pittsburgh in front of 61,545 towel-waving Steeler fans. With six minutes left in the AFC championship game, quarterback Stan Humphries scored a 43-yard touchdown and the nine-point underdog Chargers went ahead 17 to 13. Charger flags flew over San Diego and preparations were made for the trip to Miami. The San Francisco 49ers, seasoned Super Bowl contenders, played with experience and defeated the jittery Chargers 49–26 on January 19, 1995, in Super Bowl XXIX.

In a coaching shake-up, Bobby Ross was fired at the end of the 1996 season and the Chargers hired successful Oregon State University head coach Mike Riley, who failed to field a winning team. He was replaced by former Washington and Kansas City head coach Marty Schottenheimer, who had little luck in his first two seasons. Owners Alex and Dean Spanos and General Manager A.J. Smith remained optimistic about the 2004 season with number one draft pick quarterback Phil Rivers. After a slow start, veteran quarterback Drew Brees, teaming up with running back LaDainian Tomlinson and tight end Antonio Gates, led the Chargers to the AFC West Championship for the first time since 1995.

The America's Cup

San Diego Bay has always been well known along the California coast as a mecca for yachtsmen with a number of yacht clubs competing in local regattas. During the late 1980s, however, the city became

1992 America's Cup (inset) competitors on San Diego Bay. *Photo by Bob Greiser.*

internationally recognized as a result of worldwide media coverage highlighting San Diegan Dennis Conner's successful defense of the America's Cup. Ironically, Conner had become the first American yachtsman to lose the cup in 1983, but in so doing intensified the public's interest in yachting as a competitive sport. In 1987, in Fremantle on the Western Australian coast, Conner's *Stars & Stripes* defeated the Australian contender in the finals to bring the Cup home to the San Diego Yacht Club.

The San Diego Yacht Club held the trophy for eight years, successfully defending it twice. It faced its first challenge only a year after the Fremantle victory, when New Zealand's Sir Michael Fay lodged his "Big Boat" challenge in 1988. This surprise challenge was met by Dennis Conner's *Stars & Stripes* catamaran, a mismatch that was dragged through an endless succession of court battles. Conner's victory allowed plans to go forward for the 1992 race hosted by the San Diego Yacht Club.

The 1992 challenge off the coast of San Diego little resembled the simple races that began in 1851. With boats costing $20 million instead of $20,000, the stakes became considerably higher. By the time the final defender trials came to a close, only the challenger boats from New Zealand and Italy were left. The Italian boat *Il Moro di Venezia* with skipper Paul Cayard became the favorite in the duel for the Cup and San Diego became the site of world media coverage.

United States contender Bill Koch's high-tech effort *America3* eliminated Dennis Conner and then defeated *Il Moro di Venezia* for the coveted Cup. Amidst the celebration, members of the San Diego Yacht Club, where the America's Cup remained, began making plans to host the rematch in 1995. Unfortunately, San Diegans lost the next America's Cup race to Team New Zealand, who kept the Cup in Auckland until 2003, when the Alinghi Team of the Swiss Société Nautique de Genève won the Cup, becoming the first landlocked nation to do so. The America's Cup race in 2007 was held in the Mediterranean Sea off Valencia, Spain.

San Diego's International Airport and Regional Authority

Lindbergh Field, built on dredged fill from San Diego Bay on the outskirts of downtown in 1928, is a living monument to aviation history in California. With the growth of San Diego County, however, the convenient airport, one of the smallest metropolitan airports in the country, has become inadequate. It covers a mere 526 acres and serves 15 million passengers per year. Plans to expand and/or relocate it have been discussed and researched continuously since the early 1950s, when it became obvious that its potential for growth was limited by geography. In 1999, the Joint Airport Advisory Committee was formed as a partnership between the San Diego Association of Governments (SANDAG) and the airport's governing body, the San Diego Port District. The committee reached the conclusion that if no changes were made to air transportation services, the region would continue to grow at a much slower rate than would be possible with a new or greatly expanded facility.

In January 2002, the San Diego Port District handed off gradual responsibility for Lindbergh Field to a nine-member San Diego County Regional Airport Authority, which took over operational control in January 2003 and gained complete control in July 2005.

View of Naval Training Center housing at Liberty Station from Point Loma.

Under the state law that created it, the authority became the lead land-use planning agency for the county's airports, which number sixteen (one international, four military, and eleven general aviation) as well as for the property near them.

The changeover has concerned some San Diego city officials involved in the former Naval Training Center redevelopment project, which borders the airport. The authority must determine whether development proposals comply with established land-use plans for each airport. Primary planning includes protecting the public on adjacent property from excessive noise and aircraft emergencies or crashes. Housing density on the former Naval Training Center site and increased traffic congestion in 2005 have brought criticism by Point Loma residents.

In the meantime, the regional authority worked on a new airport single site solution that was presented to voters in November 2006. The Airport Site Selection Program Working Group consisted of thirty-two members representing the business, ground use, environmental, and land-use sectors of the community. Consultants and staff have provided feedback on technical assumptions and objective criteria for ranking sites.

By October 2003, the authority had selected seven potential sites: March Air Reserve Base in Riverside County, Marine Corps Air Station Miramar, Marine Corps Air Station Miramar East, Marine

Corps Base Camp Pendleton, Naval Air Station North Island, a desert site in Imperial County, and expansion of Lindbergh Field. The authority later admitted that the military sites might not be a viable option in view of national defense needs. Critics ranged from environmentalists, land-use planners, and residents near the proposed sites. Studies of each site, which would take two years, would cost an estimated $1 million each.

Statewide Issues

San Diego's former mayor and US Senator from California during the 1980s, Pete Wilson, was elected governor of the state in 1990. A number of Republicans preferred that Wilson remain in the Senate, but he believed his chances for national recognition and a possible presidential nomination were better from the governor's office. Wilson faced a budget crisis and cut spending by trimming the state bureaucracy, reforming the state's workers' compensation program, pushing through tax reforms, promoting foreign investment, and keeping businesses in California. He supported NAFTA, which meant more jobs for California, and attempted to limit health care and welfare services to illegal immigrants and their families. His stand against state spending for illegal immigrants was heavily opposed by the Hispanic community.

Wilson maintained per pupil spending in California classrooms, protected public safety by increasing funding for corrections, and saved several key San Diego military bases from what many considered unjustifiable closure. San Diego County, with its 12 major bases and other facilities, has the greatest concentration of US military troops of any region in the country. The San Diego Marine Corps Recruit Depot sends recruits to Camp Pendleton and Marine Corps Air Station Miramar. Wilson was reelected in 1994 and stepped down at the end of his term in 1999 with a record of conservative spending and a budget surplus. Wilson helped lead Arnold Schwarzenegger's successful campaign to replace Gray Davis as California's governor in the recall election of 2003.

San Diego Marine Corps Recruit Depot's Command Museum.

The 1996 Republican National Convention

San Diego had never hosted a national political convention and the Republicans had not been in California since 1964 when Barry Goldwater won the nomination in San Francisco. Although considered for the convention in 1972, the city was dropped in favor of Miami and lost out to Houston in 1992. By 1996, San Diego was characterized as "fiscally conservative" and "socially moderate," both of which appealed to Republicans scheduling the event. San Diego's waterfront convention center at that time held a little under 20,000—much less than the 30,000 to 40,000 delegates and guests expected. The event, held from August 12 through August 16, 1996, proved to be a "Sail to Victory" for San Diego even though the party's nominees, Senator Robert Dole and running mate Jack Kemp, a former San Diego Chargers quarterback, did not defeat incumbent President Bill Clinton and Vice President Al Gore. The convention brought an estimated $100 million in tourism to the city.

The University of San Diego hosted a final debate between the two presidential candidates on October 16 in the form of a town hall meeting in the remodeled Shiley Theater. The number of attendees and the media attention given to the candidates once again put the spotlight on San Diego, showcasing its ability to be a part of the national political scene.

Balboa Park Expansion

By the decade of the 1990s, Balboa Park had fulfilled its goals of rebuilding those structures destroyed by fire in 1978 and restoring several others including the administration building adjoining the Museum of Man and the St. Francis Chapel. Nevertheless, work remained to be done to complete the Master Plan for Balboa Park developed in 1989 for renovating the 1915 House of Charm—now housing the Mingei Folk Art Museum—and the House of Hospitality containing the Prado restaurant, offices, and rental facilities. Despite some controversy over landscaping, the buildings, at a cost of some $30 million, still reflect the design and maintain the integrity of the 1915 exposition.

The Reuben H. Fleet Space Theater and Science Center in 1998, just two months after the museum's 25th birthday in the park, completed an ambitious 14-month, $13 million expansion project that tripled the size of their exhibit space. From the first, an aim of the Fleet Center has been interactivity in order to remain relevant to recent generations raised on ever more frenetic amusements. With its Omnimax theater as a major attraction, it has placed heavy emphasis on education while its showcase for science has soared in size to 93,505 square feet.

The San Diego Hall of Champions moved in 2001 to the Federal Building to occupy some 70,000 square feet of exhibit space. Its departure from the Casa de Balboa left more space for the Museum of Photographic Arts, which shares the building with the San Diego History Center. Showcasing sports history in San Diego, the Hall of Champions was founded by Bob Breitbard who directed or was involved in the museum's activities until his death in 2010. The San Diego Natural History Museum also underwent a complete renovation in 2001, providing a large atrium for community events, a new and dramatic entrance in the rear of the original building, expanded exhibit space, and updated education facilities. The Natural History Museum is regional in its outlook and has developed

San Diego Natural History Museum north entrance in Balboa Park.

partnerships with conservation organizations in Mexico that are protecting the natural environment of Baja California. Its Binational Advisory Board meets regularly on both sides of the border.

San Diego Zoo Plans for Expansion

Of greatest interest is a planned expansion of the world-famous San Diego Zoo, a major part of the park complex. With such popular exhibits as the Chinese giant pandas, who came to the zoo in 1996, and its unparalleled vegetation and design, the zoo's 200 acres attract crowds from all parts of the globe. In May 2001, landscape architect Steve Estrada, a critic of zoo expansion plans who was hired in 2000 to develop an acceptable plan, suggested that a parking structure be built beneath the existing lot. This project was approved by the city, but its location was changed and an employee parking structure was completed southeast of the zoo in 2015. Some critics believe that further expansion should be made at the zoo's Safari Park.

The still unsolved overall parking problem continues to plague park planners and those visiting the park on weekends and for popular events such as December Nights and summer plays at the Old Globe Theater complex. Many ideas have been proposed over the years such as a multilevel parking structure, shuttles to the park from other areas, or trolley line service from downtown. Introduced in 2003, a free tram service from the lot across Park Boulevard handles the problem sufficiently on most days. Nevertheless, the Balboa Park Committee continues to hold meetings, examine plans, and make recommendations to city planners and the city manager's office.

San Diego Moves into the Year 2000

San Diegans, like others worldwide, made the transition into the year 2000 with sighs of relief. None of the dire predictions about computer glitches, food and water shortages, and energy crises materialized. Looking back over some of the recommendations made by some of the "panic people," it is interesting to note that standard items found on Red Cross Y2K checklists included food, water, clothing, blankets, flashlights, medicines, and other essentials. One plan recommended the use of an RV packed with freeze-dried foods, powdered drink mixes, canned and packaged foods, garbage bags, candles, lanterns, and propane heaters as part of a preparedness plan. The "psychological challenges" were met by some denial, fear, anger, depression, and panic, which needed to be transformed into acceptance and cooperation, and finally by trust in competent technology. In retrospect, it is reassuring to know that proper preparations were made by computer programmers, and life continued on January 1, 2000, with hardly a noticeable change.

United States Census

According to the United States Census of 2000, the city of San Diego had 1,223,400 residents—making it the second-largest city in California and the seventh largest in the United States. The diverse racial makeup of the city was reported as 60.18% White, 7.86% African American, 0.62% Native American, 13.65% Asian, 0.48% Pacific Islander, 12.39% from other races, and 4.83% from two or more races. The Hispanic and/or Latino/a population (of any race) is 25.40%. The percentage of Hispanic or Latino/a residents is just over twice the national average (12%) and of Asians, four times the national average (3.6%).

Centro Cultural de la Raza in Balboa Park.

San Diego's economy remained strong with manufacturing its number-one source of income from high-value goods requiring research and development. Harbor-related activities constitute its second-largest economic asset—a true gateway to trade with Pacific Rim countries and a destination for cruise-ship lines. Tourism, San Diego's third-largest industry, brought in some $5 billion in 2002. Old Town San Diego State Historic Park is the third most visited state park in California—approximately seven million per year. San Diego's Lindbergh Field accommodates over 30,000 travelers daily.

Terrorist Attack on September 11, 2001

At 8:45 a.m. Eastern Standard Time, a hijacked passenger jet, American Airlines Flight 11 out of Boston, Massachusetts, crashed into the north tower of New York's World Trade Center, tearing a gaping hole in the building and setting it afire. At 9:03 a.m., a second hijacked airliner, United Airlines Flight 175 from Boston, crashed into the south tower of the World Trade Center and exploded. Both buildings burnt and thousands of lives were lost. As further tragedies took place at the Pentagon and in Pennsylvania, San Diegans listened in fear as the news continued throughout the day. In the aftermath of the attack, all Americans realized that life had changed for everyone. San Diego sent help in many ways—one of the most significant being in the days following when San Diego's rescue dogs searched for buried bodies.

After that day, new federal security measures were put in place, resulting in intensified airport searches, investigations of foreign residents, legal and illegal, and other means by which suspicious persons could be identified. All military units in the San Diego area were put on notice and have remained in a state of preparation.

Water Assured for San Diego's Future

In early October 2003, the Imperial Irrigation District board narrowly approved a landmark agreement to share Colorado River water and transfer new water supplies to San Diego County. The El Centro-based IID voted 3–2 to approve the 45-year agreement against the objections of some Imperial Valley farmers, who feared that the sale threatened to destroy the valley's farm economy. Under the agreement, IID's use of Colorado River water was capped at 3.1 million acre-feet annually.

Critics argued that the deal could adversely affect agriculture and related businesses in the Imperial Valley by fallowing, in the first 15 years of the agreement, approximately 25,000 acres of farmland, so that water could be sold to the San Diego County Water Authority. The plan, which had already been approved by San Diego, the Los Angeles-based Metropolitan Water District of Southern California (MWD), and the Coachella Valley Water District, transfers water to MWD, and raises $300 million to help preserve the threatened Salton Sea.

Although the plan, in its first stage, calls for water to be saved by letting fields remain dry, the long-range strategy envisions that farmers install conservation devices to allow them to continue to grow crops by using less water. With an annual value of $1.2 billion, agriculture is the dominant economic factor in a valley with 140,000 people and 500,000 acres of farmland.

The pact will supply San Diego with about a third of its future water needs, as much as 277,000 acre-feet of water each year. The

The All-American Canal carries water to the Imperial Valley.
Photo courtesy Imperial Irrigation District.

San Diego County Water authority will pay an estimated $6 to $9 billion to IID over the 45-year term for the water that reduces the region's reliance on the Metropolitan Water District, which will receive an additional $250 per acre-foot to ship the water through its pipelines.

For IID, the state's largest user of Colorado River water, the money pays for system and on-farm water conservation measures and offsets the economic impact of taking land out of production. Importantly, the deal provides a measure of peace for Imperial County from the relentless efforts by other agencies, the state, and federal governments to take portions of its generous supply of water.

Meanwhile, as a condition of the transfer, the Irrigation District—which owns 70 percent of California's yearly share of the Colorado River—has agreed to sell additional water to the state. The state planned to sell the water at a slightly higher price, and use the $300 million in profit to provide environmental help for the Salton Sea, which is becoming too salty to support life. As of January 1, 2016, the state had not acquired this water for Salton Sea restoration purposes.

The Imperial County Board of Supervisors filed a lawsuit, saying that the transfer was not properly reviewed under the California Environmental Quality Act. The Imperial Group, a band of Imperial

Valley farmers, also filed a number of suits, claiming that Imperial Valley's water belongs to its landowners, and the Irrigation District is merely the trustee that manages the water rights, without a right to make long-term transfers. All of the lawsuits have since been dismissed. Imperial County and IID have joined together to seek solutions to the Salton Sea environmental issues.

Meanwhile, despite all the time and effort water leaders put into making the transfer happen, and the fact that the deal has been the largest shift of water from agricultural use to urban use in United States history, few noticed when the water started to flow.

Firestorm October 2003

The San Diego County Firestorm during the week of October 26, 2003, brought on by drought conditions and, in some areas, unchecked undergrowth, was the worst in the county's history. The Cedar Fire of East County, including the areas of Ramona, Alpine, Harbison Canyon, Scripps Ranch, and Tierrasanta burned 280,293 acres, 2,232 homes, 22 businesses, and caused 14 deaths and 91 injuries. The Paradise Fire, farther to the south, burned 56,700 acres and 179 homes, causing 2 deaths and injuring 20 firefighters. In the Otay Fire, 46,291 acres burned and 1 home was lost.

In October 2004, damages in the Cedar Fire alone were estimated to have exceeded $100 million dollars. Claims were made that fire protection was inadequate and that more could have been done by government officials to prevent such extensive loss. A number of homeowners, lacking sufficient insurance or ability to rebuild, were still without homes more than a year later.

The Legacy of Joan Kroc

Joan Kroc died on October 12, 2004, at her home in Rancho Santa Fe at the age of 75. With an estimated wealth of $1.7 billion, Joan Kroc's generosity to peace and antiwar groups was unrivaled, both in the amounts she donated and in her disinterest in being hailed. Shortly after her death, the University of San Diego revealed that she had left

Joan B. Kroc Institute for Peace and Justice at the University of San Diego. *Photo by Steven Schoenherr.* Inset: Joan Kroc.

$50 million to the school to be used for a School of Peace Studies. In 2001, she had given more than $25 million to the university to build the Joan Kroc Institute for Peace and Justice, an outstanding Renaissance structure that graces the campus and serves as a conference center on peace and justice issues. She was committed to the idea that unless we teach our children peace, someone else will teach them violence.

Following the death of her husband, Ray, in 1982, Joan gave donations in the hundreds of millions to groups such as the Salvation Army, Special Olympics, Father Joe Carroll's and other homeless shelters, the Ronald McDonald hospice, and numerous relief organizations. She donated $200 million to National Public Radio for its coverage of the US war against Iraq, which she adamantly opposed.

Old Town San Diego State Historic Park

Another popular tourist destination in San Diego has been Old Town and its commercially oriented state park. The restored buildings, which include the Casa de Estudillo, Seeley Stables, McCoy House, and several adobes draw history buffs, while the colorful Mexican restaurants Casa de Bandini, Casa de Pico, and Rancho el Nopal have attracted over a million visitors annually. These restaurants, plus a shopping complex known as Bazaar del Mundo located on the grounds of the historic Casa de Pico Motor Hotel, have been a part of San Diego since the beginnings of the park in 1969.

In what came as a shock to many San Diegans, as well as to out-of-town visitors, the park's major leaseholder, Diane Powers, creator of the Mexican-like atmosphere in the Bazaar del Mundo and adjoining restaurants, became the victim of a decision by the State Department of Parks and Recreation under former governor Gray Davis. Delaware North, an eighty-nine-year-old company based in Buffalo, New York, with experience operating concessions in Petco Park, Yellowstone and Yosemite National Parks, took over the major Old Town leases in May 2005. By 2009, Delaware North's revenue from its Old Town operations declined 66 percent over what Powers was producing. The company fled Old Town, turning over the operation to a local restaurateur.

City Politics

Former superior court judge Dick Murphy took the oath as the 33rd mayor of San Diego in December 2000. Although he had previously served one term on the San Diego City Council, many considered him a fresh face in the world of San Diego politics. His varied career included service in the US Army and as an attorney at the law firm of Luce, Forward, Hamilton & Scripps. In 1985, he was appointed municipal court judge by Governor George Deukmejian and, in 1989, became a superior court judge.

Murphy served on the San Diego City Council from 1981 to 1985, chaired the Mission Trails Regional Park Task Force and the Metropolitan Transit Development Board, and led the effort to build the East Line of the San Diego Trolley. At his first state of the city address, Mayor Murphy set forth a bold agenda to make San Diego "a City worthy of our affection." His ten goals for the city included plans to reduce traffic congestion, clean up the beaches and bays, complete the ballpark, and improve the library system.

Murphy's first term was tainted by the indictment of three council members for allegedly taking bribes to relax the city's "no-touch" regulations regarding strippers. The rules, which remain in effect,

Mission Trails Regional Park Visitors Center.

ban the risqué performances known as lap dances, giving a boost to freewheeling strip clubs in other cities.

Despite its reputation as "America's Finest City," San Diego has had its share of mismanagement of government affairs. Local historian Mike Davis, coauthor of a muckraking book, *Under the Perfect Sun: the San Diego Tourists Never See* (2003), has claimed that San Diego from its early years has been a rough-and-tumble seaport with scandals in the 1960s, 1970s, and 1980s. In a 2004 interview Davis called San Diego "the most corrupt city on the West Coast by any measure of white-collar crime, municipal corruption, or indictment of public officials."

On the positive side of Mayor Murphy's first term in office have been an open space acquisition north of Mission Trails Regional Park and the creation of the San Diego River Conservancy with plans for a river park. New branch libraries were completed in Mission Valley and Point Loma and plans for a new main library designed by Rob Quigley received approval for construction in 2004. The city also adopted a $300 million plan to rebuild and expand 24 branch libraries over the next ten years.

Plans to double the number of SENTRI lanes (fast border crossing with permits) were made with corresponding Mexican officials to ease the border wait. Nevertheless, other border issues including illegal immigration, environmental concerns, and updated cultural and political exchange mechanisms were still subjects of concern.

Voters deemed Murphy's administration only a partial success by writing in city council member Donna Frye in the November 2004 election. County Supervisor Ron Roberts, Murphy's "official" opponent, also received a significant number of votes. Murphy was declared mayor in January 2005 despite lawsuits challenging the elimination of write-in votes that were not accompanied by a filled-in "bubble" by Frye's name. The city's pension fund and financial rating remained under a cloud while the indictments of two councilmen were being settled.

KUSI weatherman Dave Scott reports on Mission Valley flooding March 5, 2005.

La Jolla Beach & Tennis Club and the Marine Room, La Jolla, California, experience the battering of waves during storms accompanied by high tides. *Photo by John Trifiletti.*

Chapter XIII

SAN DIEGO GOES GLOBAL
2005–2015

San Diego's reputation as a livable city is often based on its nearly perfect weather. San Diego is blessed with what is termed a Mediterranean climate tempered by the Pacific Ocean, with the result that summers are cool and winters warm in comparison with other places along the same general latitude. The annual average high temperature is 71°F, and annual rainfall averages close to 10 inches. The bays and beaches are perfect for maritime and aquatic activities, while the nearby mountains, which experience occasional winter

View of the San Diego Convention Center. ©2016 Ted Walton.

snows, are easily accessible for camping and hiking. Nevertheless, global warming threatens to bring higher temperatures, less rainfall, and rising sea levels. From time to time the El Niño phenomena warms the ocean and produces intermittent heavy flooding and winter rains.

As 2005 began, San Diego's weather pendulum swung once again to the rainy side. Recorded rainfall reached nearly 20 inches, third highest in recorded history. Heavy flooding and mudslides pushed homes off their foundations, engulfed yards and home interiors, and caused several road closures. The swollen San Diego River reoccupied much of its former channel while dams throughout the county spilled over. On the positive side, local reservoirs received a much-needed refill, and burned-out areas blossomed with vegetation. On the whole, the rains were a welcome relief after years of drought.

San Diego's Economic and Political Outlook

Despite the city's financial setbacks resulting from an underfunded pension plan, most San Diegans believed their financial future was secure. On April 25, 2005, Dick Murphy announced that he would resign as mayor of San Diego effective July 15. City council member Donna Frye received a plurality of votes in the July primary, but the runoff election held on November 8, 2005, brought former chief of police Jerry Sanders into the top city office under the strong-mayor form of government. This produced a dramatic change in city government as approved by the voters on the same ballot. Soon gaining a reputation as a problem-solving mayor who could handle the heavy burden of enormous debt, Sanders quieted the fears of those involved in city government.

Nevertheless, financial problems, as well as immigration issues, were difficult to solve and mirrored the issues faced by the state of California under Governor Arnold Schwarzenegger, who was reelected in 2006. An increase in arrests at the US-Mexico border sparked a controversy with suggestions that the state senate adopt a guest worker program similar to the Bracero Program used during World War II. Around 1,100 students from the San Diego Unified School District

Mayor Jerry Sanders (center) congratulating the San Diego Maritime Museum at the laying of the keel for the *San Salvador* on April 15, 2011. To his left is Councilman Kevin Faulconer and to his right is County Supervisor Greg Cox and Kumeyaay representative Anthony Pico. *Photo by Maggie Walton.*

blocked the area of Chicano Park to protest a bill restricting immigration.

At the close of 2005, the economy had heated up with the sale of homes peaking in midyear. Approximately three million people living in San Diego County held an estimated 1.5 million jobs with a median annual income of $69,530. The median price of a home had reached $517,500 in November. Since San Diego had several highly concentrated areas of active duty military personnel, the city ranked the federal government as its number one employer. As the year 2006 began, more than 95,000 sailors and marines called San Diego home, and the military was responsible for $18.3 billion in gross regional product. These figures were not without an effect on politics. Data from the Public Policy Institute of California indicated that San Diego ranked as the most conservative of the major cities on the West Coast. With Mayor Sanders continuing in office for a second term in June 2008, San Diego became the largest US city with a Republican mayor. Perhaps the most notable news story about Mayor Sanders was a reversal of his public opposition to gay marriage before signing a city council resolution that aimed to overturn California's ban on same-sex marriage. Legislation banning the use of cell phones while driving and prohibiting adults from smoking while children were in the car had finally taken effect, though not without protests.

City council members spanning the period from 2004 to 2015 were Scott Peters, Brian Maienschein, Toni Atkins, and Jim Madaffer elected in 2004; Kevin Faulconer, Tony Young, Donna Frye, and Ben Hueso elected in 2006; Todd Gloria, Carl DeMaio, Sherri Lightner, and Marti Emerald elected in 2008; Lorie Zapf and David Alvarez, elected in 2010; Mark Kersey in 2012 and Chris Cate, 2014.

Problems of Water

As President Barack Obama and Vice President Joe Biden were inaugurated in January 2009, California water scarcity was still a major problem for the state. Governor Arnold Schwarzenegger introduced his "Green Crusade" and was praised for his efforts in the "war on carbon." Despite the ongoing water shortage, Mayor Sanders was not ready to support the mixing of treated wastewater with other water in the city reservoirs. The San Diego County Water Authority won an ongoing battle with the Metropolitan Water District over water rates in mid 2014 and received a judgment totaling $188.3 million in contract damages. By 2015, the city council had approved recycling wastewater for potable use as part of its water conservation measures. When Governor Schwarzenegger termed out in 2010, former governor Jerry Brown returned to the state's highest office. Brown issued executive orders aimed at forcing greater water conservation and targeted some San Diego districts continuing to water their abundant landscaping.

San Diego Politics

The *Wall Street Journal* of September 6, 2010, reported that San Diego had quadrupled its funding to the pensions by deferring road maintenance, skimping on library funding, and reducing municipal recreation programs. Mayor Sanders's accomplishments ranged from attention to environmental concerns to promoting city opportunities

County Supervisor Ron Roberts, City Councilman Todd Gloria, and County Supervisor Greg Cox celebrate the city's partnership with the county on Live Well. *County News Center.*

for small business contractors. After the city's financial crises of the previous several years, his proposal for a new city hall was defeated by concerns over cost and projections about future space needs. The issue remained controversial while the $1.2 billion deficit in the city's pension fund continued to burden the city, although the introduction of 401k pensions for new hires was a partial solution. Also on the positive side, San Diego reached a plateau regarding recycling in 2009. Recycling rates saw a significant increase to 64 percent of waste materials and topped the state average of 59 percent. San Diego's recycle rate resulted from city residents and business owners recycling over half of their trash and reducing the burden on local landfills. Plans for a new downtown library in combination with a charter school were also approved in 2010. An extension of the trolley line to the north, including the UCSD campus, was also planned to relieve freeway congestion.

The once majority Republican city of San Diego recorded more Democrats as registered voters. Mayor Jerry Sanders continued to value community service and promoted a program called "Mayors Against Illegal Guns" coalition. The adoption of the strong-mayor system of government that eliminated the city manager in 2005 in Sanders's election, made the mayor the chief executive officer of the city, but not a voting member of the city council. In this system, the strong-mayor prepares and administers the city budget, although that budget must be approved by the council, which needed an additional member to avoid a tie vote. Elected in 2010, it is the last to use the eight district boundaries created in 2000 as redistricting approved in 2010 provided a ninth district and an additional council member. District boundaries, always controversial, were redrawn to take effect in the local elections in 2012.

Despite the popularity of Republican Mitt Romney, a part-time local resident of La Jolla, election results in November 2012 saw Democrats Barack Obama and Joe Biden continue to hold the country's highest offices. The president succeeded in securing an affordable health care plan, while Republicans lobbied for its elimination. Despite opposition, California adopted its own exchanges under the Affordable Care Act and enrolled subscribers under the Covered California Plan. Representative Darrell Issa remained a powerful San Diego voice in Congress in his role as chairman of the House Oversight Committee.

Immigration and Minority Issues

From 2000 to 2010 the diverse makeup of San Diego changed from 60.18 percent non-Hispanic white to 45 percent; from 25.4 percent Hispanic or Latino/a of any race to 29 percent; from 7.7 percent African American to 6.5 percent; from 13.7 percent Asian and 0.5 percent Pacific Islander to 15.6 percent Asian alone and 0.4 percent Pacific Islander. In 2010 the percentage of Hispanic or Latino/a residents was just under twice the national average (16 percent) and of Asians, four times the national average (4.8 percent). In government, David Alvarez took over Ben Hueso's seat on the San Diego City Council in 2010. Hueso was elected to the state senate while Juan Vargas, who served on the San Diego City Council from 1993–2000, was elected to Congress in 2012 and reelected in 2014.

Mural at Chicano Park placed under the Coronado Bridge celebrates the Mexican heritage of San Diego. Verse in Spanish translates to Water Is Sacred—Water Is Life.

Despite increased participation by persons of Hispanic descent in government offices, tensions over immigration issues and the increased fortification of the border fence remained. Another controversy arose over redistricting when it became necessary to create a ninth council district. The recommendations of the Volunteer Redistricting Committee were accepted despite some protest from Rancho Peñasquitos residents whose council district placed them in the San Diego Unified School District to the south.

Minority issues continued to plague the immigrant community and burden those who searched for an equitable solution for undocumented residents. According to the American Community Survey in 2007, 23% of San Diegans were legal immigrants (about 675,000) and 45% of those immigrants were citizens. Most residents embraced the cultural contributions of the immigrant communities as exemplified in restaurants, churches, murals, architecture, and landscaping. By 2015, more than 86 different languages were spoken in San Diego County. Unfortunately, conditions for immigrants continued to worsen. Prior to 1980 the poverty rate of immigrants was 8% and those having some kind of permanent housing was 70%. In the following three decades, the poverty rate hovered around 20% and the housing rate dipped to 30%. Legislative efforts to confront issues pertaining to illegal immigration revolved around drivers' licenses, health care, education, human and drug trafficking, unaccompanied children, and stronger border protection. The city of Escondido in North County, with a significant Latino population—nearly half of its 148,000 residents—and an immigrant mayor, also adopted some of the harshest anti-illegal-immigration measures in the country. They did not welcome unaccompanied Central American minors during an influx in 2014.

Later Elections

On November 6, 2012, national elections took center stage. Barack Obama carried California and Democrats took control of the US Senate while Republicans held the majority in the House. Representative Scott Peters, a Democrat, gained District 52 and San Diego's vote by only 1% over Brian Bilbray. Issues of morality, including the death penalty, abortion, contraception, and gay marriage seemed to win out over financial concerns. Democrats Marty Block joined the state senate from San Diego and Toni Atkins was elected to the state assembly and became speaker. Dave Roberts, the first Democrat elected as a county supervisor in twenty years, replaced Pam Slater-Price in 2013 and joined longtime members Greg Cox, chairman; Dianne Jacob; Ron Roberts; and Bill Horn.

Bob Filner, a veteran Democrat who had held a number of offices, took on the role of strong mayor on December 6, 2012. The fact that charges had been brought against Filner in 2007 for assault and battery of a woman who worked for United Airlines was not well known since charges had been dropped in lieu of a fine. Almost as soon as Filner assumed office, accusations began to surface concerning allegations of sexual misconduct. On July 10, 2013, former city Council member Donna Frye handed Filner a letter requesting his immediate resignation resulting from credible evidence that the mayor had harassed multiple women. Over the next few weeks, the scandal escalated and, as more women came forward, reached national and even international news. A number of additional problems surfaced over the next few months forcing Filner to plead guilty to felony charges. Multiple legal charges by women ended in his removal as the 35th mayor, effective August 30, 2013. Council president Todd Gloria became interim mayor until a special election held on November 19 ended in a runoff. The deciding election was held in February 2014 in which former city council member Kevin Faulconer, a graduate of San Diego State University in 1990, defeated Councilman David Alvarez in a runoff mayoral election.

During his brief term, Filner raised additional controversy when he withheld his signature to authorize funding to the Tourism Marketing District. He demanded that hotel workers salaries be raised and a method be adopted to send more of the tourist tax directly to the city of San Diego. Ultimately, Filner and the tourism office compromised and the mayor authorized the funding.

A Changed Political Climate

Mayor Kevin Faulconer, a native Californian, was elected to a full term on the city council in June 2006. Reelected in June 2010 and elected mayor in a special election held in February 2014, Faulconer served the balance of Filner's term through 2016, when city elections were scheduled. Two office holders of note were Todd Gloria, former council president, who put in a bid for the state assembly in 2016, and Toni Atkins, former speaker of the state assembly, whose term expired in 2016. She planned to run for the California senate in 2016. Current state senators as 2016 began were Marty Block, Ben Hueso, Joel Anderson, and Patricia Bates. Susan Davis, Duncan Hunter, and Scott Peters were serving as members of Congress in Washington, D.C.

Population Trends in San Diego County

The county's population reached nearly 3.1 million by 2010, while the city remained at a little over 1.3 million. By 2014, the county had reached an estimated 3.26 million. Much of the county's growth was taking place east of I-5, changing the demographics from the large family homes of Del Mar, Encinitas, and Carlsbad to communities complete with new schools, parks, multiple athleltic fields, and popular strip malls. The years from 2005 to 2015 saw the population of Carlsbad in North County grow from 90,773 to 110,653 and in Chula Vista in the southern part of the county from 210,497 to 257,989. Other cities in the county showed remarkable growth as well, contributing to increased problems of freeway traffic, lack of water resources, crowded schools, and air pollution. In some communities, citizen groups were able to control the projected size of new developments and shopping centers such as One Paseo in Carmel Valley and Agua Hedionda in Carlsbad. Ballot measures have been able to control growth in some areas, but not in others, such as San Diego's Mission Valley.

In early 2015, the city of San Diego's population was estimated at nearly 1.4 million, the second-fastest growing city in California and continuing as the eighth-largest city in the United States with the third-largest homeless population. The city grew faster than suburban areas because of a regeneration and gentrification of the downtown area combined with new residents wanting to avoid freeway congestion. As the number of people commuting from the South Bay area and North County to the city center caused traffic delays, living downtown or working from home became popular.

The border between San Diego and Tijuana at San Ysidro remained the world's busiest land border crossing, with more than 30 million crossings in and out of the county each year. It is the location of the most deportations, with numbers reaching between 100 and 160 per day. Because of the prevalence of illegal drugs smuggled into the country, the city put additional resources toward the implementation of the 2012–2016 Border Patrol Strategic Plan. One of the popular methods of bringing in illegal drugs has been through skillfully dug tunnels between Mexico and the United States that are discovered and destroyed by the Border Patrol with regularity.

Native Americans of San Diego County

Casino income shared among the Native American residents of the nine Indian reservations throughout the county continued to increase (pp. 17–20). By 2010 the various bands had expanded into the hotel business, education, health clinics, golf resorts, and RV parks. These enterprises produced sufficient income for increased health care, housing, education, and retirement pensions. Kumeyaay Community College, a tribal educational institution sponsored by the Sycuan Band, has been dedicated to the research of Kumeyaay traditional knowledge. It has been designed to teach customs, traditions, and local languages to the younger generations of Native Indian peoples as well as the non-Kumeyaay population at large. Kumeyaay Community College primarily serves and relies on resources from the thirteen reservations of the Kumeyaay nation situated in San Diego County. By 2015, there were nineteen federally recognized tribal bands in the county (p. 318).

Renovation of Horton Plaza Park

Downtown San Diego, continuing its trend of high-rise condos and office buildings, completed plans in 2013 for a costly redevelopment of Horton Plaza Park, an area between Third and Fourth Avenues adjacent to the shopping mall that was originally opened in 1985 (pp. 194–196). The park's historic fountain, a powerful city icon designed by Irving Gill in 1909 and based on the fourth century BCE Choragic Monument in Athens, is admired annually by scores of visitors (p. 121). President Benjamin Harrison spoke there in 1892 and John F. Kennedy was photographed at the site while campaigning for president. The fountain was first restored in 1984 at a cost of $775,000 when it was necessary to upgrade the one-hundred-year-old interior lighting.

Fronting on Broadway across from the US Grant Hotel, the park and fountain are difficult to protect. After some delays, the California Department of Finance in 2015 approved $4.9 million in funding to move forward with development of the park project that will cost a total of $17.7 million. The approval allowed construction to proceed on the public square area. The new 1.3-acre park has been developed

Landmark fountain designed by Irving Gill in 1909 and first restored in 1984 serves as the centerpiece of the new Horton Plaza Park. *Photo by Robi Olson.*

by both the city and mall operator Westfield Group, next door to the Horton Plaza Mall. Construction actually began in 2012 on the site of the former Robinsons-May department store building that was razed to make way for the ambitious project.

The new Horton Plaza Park plan includes an amphitheater, food and retail pavilions, public restrooms, granite paving, and an interactive water feature. There are also public right-of-way improvements in the vicinity, and the existing historic park has been rehabilitated with new landscaping and restoration of the Gill Fountain. Under an agreement with the city, Westfield Group has agreed to maintain the new park for 25 years, and will be programming approximately 200 events annually at the venue, including concerts, festivals, and holiday celebrations. According to historic consultant David Marshall, this newest restoration costing about $1.6 million including the fountain, is the most accurate yet.

Neighborhood Progress

Neighborhood identity is strong in San Diego and provides a way for residents to work together on various projects. For example, Barrio Logan is the home of Chicano Park, a Chicano-themed public park created in large part by the residents (p. 199). Located at the site of a 1970s demonstration against freeway incursion, the park features more than 60 colorful murals painted on the concrete support piers for the San Diego-Coronado Bridge and Interstate 5. It was designated an official historic site by the San Diego Historic Sites Board in 1980 and listed on the National Register of Historic Places in 2013. Maritime industry interests were able to overturn its locally organized community plan to the dismay of supporters.

Smaller districts include the neighborhood of Hillcrest, known for its vibrant LGBT community, that was able to form a Hillcrest Town Council in 2007. It gave residents a voice on various issues, especially permission to fly a large, privately funded rainbow flag at the corner of University Avenue and Normal Street and to sponsor an annual Gay Pride Parade. The neighborhood of Grantville is working with the San Diego River Conservancy to protect and improve the flow of the San Diego River as it enters Mission Valley from Mission Gorge. Plans are underway for setting aside additional parkland. Liberty Station, an award-winning mixed-use development created out of the former Naval Training Center San Diego is located in the Point Loma community. In addition to a retail and commercial district, the project contains ample open space and dozens of historic buildings housing museums and other cultural institutions. It is listed on the National Register of Historic Places and contains High Tech Village, a group of public charter schools centered around High Tech High.

San Diego's City Heights neighborhood received recognition in 2011 for supporting its refugee population with an innovative farm program called New Roots. The program provides growing spaces for 85 families from 12 different countries in the heart of the city. Many of the participants were farmers in their home countries and were given an opportunity to reconnect with the land as well as

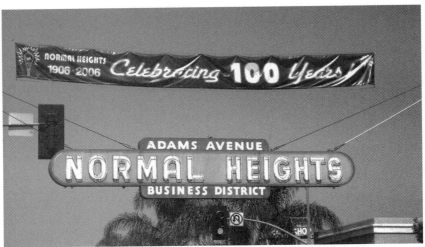

Banner celebrating 100 years of Normal Heights designation as a neighborhood business district on Adams Avenue. *Photo courtesy of Suzanne Ledeboer.*

increase their family's food security by gaining access to proper nutrition. New Roots, begun among refugee farmers in the Fresno area in the late 1970s, was started at the request of the Somali Bantu community with the help of Bilali Muya. New Roots provides training in soil, irrigation techniques, and climate change to help refugees develop their gardens into independent farms.

Another educational program in City Heights, centered in the Ocean Discovery Institute, serves 6,000 young people a year. Its goal is to understand the ocean and its problems of pollution, overfishing, temperature change, and reef protection by using a living lab created in partnership with the San Diego Unified School District. This relationship provides standards-based curriculum-aligned science education during the school day and hands-on experience at all hours. The new and expanded Copley/Price YMCA opened in 2014 in City Heights to give people of diverse backgrounds and religions a place to come together and participate in programs that emphasize youth development, healthy living, and social responsibility. City Heights has sizable immigrant populations representing many Middle Eastern, African, and South American countries.

River Conservancies in San Diego County

The San Diego River Conservancy was established by an act of the California Legislature in 2002 to preserve, restore, and enhance the San Diego River area. As stated by the conservancy, "The San Diego River Area is an historical, archeological and biological treasure of statewide significance that must be preserved." A prime example of sustainability is the nonprofit conservancy in the San Dieguito River watershed that is dedicated to management of the natural resources along the river's corridor. Land has been set aside within a 92,000 acre river park area that extends seventy-one miles along the Coast to Crest Trail from the ocean at Del Mar to Volcan Mountain north of Julian. The conservancy is led by a citizen board of directors and is supported by more than 1,300 members from throughout the county. Protection of the river, along with the preservation of the natural and cultural resources of the area, is a collaborative effort with the greater San Diego community and stands as a landmark in the use of local park lands. Volunteers work to restore habitats, lead hikes, and educate residents of the region in order to protect the remaining open space within San Diego County. In addition to the example of the San Dieguito River Conservancy, the success of river conservancies has inspired the similar efforts of those involved with the Sweetwater and Otay River valleys. Ongoing volunteer efforts have been protecting the habitats of endangered species in the southeastern portions of the county.

Tourism in San Diego

San Diego hosted over 32 million tourists in 2012 despite a weak economy and the decrease in the number of cruise ships to Mexico stopping at the port. Nevertheless, a surge of new visitors was realized for the 2015 centennial celebration of the 1915 Panama-California Exposition in Balboa Park. A concept to remove parking and vehicles from the Plaza de Panama by modifying the Cabrillo Bridge entrance was eventually approved in its original form, but an alternate and less

The County of San Diego Water Park on Harbor Drive with San Diego Bay in the background. *Photo by Jessica Piatt.*

costly redirection of traffic was accomplished by Mayor Filner. The newly cleared plaza allowed the possibility for new events in the area. Proposals for paid parking continued to be an issue in Balboa Park since the 1870 Trust Dedication of the City Park promised entry would be forever free to all. No cars were involved in 1870, but increased visitation has created a modern parking issue.

On July 4, 2013, San Diego's Big Boom Fireworks Show received national publicity because of its failure. A glitch in pyrotechnics caused all of the fireworks to explode at once, giving a 15 second moment of triumph. The "fizzle" was broadcast over numerous television networks and the Internet, adding to San Diego's embarrassing episode. The fireworks show worked perfectly the next year. Other tourist destinations such as the Gaslamp Quarter, Seaport Village, Midway Museum, *Star of India*, and County Water Park on Harbor Drive all brought a steady stream of tourists to the downtown waterfront area. The historic San Diego Police Headquarters, remodeled and modernized as a site for restaurants and retail, created a new favorite stopping place for tourists. Old Town San Diego continued to draw out-of-town visitors despite a slowdown by local residents who opposed a change in leaseholders (p. 246) and the relocation of Diane Powers's popular Bazaar del Mundo to Taylor Street and Casa de Pico restaurant to Grossmont Center.

SeaWorld's Changing Status

The year 2006 saw the first incident that would bring San Diego's popular marine park SeaWorld under scrutiny. In November, a killer whale named Kasatka grabbed trainer Ken Peters and dragged him deep into the tank, keeping him underwater for about half a minute until other SeaWorld trainers were able to persuade the whale to surface. This allowed the trainer to take a breath of air before being dragged under again for a full minute. The trainer fully recovered, suffering only a broken foot, but the event made headlines and called the attention of many to some possible dangers at SeaWorld, which did not bode well for the park's future reputation.

A movie released in 2013 called *Blackfish* focused on some alleged consequences of keeping whales in captivity. Tilikum, an orca captured

Dolphins have been performing at SeaWorld's popular marine show in San Diego since 1964. *Photo by ISO Europe International Student Office.*

in 1983 off the coast of Iceland, performed at SeaWorld's park in Orlando, Florida. The movie falsely claimed that Tilikum was involved in the deaths of three trainers due to stress resulting from the whale's treatment at SeaWorld. The film presented a strong bias against SeaWorld. After the movie (incorrectly categorized as a documentary) was released, past and present SeaWorld trainers insisted that after the tragic death of Orlando employee Dawn Brancheau, the trainer dragged underwater, SeaWorld changed the facilities, equipment, and procedures of the killer whale habitats to make them safer. None of the ongoing work of conservation was portrayed in the movie, but SeaWorld did not think it necessary to produce a documentary to clarify the false claims against the park. Overall attendance at SeaWorld declined while California Assemblyman Richard Bloom introduced the Orca Welfare and Safety Act that would ban entertainment-driven orca captivity and retire all current whales. In 2015, the California Coastal Commission ruled that SeaWorld could no longer breed whales in captivity. SeaWorld protested this ruling but has proposed a new plan that would close the orca facilities by 2017. They have terminated the whale breeding program and SeaWorld remains heavily involved in rescuing wounded and sick sea animals in nearby coastal waters.

San Diego Maritime Museum Re-creates the *San Salvador*

A full-sized, fully functional, and historically accurate replica of Juan Rodríguez Cabrillo's flagship, the *San Salvador*, began to take shape in public view at San Diego's Spanish Landing park area in 2011. Based upon sixteenth-century documents, descriptions of similar galleons, and a thorough research of the wood available, the ship emerged as close as possible to the original that arrived in San Diego on September 28, 1542. This event predated the settlement of Jamestown in 1607 and the arrival of the Pilgrims at Plymouth Rock in 1620 by nearly seventy years. Under the direction of Maritime Museum president Dr. Ray Ashley and naval architect Douglas Sharp, the goal of the museum was to build a ship accessible for visitors to

The newly launched *San Salvador* with the San Diego skyline in the background on September 4, 2015.

understand the role of San Diego in the country's origin story. A fund-raising campaign was begun with aid from the California State Coastal Conservancy and a number of local donors.

Sixteenth-century documents and charts had been studied for several years, so the galleon's shape and approximate dimensions were well understood when the keel was laid in a ceremony on April 15, 2011. The formal technical design process started with a digital hull surface model so its measurements could be worked out in modern terms. A Kumeyaay village was created at the building site to give visitors an opportunity to learn about the Native Americans who interacted with the Spaniards during their five-day visit to San Diego in September 1542 (pp. 36–39).

During 2015, as the ship was readied for launching, Canadian researcher Wendy Kramer found several documents clarifying long-standing questions about Cabrillo's nationality. These included sworn testimony by Cabrillo himself that he was born in Palma del Rio, a small town in southern Spain near Córdoba. Although he may have had Portuguese ancestors, San Diego's first European visitor listed himself as Spanish. The *San Salvador* launching took place in Chula

Vista on July 22, 2015, with full rigging completed at the Maritime Museum in early spring 2016. The ship serves as a floating classroom for students and visitors up and down the coast.

Plans for the Embarcadero

On September 4, 2015, Manchester Financial Group finalized a settlement agreement with the California Coastal Commission regarding development of an eight-city-block area fronting on San Diego Bay at Broadway and Harbor Drive. Eight years in negotiations, the Manchester Pacific Gateway Project included a new NAVFAC Government Administration Class A office building for the US Navy (replacing the navy complex occupying the foot of Broadway since the 1920s); a 1.9 acre waterfront park; and cultural museum, restaurants, entertainment, retail, public parking, and new waterfront access embracing the city's North Embarcadero Visionary Plan on San Diego Bay. Its proposed completion date is subject to market conditions and is projected for the mid-2020s.

Further to the north, the historic Anthony's restaurant owned by pioneer Italian settlers of the Ghio family, and fronting on San Diego Bay for the past seventy years, gave way in late 2015 to the Brigantine restaurant chain. A new eating establishment with an 85-foot boat dock, built by the local Michael Morton family of Point Loma, will stand next to the San Diego Maritime Museum's *Star of India*. To the south, Seaport Village plans an extensive redevelopment when its lease expires in 2017.

Advances in Science

San Diego is ranked fourth nationally in the development of biotechnology. In 2012, Nasseo Inc., a medical device company providing clinicians and patients with dental and orthopedic implant treatment options, made history with its biomedical breakthrough in dental implants. Also in 2012, the Salk Institute was named the SDG&E Energy Champion for its efforts in conservation and energy efficiency. The Campaign for Salk, a fund-raising plan to support the

Craig Venter, award-winning founder of J. Craig Venter Institute, La Jolla, California.

four major scientific fields of cancer, genomic medicine, healthy aging, and the dynamic brain raised record amounts in 2012. Salk takes advantage of the strategies and technologies helpful in conducting research at the molecular and cellular level for learning more about disease. New techniques also show how to grow plants that can withstand environmental challenges from infestation and climate change. On November 18, 2015, the Salk Institute named Nobel Prize-winning scientist Elizabeth Blackburn, a pioneering molecular biologist, as president.

Another institution doing major research is the Sanford-Burnham-Prebys Medical Discovery Institute, which has more than 850 scientists doing fundamental studies, especially with drugs to address needs in the areas of cancer, neuroscience, immunity, and metabolic disorders. All branches of Scripps hospitals and the Institution of Oceanography are also dedicated to this work. The University of California San Diego and the University of Southern California extracted themselves from a complex struggle in 2015 over who would administer grants for research on Alzheimer's disease. After a series of threats resulting in a lawsuit, the two universities agreed to work jointly to solve issues of research funding. Acquisitions and mergers involving biomed companies have continued throughout the decade.

La Jolla resident J. Craig Venter was included among *Time*'s list of the 100 most influential people—second under scientists and thinkers—in 2007. Venter, variously described as a biotechnologist, biochemist, geneticist, and entrepreneur, has been recognized as one of the first to sequence the human genome and the first to transfect a cell with a synthetic genome. Born in Utah in 1946, Venter received a BS in biochemistry in 1972, and a PhD in physiology and pharmacology in 1975, both from UCSD. He became interested in genomic research because he recognized his own ADHD behavior in adolescence, and later found ADHD-linked genes in his DNA. In June 2005, Venter cofounded Synthetic Genomics, a firm dedicated to using modified microorganisms to produce clean fuels and biochemicals. In July 2009, ExxonMobil announced a $600 million collaboration with Synthetic Genomics to research and develop next-generation biofuels. In May 2010, a team of scientists led by Venter became the first to successfully create what was described as "synthetic life." By 2015, it was the largest and most complex lab making synthetic DNA in the nation.

Venter is seeking to patent the first partially synthetic species, possibly to be named *Mycoplasma laboratorium*. This research could lead to producing bacteria that have been engineered to perform specific reactions, for example, to produce fuels, make medicines, and combat global warming. Venter developed the prototype of a digital biological converter and continues to conduct lifesaving work.

A New Central Library and Charter School

After some 30 years of planning, extensive private donations, principally by Irwin and Joan Jacobs, state bond funds, and with the cooperation of existing libraries, a nine-story Central Library designed by Rob Quigley was built in the East Village area of downtown San Diego. It was dedicated on September 30, 2013. This state-of-the-art facility is located halfway between Balboa Park and San Diego Bay with easy trolley access and suitable parking. Connected to the 35 branch libraries by its online Library Catalog and Database, the new facility shares resources, provides technology, and makes information services available to all residents. Access to a bank of computers is

The San Diego Central Library designed by Rob Quigley was dedicated on September 30, 2013, at 330 Park Boulevard in the East Village neighborhood. ©*2016 Ted Walton.*

available to all library visitors. The library also encompasses a charter school—e3 Civic High School—that opened in September 2013 with an initial enrollment of 260 students in the ninth and tenth grades. E3 stands for "engage, educate, empower." The school serves students in the downtown neighborhood as well as those throughout the county. Most of the rooms have modular glass walls and movable furniture to encourage collaboration among students and teachers. The target enrollment in 2015 reached 500 students.

The library's unique metallic dome was constructed of more than 3,000 individual members of steel and clad in 1,500 perforated aluminum panels to provide necessary shade. It is larger in size than the US Capitol dome and comparable to the Pantheon dome in Rome that measures 142 feet. The latticework design of the dome creates the impression that it is unfinished and remains, like human knowledge, in the perpetual act of becoming. Another design challenge was the 8th floor Helen Price Reading Room providing a spectacular view of the city and harbor. To provide shade to this three-story, 2,000 square foot space surrounded by glass walls, the metallic dome was hoisted into place atop the reading room 221 feet above street level. This massive, architecturally magnificent structure has become a city icon.

Governor Jerry Brown (left) seated with Mayor Kevin Faulconer praises San Diego for water conservation on August 11, 2015. *Photo by City News Service.*

Environmental Concerns

Although 2015 has been recorded as the hottest year ever in California, San Diego has had its share of intermittent rains. A decline in rainfall reaching drought proportions early in the decade, however, created an ongoing fire danger in most of California. San Diego's wildfires in the fall of 2007 were among the worst on record. Eleven wildfires occurred during the summer and autumn months that killed fourteen, injured at least 160, and burned 970,977 acres costing the state 1.4 billion dollars. The October Witch Creek and Harris Fires in the county were the largest in California. The Harris Fire began in Potrero near the Mexican border a few miles north of Tecate. The total for San Diego County reached 400,000 acres burned, and nearly 3,000 structures destroyed. The number of people evacuated throughout the county exceeded the numbers evacuated in New Orleans during Hurricane Katrina. The damage in East County, in terms of personal suffering, was impossible to measure. Governor Schwarzenegger made a personal visit and talked with many families burned out in Harbison Canyon. President George W. Bush also toured the scorched areas to offer support.

Wildfires continued to be a constant threat to San Diego County throughout the decade. New preventative policies such as cutting back the brush were introduced. Unfortunately, serious drought conditions made preventing fires extremely difficult. During the fire season of 2014, a series of 14 wildfires erupted in the month of May. Santa Ana wind conditions made controlling the fires even more difficult. On May 14, Governor Jerry Brown declared a state of emergency with the most severe damage resulting from fires in the Rancho Bernardo area, Bonsall, Fallbrook, Oceanside, and Twin Oaks near Escondido. By the end of May, some 26,000 acres had burned with an estimated 65 structures destroyed at a cost of close to $60 million. In 2015, the continuing drought caused an ongoing "fire season" with firefighters battling outbreaks all year long. A slight increase in rainfall by late November and early December lessened the wildfire toll. The 2015–2016 El Niño weather conditions brought a temporary respite to the growing concern about climate change even though underground water remained in short supply.

Earthquakes are a familiar phenomena to San Diegans, but damages have been less severe than those sustained outside the region. On April 4, 2010, downtown high-rises and homes throughout the county swayed back and forth as a magnitude 7.2 earthquake centered near Mexicali caused considerable damage in Imperial County and areas south of the border. The Sheraton Harbor Island Hotel and Lindbergh Field terminals, among other buildings near San Diego Bay, were evacuated. San Diego Gas & Electric reported power outages throughout the county including disruption of San Diego's trolley service. Fortunately San Diegans were spared major damage except for some resulting fears of another quake. It was proposed in April to schedule regular earthquake drills periodically throughout the county.

Challenges to the Electric Power Grid

In April 2011, San Diego Gas & Electric signed a twenty-year contract with Sempra Generation to obtain power generated by the Energía Sierra Juarez Project, a wind farm including 450 wind turbines in Baja California. This was a small step toward solving overall problems of power. On September 8, 2011, San Diego County, Baja California, and parts of Arizona, totaling some five million people, suffered the loss of electricity. The outage began at 3:38 p.m. after a 500-kilovolt high voltage transmission line from Arizona to California failed, triggering a cascade of events that knocked the San Onofre nuclear power generating plant offline. Within the next two years, a leak in the San Onofre plant forced its complete closure. Southern California Edison formally notified the Nuclear Regulatory Commission (NRC) on June 12, 2013, that it had permanently ceased operation of Units 2 and 3 on June 7, 2013. San Diego ratepayers have filed a lawsuit against SCE and the California Public Utilities Commission over the more than $3 billion in costs to close the plant. The ongoing legal action has yet to be settled.

The 2011 blackout forced closure of all San Diego County public and private schools, including the major universities. All the beaches north of Scripps Pier received warnings for sewage contamination since treatment plants were shut down. In the city, all major hospitals remained open through the use of backup generators while Lindbergh Field, Amtrak, Coaster and Sprinter trains remained in full service. There were airline travel cancellations, blacked-out traffic lights, and trapped elevator passengers. Power returned to Orange County and parts of San Diego County by late Thursday evening as power substations were rebooted one by one. The blackout served as a reminder of how quickly the city and country could be paralyzed by a loss of electricity. Ted Koppel's 2015 publication *Lights Out* warns of future dangers resulting from power failures.

On a positive note, San Diego ranks second among major cities nationwide in the number of solar panels installed during the past decade. Mayor Kevin Faulconer and Councilmember Todd Gloria have been aggressively pushing forward on solar-energy initiatives by promoting streamlined and easily obtained permitting fees. According to Faulconer, "Solar energy is a key element to the city's proposed Climate Action Plan, which calls for 100 percent renewable energy use in the city by 2035." According to researchers who

Poseidon Water, a desalination plant in Carlsbad completed in 2015 to supplement water resources for San Diego County. *Photo by Snapfish September Aerial 4.*

examined solar power installations in 65 American cities in nearly every state, San Diego had enough solar energy online at the end of 2014 to power just over 32,000 homes.

Desalination Project

Peter MacLaggan, senior vice president of Poseidon Water, was named Businessperson of the Year 2015 by the Carlsbad Chamber of Commerce for his role in bringing into operation the largest project in North America to remove salt from ocean water. The project provides a new source of supply to drought-ridden San Diego County and has set the stage for similar plants throughout the state. The privately financed project produces enough drinking water to serve 300,000 San Diegans and could provide the county with some 7 percent of its total water needs by 2020. Poseidon created 2,500 jobs during construction and will maintain 25 full-time employees as well as 175 indirect jobs once the facility is in full operation. For the region, the Carlsbad plant creates a more secure and reliable water future while working to protect disrupted natural ocean habitats.

Sports Spanning the Decade

San Diego's "Mr. Padre" Tony Gwynn in his familiar left-handed batting stance at Petco Park during his 20 seasons in San Diego from 1982 to 2001.

The San Diego Chargers began a series of seemingly unwise decisions at the beginning of 2006. Coach Marty Schottenheimer was fired in February as Chargers head coach despite a 14–2 record with outstanding players Ladanian Tomlinson and Antonio Gates. Losing in the playoffs that year sealed the deal. For the remainder of the decade, despite winning the AFC conference championship in 2007, the Chargers lost in the playoffs four more times under coaches Norv Turner (2007–2012) and Mike McCoy (2013–2015). The Chargers' 2015 losing season was overshadowed by speculation about the team's relocation to Carson, a city south of Los Angeles, and sharing a new stadium with the Oakland Raiders, or moving to another site in conjunction with the former St. Louis Rams who were approved by the NFL owners to move to Los Angeles. The inability of San Diego to field an offer for a new downtown stadium left Chargers' management blaming the city despite Mayor Faulconer's best efforts. Taxpayers balked at the idea of a new stadium and preferred the Qualcomm Mission Valley site over a downtown location. At the beginning of 2016, the Chargers elected to remain in San Diego for at least one year and negotiate for a new stadium.

Another unfortunate sports statistic was the inability of Junior Seau to play out his last few years in San Diego. This decision became even more poignant when the all-pro linebacker took his own life five years later in 2012. National Football League (NFL) administrators for years had been downplaying the effects of concussions on players as well as mitigating their legal position on the aftereffects of these injuries. With accumulated medical evidence, the league established funds for afflicted players. By 2015, the NFL had reached a $765 million settlement with families of former players who suffered various conditions involving brain damage and degeneration. *Concussion*, a movie released in 2015 by Columbia Pictures, is a biographical sports medical dramatization of alleged NFL suppression of research into brain damage suffered by football players.

The San Diego Padres had a mixed record under manager Bruce Bochy (1997–2006), despite winning conference championships in 2005 and 2006. One of the team's most beloved players, Anthony Keith "Tony" Gwynn Sr., nicknamed "Mr. Padre," passed away on June 16, 2014. Gwynn, a graduate of San Diego State University, was a right fielder who played 20 seasons (1982–2001) in Major League Baseball for the San Diego Padres. Gwynn was elected to the Baseball Hall of Fame just the year before in 2013. Another Hall of Famer, Jerry Coleman, former Yankees second baseman, World War II hero, and the voice of the Padres for more than four decades, died in early 2014 at the age of 89. Jeff Moorad, former CEO of the Arizona Diamondbacks, purchased the Padres from John Moores in February 2009 for a reported $500 million. After little success in the following seasons under manager Bud Black (2007–2015), the Padres hired new manager Andy Green, a 38-year-old former third-base coach for the Arizona Diamondbacks in mid-season 2015. Matt Kemp became the first Padre in franchise history to hit for the cycle in the club's 7,444th game. Veteran broadcaster Dick Enberg retired at the end of the 2015 season and the San Diego Padres once again looked forward to a winning season.

Local sporting events such as soccer, surfing, and sailing continued to be popular San Diego pastimes. Various running events, which combine competition with fund-raising for local charities, increased in popularity. Such events as the America's Finest City Half Marathon, the Run for the Hungry 10K and 5K, Father Joe's Villages 5K, the Rock 'n' Roll Marathon, and other annual runs take place every weekend somewhere in San Diego County. Local runner Mebrathom "Meb" Keflezigi, a native of Eritrea and former San Diego High School student, won the 2009 New York City Marathon and the 2014 Boston Marathon. All high school and university sports teams continued to be well supported by San Diego residents. At the end of 2015, John Moores was looking toward the acquisition of a major league soccer team with the possible adaptation of Qualcomm Stadium for use by San Diego State University and professional soccer games.

Crime in San Diego

On November 28, 2005, United States Congressman Randy "Duke" Cunningham resigned after conviction on federal bribery charges. He had represented California's 50th congressional district, which included much of the northern portion of the city of San Diego, from 1991 to 2005. In 2006, Cunningham, a decorated United States Navy veteran, was sentenced to a 100-month prison sentence. Copley News Service received a Pulitzer Prize for exposing his wrongdoing. Cunningham was released from confinement on June 4, 2013.

San Diegans were hit hard by the news of the disappearance and murder of Poway High School senior Chelsea King on February 25, 2010, at Rancho Bernardo Community Park. After Chelsea's body was found near Lake Hodges, an investigation led to the arrest and eventual confession of John Albert Gardner III. In a surprising turn of events, Gardner also confessed to the murder of Amber DuBois of Escondido that he had committed in 2009. Gardner was sentenced to two life sentences without possibility of parole. As a result, the King family was able to secure legislation known as Chelsea's Law passed in September 2010 that increased penalties, parole provisions, and oversight for the worst sex offenders in society—the violent sexual predator who attacks children.

Despite these well-publicized crimes, San Diego in 2010 had its

Police Chief Shelley Zimmerman at police headquarters. *Photo courtesy of Jewish World News.*

lowest crime rate in ten years for murder and rape and was listed as the ninth-safest city in the United States by *Forbes* magazine. By 2013 San Diego was ranked as the twentieth-safest city in America by *Business Insider.* Shelley Zimmerman, a native of Cleveland hired in 1982 by the San Diego Police Department, became the first female chief of police in San Diego on March 4, 2014. A graduate of Ohio State University with a degree in criminal justice, she had worked in several departments, specializing in planning security details for major events. The use of body cameras in 2015 by about one-third of the police department under Zimmerman's direction has achieved mixed results.

News by Way of the Local Newspapers

San Diego's historic newspaper, first called *The San Diego Union,* was founded in 1868 by Jeff Gatewood in Old Town San Diego (pp. 85–86). The Copley Press, a family-controlled company that bought the paper in 1928, used the name *San Diego Union-Tribune* after a merger with their *Evening Tribune* in 1992. The paper was then sold by David Copley, successor within the Copley family, to Platinum Equity of Beverly Hills in 2009, who retained the name. It was in turn sold by Platinum Equity to local developer Doug Manchester for "above" $110 million including its building in Mission Valley. A number of changes were made, including the name to *U-T San Diego*, and many longtime staff members were laid off. This transaction, however, was only a stepping-stone for the Manchester Financial Group, who would in 2015 sell the paper for $85 million to Tribune Co., a subsidiary of Tribune Publishing, while retaining the newspaper's real estate in Mission Valley. The name of the paper was returned to *The San Diego Union-Tribune* at that time. While the *San Diego Daily Transcript* ceased publication in 2014, the weekly *San Diego Reader*, *San Diego Business Journal*, and *CityBeat* have survived (pp. 213–214). Voice of San Diego is a nonprofit online-only news source covering government, politics, local events, neighborhoods, and the arts. Founded in 2005 by journalist Neil Morgan and businessman Buzz Woolley, who provided much of the seed money, it has moved its headquarters to downtown San Diego. Investigative News Source (INews) is another nonprofit news organization housed at San Diego State University and partnered with KPBS, San Diego's most respected news source.

Despite the fact that only 55 percent of Americans said they enjoyed reading a daily newspaper, and high school and college audiences preferred the Internet for their major news, *The San Diego Union-Tribune* continued as a popular source of local news throughout the county. Amid the controversy over the increasing impact of technology was the death of Apple CEO and company founder Steve Jobs on October 5, 2011, at the age of 56 from pancreatic cancer. Jobs, whose innovative thinking revolutionized the world of communication, was responsible for combining MP3 technology developed in San Diego with cell phones to create such popular devices as the iPhone and iPad.

Craft Beer

San Diego's reputation as a center for the production of a variety of craft beers has been one of the city's best-known success stories. Beer

Home Brew Mart and Ballast Point showroom at first location on Linda Vista Road across from the University of San Diego.

has been brewed in San Diego since 1868 when Austrian immigrant Conrad Dobler (Doblier) began brewing beer at his homestead in the Chollas Valley (present day I-15 and SR 94) in small quantities from European recipes. Beer has been brewed locally ever since. A change in federal regulations in 1978 allowed for the individual production of alcoholic beverages for personal consumption and a robust home-brewing community developed in San Diego, providing the foundation for what would grow to be one of San Diego's most thriving industries.

California state legislation in 1982 granted commercial production of small amounts of beer and opened the door for commercial brewing. The Karl Strauss Brewing Company sold the first commercially produced beer in San Diego after Altes Brewing closed in 1953. As a result, home brewers opened breweries of their own featuring all styles of beers—both ales and lagers—but India Pale Ales (IPAs) are a favorite. Brewers like Greg Koch and Steve Wagner (Stone), Gina and Vince Marsaglia (Pizza Port), Jack White and Yuseff Cherney (Ballast Point), Skip Vergilio (AleSmith), Pat MacIlhenney (Alpine), and Paul Segura (Karl Strauss) perfected their West Coast IPAs (for which San Diego is now famous) and delivered them to customers through bars and restaurants.

Comic-Con attendees dress for the celebratory get-together at the San Diego Convention Center in 2014. *Photo by Allen Wynar.*

It took the enterprising spirit of Stone brewers, in the mid-1990s, to distribute their own beer and, in the process, help to sell their competitors' beers as well. In concert with the newly formed San Diego Brewers Guild—local brewers who promote awareness of craft brewing—aspiring professional brewers can exchange ideas and produce beer in San Diego that maintains a high quality and gains the appreciation of the public at large. By 2015, the craft beer industry generated almost $966 million in sales from 114 county breweries. So promising is the future of craft beer that one of San Diego's pioneer breweries, Ballast Point, was sold to Constellation Brands for one billion dollars in December 2015.

Pop Culture Events

One of the most important events held yearly in San Diego is Comic-Con International, founded in 1970 by a group of San Diegans as the Golden State Comic Book Convention. The original five—Shel Dorf, Richad Alf, Ken Krueger, Mike Towry, and Greg Bear—considered it a success when they drew 300 people to the US Grant Hotel. Several other locations hosted the increasingly popular event until it moved to the San Diego Convention Center in 1991. The convention, the largest held in San Diego, is organized by a panel of 13 board members with a mere 18 to 20 employees and some 80 volunteers. Despite several proposals to move to other cities, Dorf has remained loyal to San Diego—at least through 2017. Drawing some 130,000 attendees, the annual regional economic impact is estimated at $162.8 million. Traditions include costumes worn by attendees both in and out of the Convention Center, an eclectic film program, gaming, exhibitions, an autograph area, free sketches, and academic presentations featuring comics as a medium. Television shows produced on the spot outpace the number of movies filmed at the convention 3 to 1. Comic-Con is referred to or mentioned briefly on both network and cable TV shows and is well known throughout San Diego. While this event is taking place, hundreds of people dressed up like superheroes, villains, and comic book characters stroll throughout downtown. To get a ticket to attend, one must be alert when the announcement of availability is made, since tickets sell out almost immediately.

While Comic-Con has increased in numbers of attendees every year, San Diego's largest and oldest annual rock music festival, Street Scene, ended its long run in 2009. Since 1984, Street Scene had assembled two stages each year on Fifth Avenue between J and K Streets. In 1987, the popularity of the music festival began to grow as new acts and genres caused the celebration to spill over into additional blocks. The city's difficult economic situation was cited as the reason for cancellation of the popular event.

The 2015 Panama-California Centennial Exposition

The completion of the Panama Canal in 1914, making San Diego the first port of call in the United States for ships using the new waterway, inspired San Diego to plan an international exposition to celebrate the event that put Balboa Park on the map in 1915. The idea of a 100th anniversary of the fair allowed many San Diegans to offer ways that the 2015 Panama-California Centennial Exposition could be

Betty Peabody, "Mrs. San Diego," accompanied by Vicente Rivera, rides the re-created Electriquette to celebrate the 2015 Centennial of the Panama-California Exposition.

promoted. Because of difficulties with city sponsorship, planning for the celebration that opened on January 1, 2015, was slow to get underway. A number of volunteer committees had been formed as early as 2010 by local museum, business, and university personnel to plan the celebration, but the mayor's office selected an "official" planning committee funded by the city to design the plan and disregard all previous work. After spending millions of dollars on a logo, a video, and a theme that was ultimately rejected by the majority of Balboa Park interested parties, the committee disbanded after having accomplished little.

The San Diego Park and Recreation Department, local museum directors and their staffs, plus volunteers stepped forward and planned individual exhibits in each of the venues. Although off to a late start, most were among the original planners who had begun several years in advance to plan for the 2015 fair. The local newspaper, then the *UT-San Diego*, featured a historic tribute each day for 100 days from April to July 2015 to celebrate the activities of 1915 and honor the Patrons of the Prado for their support of Balboa Park institutions. The city of Panama became a sister city of San Diego on July 22, 2015, as Mayor José Isabel Blandón exchanged signatures with Mayor Kevin Faulconer.

The celebratory exhibit at the San Diego History Center, entitled *San Diego Invites the World,* featured a re-created Electriquette, a magnificent guest book with signatures of original attendees, a working model of the Panama Canal, colorful banners of the 1915 buildings taken from postcards, and a timely film that presented the park's history from its conception in 1870 through the present. Art works—mostly plein air paintings from the 1915 exhibit—were also shown. The San Diego History Center teamed with *The San Diego Union Tribune* to produce a popular documentary called *Balboa Park: The Jewel of San Diego* that was shown daily in the History Center. The Cabrillo Bridge was given a $30 million renovation and restoration by CalTrans plus new and permanent lighting while the Museum of Man opened its iconic California Tower to the public. By climbing the 125 steps, visitors once again could witness a remarkable citywide view. Exhibits at

The Cabrillo Bridge remains as a San Diego icon with its original landscaped center divide for the enjoyment of commuters between downtown and Mission Valley. ©*2016 Ted Walton.*

The Cross-Border Express Terminal between San Diego and Tijuana. It is the first binational airport terminal in the United States.

the San Diego Museum of Art, Museum of Photographic Arts, Automotive Museum, Natural History Museum, Air and Space Museum, and others brought back memories of an earlier time.

The various animals shown in cages around the grounds at the 1915 fair were designated for a permanent home in the San Diego Zoo founded in 1916 while the original fair continued for another year. The centennial celebration of the zoo's founding, *It All Began with a Roar*, was planned as a highlight exhibit in 2016 at the San Diego History Center as well as at the zoo itself.

Improvements in Air Travel

San Diego's International Airport—Lindbergh Field—completed a $1 billion Terminal 2 expansion in 2015 and moved immediately to finalize plans for a $2 billion replacement for Terminal 1. New restaurants and retail shops were added. The airport also completed a new consolidated Rental Car Center (RCC) on the north side of the airfield in January 2016. Construction of the facility began in October 2013 and can be seen from I-5 interstate just north of downtown. The center houses rental car companies in a single building, including national brands as well as local independent and small business rental car companies. Additional parking facilities are also planned to serve Terminal 2.

Further to the south, the Tijuana Cross-Border Terminal, also called the Cross Border Xpress, is the world's first binational airport passenger terminal. Construction began on both the Tijuana and San Diego sides in October 2013, and was completed in December 2015. It connects passenger terminals between Mexico and the United States—spanning the international border by a pedestrian bridge of approximately 525 feet (160 m). It allows passengers to check in on the US side and continue to the Tijuana terminal. Arriving passengers can clear US customs and passport control, and exit on the US side. Only ticketed passengers are allowed to cross for the nominal fee of $18.00 per person.

The terminal building in Otay Mesa serves only as a check-in and processing facility for departing and arriving passengers. It has its own parking, check-in stations, and customs offices, but no gates, departure, or arrival facilities. The structural scheme allows greater access to flights out of the Tijuana Airport for both domestic and international air carriers. The project cost an estimated 78 million U.S. dollars, funded by Mexican and US private investors and Grupo Aeroportuario del Pacífico. Building E of Tijuana's Terminal 1 is undergoing restructuring to support the new bridge structure on Mexican soil. The design of Terminal 2 is the work of late Mexican architect Ricardo Legorreta.

The seal of the city of San Diego superimposed on the downtown skyline.

The statue of first visitor Juan Rodríguez Cabrillo overlooks North Island Naval Air Station and the city of San Diego as they appeared in 2015. *Photo by James Blank.*

A Future Outlook in 2016

The decade beginning in 2005 brought heavy storms in early January. During the following years, however, a lack of rainfall causing severe drought was the dominant weather pattern. Again, at the beginning of 2016, heavy rainfall lessened the severity of the drought and promoted downtown development of new high-rise building projects. The San Diego Port District approved a new harbor-front design in late 2015 to enhance access to the port for pedestrians and watercraft, in addition to planning new restaurant and park facilities for residents and visitors.

As it had since the city's founding, San Diego's harbor continued to exert a significant impact on the local economy. An important global link in the nation's international shipping trade with growing cruise ship operations, the San Diego Port District is a major contributor to the region's success. As headquarters for the Eleventh Naval District, the harbor remains home base for the U.S. Navy Pacific fleet with the overall military/defense industry contributing more than $13 billion to the economy annually. Both the city and county welcomed 2016 with a solid basis in economic and educational progress, a viable and growing tourist industry, and a people proud of their cultural and intellectual achievements. San Diego, as always, continued to embody its legacy as California's Cornerstone.

San Diego Chronology

Prehistory

15,000 BCE Hunting peoples of northeast Asia cross the present-day Bering Strait; they move south along ice-free corridors into the American continents as far east as the Atlantic Ocean and as far south as Tierra del Fuego in South America.

13,000 BCE to 7000 BCE Migration southward along the California coast; original inhabitants of the San Diego area known as the San Dieguito Paleo-Indian people.

7000 BCE to 1000 BCE La Jolla people assimilate original San Dieguito people.

1000 BCE to 1600 CE Yuman (Ipai) and Shoshonean-speaking (Luiseño and Cahuilla) groups migrate to San Diego area; Yuman speaking Kumeyaay (earlier Tipai) occupy the area south from Mission Valley into Baja California.

1492–1541

The empire of Spain reaches a zenith under the Habsburg monarchs; discovery and exploration of the New World is carried on by Spain, Portugal, and other European powers; Spaniards introduce the horse and the planting of wheat, vineyards, sugar cane, and other products into America; the Indians give corn, tomatoes, potatoes, chocolate, tobacco, and quinine to the Europeans; heavily populated Indian civilizations are found in Central and South America.

1492   Columbus reaches New World and claims Indies for Spain; he is greeted by native Americans whose ancestors arrived 12,000 to 15,000 years before.

1513   Explorer Vasco Nuñez de Balboa discovers the Pacific Ocean.

1519   Expedition of Ferdinand Magellan, a Portuguese sailing for Spain, circumnavigates globe; Hernán Cortés conquers Aztecs of Tenochtitlán (Mexico City) and establishes Spanish control.

1533   Fortún Jiménez fails to gain foothold in Baja California.

1535   Antonio de Mendoza becomes viceroy of New Spain; Cortés attempts to colonize Baja California but is unsuccessful.

1539   Francisco de Ulloa explores Gulf of California and west coast of Baja California, proving California not an island, but idea remains.

1540   Francisco Vásquez de Coronado explores southwest as far as Kansas; Melchior Díaz reaches Colorado River and crosses into Alta (Upper) California; Hernando de Soto explores southeast from Florida to Mississippi River.

1541   The name California comes into use.

1542–1700

England, France, and the Netherlands gain New World holdings; Roman Catholic missions established to Christianize Native Americans; Spain opens a Pacific route used by Manila galleons sailing between Philippine Islands and Acapulco; England challenges Spain's power in New World and Europe; France gains territory in Canada and explores Mississippi Valley.

1542   Spanish explorer Juan Rodríguez Cabrillo sails into San Diego Bay on September 28, names port San Miguel.

1553   University of Mexico founded in Mexico City.

1565   Spain extends conquest to Philippines; St. Augustine, Florida, founded by Spanish soldiers.

1571   Manila founded by Miguel López de Legaspi.

1579   Francis Drake lands on coast of California and names area near San Francisco Bay "Nova Albion."

1588   San Diego de Alcalá (St. Didacus) canonized in Rome; English defeat Spanish armada.

1595   Sebastián Rodríguez Cermeño explores California coast, wrecks galleon near Drakes Bay.

1602   Sebastián Vizcaíno heads expedition to explore California, sails into Cabrillo's San Miguel and names port San Diego de Alcalá to honor saint whose day is celebrated November 12; First Roman Catholic mass celebrated by Father Antonio de la Ascensión at today's Ballast Point.

1607   English found Jamestown Colony on Chesapeake Bay.

1608   French establish Quebec on St. Lawrence River.

1609   Santa Fe founded by Spain in New Mexico.

1615   Private entrepreneurs seek wealth in Baja California through pearl fishing; pearls too few for sufficient profits.

1683   Father Eusebio Francisco Kino and Isidro Atondo y Antillon attempt to establish settlement at San Bruno, Baja California, and cross peninsula overland to Pacific coast.

1697   Jesuit missionaries under Father Juan María Salvatierra establish first permanent settlement in Baja California with Mission Nuestra Señora de Loreto.

1701–1770

The throne of Spain passes to Bourbons; colonial rivalries continue among European powers in Americas, Asia, and Africa; the thirteen English colonies solidify position on East Coast of North America; Vitus Bering explores strait separating Asia from North America; George III becomes king of Great Britain and Carlos III king of Spain; Carolus Linnaeus of Sweden develops system of scientific nomenclature; Eighteenth-century enlightenment felt on both sides of the Atlantic.

1701   Father Kino reaffirms that California is not an island after exploring the area at the headwaters of the Gulf of California; Jesuit missionaries found ten missions in southern portion of Baja California peninsula.

1735   Indians at four Baja California missions lead uprising against Spaniards.

1746   Jesuit Father Fernando Consag explores northward along gulf coast of Baja California in search of mission sites.

1763   Treaty of Paris ends Seven Years' War; France expelled from North America, Louisiana ceded to Spain, Florida passes to Great Britain.

1766   Jesuit Father Wenceslaus Linck explores Baja California's northern portions.

1767   Santa María de los Angeles, northernmost Jesuit mission in Baja California, founded; Gaspar de Portolá appointed governor of Baja California with headquarters at Loreto.

1768   Jesuit missionaries expelled from Baja California for political reasons and replaced by Franciscans.

1769   Arrival in San Diego of maritime and land expeditions gives Spain foothold in Alta California; Father Junípero Serra blesses Presidio Hill as site of Mission San Diego de Alcalá July 16.

1770   Spanish soldiers and priests found both Presidio of Monterey as capital of Alta California and Mission San Carlos Borromeo June 3.

1771–1780

British colonies in North America declare independence July 4, 1776; separate viceroyalties set up by Spain for La Plata (Argentina) and Nueva Granada (Colombia, Venezuela, and Ecuador) to join viceroyalties of Peru and New Spain; Daniel Boone leads settlers westward into Kentucky; Captain James Cook, English navigator, discovers Hawaiian Islands and visits Pacific Northwest coast.

1772   Spain divides missions of Baja California and Alta California between Dominican and Franciscan Orders at a point just south of present boundary between United States and Mexico.

1774   In August, Mission San Diego de Alcalá moves to present site six miles inland from presidio; Juan Bautista de Anza opens an overland route to California between Arizona and California; Juan Pérez sails to 54°40' north latitude to claim the Pacific Northwest for Spain.

1775   Local Indians attack and burn Mission San Diego, killing Father Luis Jayme November 5.

1776   Anza travels overland to Mission San Gabriel from Tubac, Arizona, with colonists destined for Monterey and San Francisco; San Francisco Presidio and Missions San Francisco de Asis and San Juan Capistrano founded; first baptism at rebuilt Mission San Diego held in December.

1777   San José de Guadalupe, first civilian settlement in Alta California, founded.

1779   A Reglamento (code) for governing California issued by Governor Felipe de Neve.

1781–1790

Treaty of Paris of 1783 recognizes American independence and returns Florida to Spain; Spaniards expand mission efforts in northern Mexico and Californias; Russians establish trading post on Kodiak Island; United States Constitution adopted (1787); Royal Botanical Garden founded in Mexico City.

1781   California's second town, El Pueblo de Nuestra Señora la Reina de Los Angeles, founded September 4; Indians at Yuma attack Spanish colonizing party, closing overland route from Arizona to California.

1783   Father Fermín Francisco de Lasuén reports 966 baptisms, 232 marriages, and 210 deaths at Mission San Diego.

1784   Father Junípero Serra dies at Mission San Carlos Borromeo (Carmel); Governor Pedro Fages grants the first private ranchos in California to José Verdugo, Juan José Domínguez, and Manuel Nieto, soldiers having served at San Diego Presidio.

1785   Father Lasuén becomes Father President of the California missions.

1786   French Count of La Perouse, first foreign visitor in California.

1788   First American ships, *Columbia* and *Lady Washington*, sail to Pacific Northwest coast.

1790   San Diego Presidio has population of 212; Mission San Diego houses 933 Indians.

1791–1800

George Washington and John Adams become presidents of United States; French Revolution occurs in 1792, Napoleon rises to power; Spaniards withdraw from Nootka Sound on Vancouver Island because of British pressure; Russians establish post at Sitka, Alaska; Treaty of San Ildefonso in 1800 returns Louisiana to France from Spain.

1791   Spanish expedition of Alejandro Malaspina surveys California to gather scientific information on around-the-world journey.

1793   British Captain George Vancouver visits San Diego and finds it poorly protected.

1795   Padres discover spring near Mission San Diego to increase water supply; school at San Diego Presidio has 22 pupils under Sergeant Don Manuel de Vargas.

1796   *Otter* from New England arrives in Monterey to establish trade with California; construction begins on Spanish Fort Guijarros at Ballast Point.

1797   Mission San Diego becomes most populous in California with 1,405 Indians.

1798   Wine is pressed from local grapes at Mission San Diego; Mission San Luis Rey de Francia founded June 13; Dominican missionaries from Baja California visit San Diego.

1800   First American ship, the *Betsy*, arrives in San Diego.

1801–1810

Thomas Jefferson and James Madison serve as US presidents; most of Europe begins to unite against Napoleon; French place Joseph Bonaparte on throne of Spain; United States purchases Louisiana from France; Lewis and Clark reach the mouth of Columbia River overland; Daniel Boone leads settlers to Missouri; Father Miguel Hidalgo issues call for Mexican independence at pueblo of Dolores near Querétaro.

1803   American brig *Lelia Byrd* fired upon from Point Guijarros (Ballast Point); called the Battle of San Diego.

1804   Lieutenant Manuel Rodríguez, commandant of San Diego Presidio, supervises reburial of bodies of Fathers Luis Jayme (d. 1775), Juan Figuer (d. 1784), and Juan Mariner (d. 1800) between two altars of new church April 26; missionaries continue to work on dam and aqueduct system to obtain good water supply from San Diego River.

1806–1810 Lieutenants Francisco María Ruiz and José de la Guerra y Noriega and Captain José Raimundo Carrillo serve as presidio commanders at San Diego.

1808   Construction of new San Diego Mission church structure.

1809   Russians establish a few buildings at Bodega Bay.

1810   San Diego's presidial population approximately 350, with 1,611 Indians at Mission San Diego and 1,517 at Mission San Luis Rey.

1811–1820

United States and Great Britain fight War of 1812; James Madison and James Monroe serve as US presidents; Napoleon defeated at Waterloo; Fernando VII resumes throne of Spain; Mexico begins fight for independence with most of South America; the Missouri Compromise allows entry of Maine as free state and Missouri as slave state.

1812   Earthquake shakes much of California causing major destruction at Mission San Juan Capistrano; Russians found a colony at Fort Ross, north of San Francisco.

1813   Church at Mission San Diego completed and dedicated by Father José Barona; Padres and Indians begin dam in Mission Gorge and aqueduct system to supply the mission with water.

1816   *Asistencia* (sub-mission) founded at San Antonio de Pala (and continues today to serve Indians in district).

1818   *Asistencia* founded at Santa Ysabel with oldest two bells in California (1723 and 1767); Hipolyte de Bouchard attacks California coast in name of independence from Spain.

1819   Adams-Onis Treaty transfers Florida and Spain's claim to Pacific Northwest (54°40') to United States.

1820   Kumeyaay Indians at Mission San Diego number 1,567; Luiseño Indians at Mission San Luis Rey total 2,603.

1821–1830

Mexico achieves independence from Spain in 1821; James Monroe, John Quincy Adams, and Andrew Jackson are US presidents; Santa Fe Trail opened between Missouri and New Mexico; Americans move into Texas; Monroe Doctrine formulated; Boston trading ships sail along Pacific coast.

1822   California swears allegiance to government of Mexico; Luis Argüello becomes first elected native-born governor of California; Presidio families begin move down the hill to build houses below (Old Town) in San Diego County.

1823   First private rancho in San Diego County (*Los Peñasquitos*) granted to Francisco María Ruiz.

1825   Governor José María Echeandía moves capital of California from Monterey to San Diego.

1826   Jedediah Smith, fur trapper, first American to arrive in San Diego via overland route.

1827   French sea captain Auguste Bernard du Haut-Cilly visits San Diego in *Les Heros.*

1829   Fur trapper James Ohio Pattie imprisoned at San Diego presidio; first hide house built at La Playa (Point Loma); Boston trader Henry Delano Fitch elopes with Josefa Carrillo.

1830   San Diego's presidial population 520; 7,294 Indians in district; Mission San Diego lists 1,544 and Mission San Luis Rey 2,776 residents; Mission San Diego has 7,630 head of cattle and 16,120 sheep; Mission San Luis Rey has 25,000 head of each and 2,210 horses.

1831–1840

Andrew Jackson and Martin Van Buren are presidents of United States; Antonio López de Santa Anna dominates Mexican politics; American settlers move into Oregon Territory; Texas declares independence from Mexico; American trappers enter California from east.

1831   Jonathan Trumbull (later Juan Jose) Warner reaches California; capital of California returned to Monterey; rivalry develops between northern and southern California.

1832   Father Antonio Peyri leaves Mission San Luis Rey for Spain.

1833   Act to secularize California missions passed in Mexico.

1834–1836 Secularization of Missions San Diego and San Luis Rey provides land for granting ranchos; Juan Osuna elected Alcalde (mayor) of the pueblo.

1835   San Diego officially becomes a pueblo (town); Presidio effectively abandoned; Richard Henry Dana visits San Diego aboard a hide and tallow trader from New England.

1836   Indians attack rancho settlements.

1838   San Diego loses pueblo status and becomes subprefecture of Los Angeles.

1839   Russians sell Fort Ross to John Sutter who moves it to confluence of the Sacramento and American Rivers.

1840   San Diego's population is 150; 2,250 Indians still live in the
        area of the former mission.

1841–1850

William Henry Harrison, John Tyler, James K. Polk, and Zachary
Taylor serve as US presidents; "Manifest Destiny" becomes theme for
westward expansion; Mormons reach Utah; US and Great Britain
settle the Oregon boundary question at 49th parallel; US and Mexico
go to war over Texas boundary dispute in May 1846; Samuel Morse
invents telegraph; California has population of 92,597 in 1850.

1841   First American immigrant wagon train reaches California over
        Sierra Nevada; Bishop Garcia Diego y Moreno, first bishop
        of California, visits San Diego and confirms 125 people at
        old presidio chapel.

1842   Governor Manuel Micheltorena visits San Diego on way from
        Mexico to Monterey.

1844   John C. Fremont's US military mapping expedition reaches
        Sutter's Fort.

1845–1846 Donner party suffers serious losses on overland trek to
        California.

1846   American settlers declare California's independence as Bear
        Flag Republic June 14; Commodore John D. Sloat raises US
        flag at Monterey July 2; US flag raised in San Diego July 29;
        Fort Stockton built on Presidio Hill; Battle of San Pasqual
        fought near Escondido December 6.

1847   Capitulation of Cahuenga ends Mexican War in California
        January 13; Mormon battalion arrives in San Diego January 27.

1848   Gold discovered at Sutter's Mill by James Marshall January
        24; Treaty of Guadalupe Hidalgo signed February 2 ends
        US-Mexican War; California becomes part of United States.

1849   US Boundary Commission arrives in San Diego.

1850   California admitted to Union September 9 as 31st state;
        County of San Diego incorporated (with population of 650),
        as first county created by California legislature; Joshua Bean
        becomes first American mayor of San Diego; William Heath
        Davis starts New San Diego by waterfront.

1851–1860

Millard Filmore, Franklin Pierce, and James Buchanan are US presidents; Peter H. Burnett is first American governor of California; Gadsden Purchase brings southern Arizona into Union; several transcontinental railroad surveys made; Commodore Perry opens trade with Japan; expansion of slavery issue becomes irrepressible conflict; silver discovered in Nevada; California's population reaches 379,994 in 1860.

1851   San Diego *Herald* begins publication; Indians led by Antonio Garra attack Warner's Ranch; first Masonic Lodge organized on November 20.

1852   Phineas Banning and D.W. Alexander start stage line between Los Angeles and San Diego.

1853   Lieutenant George Derby plans to divert San Diego River into False (later Mission) Bay.

1854   San Diego & Gila, Southern Pacific & Atlantic Railroad organized; county public school system organized.

1855   Heavy rains wash out dam on San Diego River.

1856   Whaley House, oldest brick structure in San Diego, built by Thomas Whaley in Old Town.

1857   James Birch opens first transcontinental overland mail route (Jackass Mail Line) from San Antonio to San Diego.

1858   Butterfield Overland Stage begins regular service from Missouri to San Francisco; Church of the Immaculate Conception dedicated in Old Town.

1860   San Diego's population is 731; county totals 4,324 (1,249 white, 8 black, 3,067 Indian).

1861–1870

Abraham Lincoln serves as president until his assassination April 1865; Jefferson Davis becomes president of Confederacy; Civil War ends with Lee's surrender at Appomattox; Andrew Johnson succeeds Lincoln and fights with Congress over Reconstruction; French intervene in Mexico; US purchases Alaska from Russia; transcontinental railroad completed from Council Bluffs, Iowa, to San Francisco.

1861   All stage travel over the southern route discontinued as Civil War begins; storms, earthquakes, and flood tides damage San Diego.

1862   Abraham Lincoln signs order returning title to mission buildings at San Diego to Catholic Church together with 22.2 acres of surrounding lands; drought, smallpox epidemic, and locust plague hit San Diego area.

1863   *Star of India* launched as *Euterpe* at Ramsey, Isle of Man (England).

1865   President Lincoln signs order returning mission buildings at San Luis Rey to Catholic Church together with 64 acres of surrounding lands.

1866   General William Rosecrans surveys San Diego for railroad depot.

1867   Alonzo Horton arrives April 15 and, by May 10, has purchased 960 acres of New Town for $265.

1868   Construction begins on Horton's Wharf; Kimball brothers lay out National City on northwestern corner of old Rancho de la Nación; first school opened in New San Diego; land (1,440 acres) set aside for large city park (later renamed Balboa Park).

1869   First US post office established in San Diego with Jacob Allen as postmaster.

1870   San Diego Chamber of Commerce founded in January; Alonzo Horton opens the Horton House Hotel on D Street (now Broadway); gold discovered near present-day Julian; San Diego's population is 2,300; there are 4,324 people in county and 560,247 in state.

1871–1880

General Ulysses S. Grant and Rutherford B. Hayes serve as US presidents; reconstruction ends; Salvation Army is organized; first major baseball league is formed; Alexander Graham Bell invents telephone; F.W. Woolworth opens five- and ten-cent store.

1871   County seat moves to Horton's Addition (New Town); San Diegans lay cornerstone for new county courthouse; *The San Diego Union* begins daily publication March 20; Mt. Hope Cemetery established.

1872   First Jewish synagogue organized in Marcus Schiller's home; fire destroys much of Old Town in April; San Diego Fire Engine Co. #1 organized; tourmaline discovered near Pala.

1873   San Diego Water Company formed.

1874   City receives its final patent to pueblo lands; San Diego Society of Natural History founded.

1875   Chamber of commerce arranges for US Cavalry post.

1876   Southern Pacific Railroad connects San Francisco with Los Angeles.

1877   San Diego River diverted into False Bay; severe drought hits.

1878   First telephone demonstrated in city.

1879   California adopts new state constitution.

1880   San Diego's population reaches 2,637; there are 8,618 people in county and 864,694 in state.

1881–1890

James A. Garfield, Chester A. Arthur, and Grover Cleveland are US. presidents; Clara Barton establishes Red Cross; Apache chief Geronimo finally captured in Arizona; American Federation of Labor and Interstate Commerce Commission formed; Chinese Exclusion Act passed.

1881   San Diego Gas Company organized.

1882   San Diego's first public library opened; San Diego Telephone Company organized; California Southern Railroad service begins with San Diego's connection to Santa Fe Railroad.

1883   Kate Sessions becomes principal of Russ School; Leach's Opera House, first in the city, opened; John Montgomery makes first controlled glider flight.

1884   First transcontinental railroad reaches San Diego; Helen Hunt Jackson publishes novel *Ramona* to call attention to plight of Indians.

1885   Group of German-Americans found Olivenhain.

1886   Construction begins on Hotel del Coronado; electric lights installed in downtown; San Diego Yacht Club founded.

1887   National City incorporated; San Diego and Old Town electric street cars begin operating; Chamber of commerce urges engineering plan for 1,400-acre city park (Balboa Park); the *Golden Era* magazine promotes San Diego; Jesse Shephard builds the Villa Montezuma in Sherman Heights.

1888   Cities of Escondido and Oceanside incorporated; San Diego High School organized; Sweetwater Dam and San Diego Flume completed; Hotel del Coronado opens; Ed Fletcher arrives.

1889   San Diego becomes fourth-class city under new charter; Douglas Gunn elected mayor; San Diego Trust & Savings Bank founded.

1890   San Diego's population declines from estimated 40,000 in 1887 to 16,159; 34,987 in county and 1,213,398 in state.

1891–1900

Benjamin Harrison, Grover Cleveland, and William McKinley are US presidents; Marconi patents wireless; Panic of 1893 results from economic depression; automobiles begin to be manufactured in Detroit; Spanish American War is fought over Cuba and United States annexes Philippines, Puerto Rico, and Guam as a result; Hawaii also becomes a part of United States.

1891   City of Coronado secedes from San Diego; W.H. Carlson elected mayor; San Diego County Law Library founded May 6.

1892   John D. Spreckels buys transit system; Klondike gold rush begins; Fisher Opera House opens; first Cabrillo celebration held on September 28–30 to celebrate 400th anniversary.

1893   Riverside County is formed from large slice of San Diego County.

1894   Chamber of commerce urges establishment of State Normal School.

1895   The San Diego *Evening Tribune* founded.

1896   Harbor fortifications begun at Point Loma.

1897   Cornernerstone laid for Katherine Tingley's School of Antiquity; Hotel Robinson opened in Julian by former slave Albert Robinson and wife Margaret Tull.

1898   D.C. Reed elected mayor; one of first movies, *San Diego Street Scene*, filmed in city; State Normal School opens.

1899   Edwin M. Capps elected mayor; the Bar Association of San Diego formed on April 22; State Normal School, predecessor of San Diego State College, opened.

1900   John D. Spreckels opens Tent City in Coronado; San Diego's population reaches 17,700; the County numbers 35,090.

1901–1910

William McKinley (assassinated 1901), Theodore Roosevelt, and William Howard Taft are US presidents; Henry Ford organizes motor company and Wright Brothers complete successful flight; San Francisco earthquake and fire of 1906 kill 452 people; Admiral Robert E. Peary reaches North Pole; California population is 2,377,549 in 1910.

1901   Imperial Valley canals filled from Colorado River; San Diego purchases water systems within city.

1903   Marine Biological Assocation, later Scripps Institution of Oceanography, formed; San Diego County Hospital built.

1904   Cupeño Indians are expelled from their traditional home at Warner's Ranch and marched to Pala Reservation.

1905   USS *Bennington*'s boiler explodes in San Diego harbor, killing 60 and injuring 47.

1905–1906 Flood waters pour through the Colorado River bank for 16 months to create Salton Sea.

1906   John D. Spreckels and others plan San Diego, Arizona & Eastern Railroad; Dr. Lee DeForest operates first wireless in San Diego; chamber of commerce appropriates funds for harbor improvements.

1907   Imperial County formed from 4,089 square miles of San Diego County.

1908   Cities of El Centro and Calexico incorporated; chamber of commerce board increased from 21 to 30 to include representatives from county communities; Nolen Plan for city development presented for approval; US Navy's Great White Fleet visits San Diego December 5.

1909   Historian William E. Smythe begins Little Landers Colony in the South Bay area.

1910   US Grant Hotel, dedicated October 15, replaces Horton House; City Park renamed Balboa Park; San Diego's population reaches nearly 39,578; San Diego County numbers 61,665.

1911–1920

Woodrow Wilson follows Taft as president in 1912; Mexican Revolution of 1910 ousts Porfírio Díaz and pledges social reform; National Association for the Advancement of Colored People (NAACP) begins and Boy Scouts of America founded; Congress institutes federal income tax; Panama Canal completed and World War I begins in Europe; 18th amendment (Prohibition) is ratified; women achieve right to vote; League of Nations formed but US refuses to join; Roald Amundsen reaches South Pole.

1911   City of Chula Vista incorporates; Glenn Curtiss starts flying school on North Island and makes first successful seaplane flight; American Film Company (Flying A) sets up studio in Lakeside, then La Mesa; voters approve harbor development bonds.

1912   El Cajon and La Mesa incorporated; Essanay Western film company shoots movies in La Mesa while Ammex produces movies in National City; the IWW free speech controversy climaxes with expulsion of Emma Goldman; Spruce Street suspension bridge completed between Brant and Front.

1913   Congressman Wm. Kettner and chamber of commerce help obtain appropriations for naval coaling and radio stations; Cabrillo Monument founded on October 14.

1914   Morena Dam purchased by city for $1.5 million.

1915   Panama-California Exposition dedicated January 1 and Balboa Stadium opens in Balboa Park; Rainmaker Charles Hatfield commissioned to fill Morena Reservoir.

1916   Heavy flooding washes out Otay Dam and Old Town Bridge; San Diego Zoo begins with animals from closing of Balboa Park exposition.

1917   Louis J. Wilde (Smokestacks) defeats George Marston (Geraniums) for mayor; Camp Kearny established; US Marine

Base and Naval Hospital approved; Rockwell Field and Naval Air Station set up on North Island; San Diego enters WWI.

1918   Chamber of commerce raises $280,000 to buy land for first major US Navy base; World War I ends on November 11.

1919   San Diego, Arizona & Eastern Railroad completed.

1920   Phil D. Swing of Imperial County elected to Congress; San Diego's population reaches 74,683; San Diego County is 112,248.

1921–1930

Warren G. Harding, Calvin Coolidge, and Herbert Hoover serve as US presidents; *Time* magazine and *Readers Digest* begin publication; first all-weather transcontinental highway dedicated; J. Edgar Hoover appointed to head FBI; Mickey Mouse created by Walt Disney; the Roaring Twenties end abruptly with the stock market crash October 29, 1929; California has 5,677,251 people in 1930.

1921   Edward, Prince of Wales, addresses 25,000 San Diegans in Balboa Stadium.

1922   Nine radio stations licensed in San Diego; only KFBC (KGB) remains continuously on air; county population reaches 100,000; Barrett Dam completed on Cottonwood Creek; US Navy dedicates hospital in Balboa Park.

1923   Lieutenants Oakley Kelly and John Macready make first non-stop transcontinental flight from New York to San Diego in 26 hours and 50 minutes; Marine Corps Recruit Depot opens; Naval Training Center commissioned with 10 officers.

1924   Electric railway line opened to Mission Beach and La Jolla; the San Diego Yacht Club hosts the Southern California Yachting Association regatta.

1925   Ryan Airlines establishes first regular air passenger service in the US between Los Angeles and San Francisco; Mission Beach Amusement Center (Belmont Park) opens.

1926   Radio station KFSD (KOGO) begins broadcasting from the US Grant Hotel.

1927   Fine Arts Gallery (San Diego Museum of Art) designed by William Templeton Johnson opens in Balboa Park; Charles

Lindbergh completes his flight from New York to Paris in *Spirit of St. Louis*, built by Ryan in San Diego; El Cortez Hotel opens; *Star of India* towed to San Diego.

1928   Ira C. Copley purchases *The San Diego Union* and *Evening Tribune*; Lindbergh Field, San Diego's new municipal airport, dedicated; San Diego Trust and Savings Bank completed at 6th and Broadway.

1929   San Diego Historical Society incorporated December 13; Presidio Park and Serra Museum dedicated July 16; $1.8 million Fox Theater dedicated.

1930   Dr. Albert Einstein visits San Diego; county population reaches 209,659; the city numbered 147,995.

1931–1940

Franklin D. Roosevelt serves as president of US; Adolph Hitler becomes chancellor of Germany and Benito Mussolini rises to power in Italy; Congress creates Social Security system; Prohibition ended by 21st Amendment; New York World's Fair opens; transatlantic air flights begin; Boulder Dam completed on the Colorado River; Hitler invades Poland.

1931   San Diego adopts city charter for city manager form of government; new San Diego State College campus dedicated.

1932   San Diego County has 16,000 persons unemployed and 4,000 on relief; chamber of commerce helps Consolidated Aircraft move to San Diego from Buffalo, New York, beginning aerospace industry; George Marston helps create Anza-Borrego State Desert Park.

1933   San Diego Natural History Museum completed in Balboa Park with funds donated by Ellen Browning Scripps; Long Beach earthquake kills 121 persons.

1934   The California Institute of Technology acquires 160 acres on Mount Palomar to install a telescope.

1935   El Capitan Dam, capacity of 38 billion gallons, dedicated; California Pacific International Exposition opened May 28 in Balboa Park; gambling banned in Mexico; Consolidated Aircraft dedicates new plant at Lindbergh Field.

1936   Federal government approves construction of the County Fair Grounds at Del Mar; Ted Williams plays baseball with Pacific Coast League Padres at Lane Field.

1937   The Right Reverend Charles Francis Buddy installed as bishop of the newly created Roman Catholic Diocese of San Diego.

1938   San Diego Civic Center (County Administration Center) dedicated on Harbor Drive; Old Globe Theatre built in Balboa Park.

1939   Metropolitan's Colorado River aqueduct completed to Lake Mathews; Naval Air Station Miramar developed on site of Camp Kearny.

1940   All American Canal formally dedicated in Imperial Valley. San Diego County numbers 289,348; city's population reaches 203,341.

1941–1950

US President Franklin Roosevelt dies in his fourth term and is succeeded by Harry Truman; Japan's bombing of Pearl Harbor on December 7, 1941, causes US entry into World War II; rationing of food and other essentials begins; Earl Warren becomes governor of California; Germany surrenders in on May 8 and Japan on August 14, 1945, after atomic bombing of Hiroshima and Nagasaki; Philippines granted independence; United Nations Charter adopted; India becomes independent and Israel created; US enters Korean War.

1941   San Diego Naval Air Station begins training pilots for US Air Force (a total of 31,400 during World War II.)

1942   Western Defense Command removes nearly 2,000 persons of Japanese descent from San Diego to relocation centers; wartime housing constructed at Linda Vista; Consolidated Aircraft merges with Vultee to become Convair; Camp Pendleton area (Santa Margarita Rancho) purchased by US.Navy for marine base.

1943   Chamber of commerce begins planning San Diego's postwar economy.

1944   City Manager Walter Cooper killed in airplane accident; Mayor Harley E. Knox injured; San Diego County Water Authority formed with nine member agencies.

1945 US ratifies a treaty giving portion of Colorado River water to Mexico; voters approve bond issue of $2 million to develop Mission Bay; San Diego experiences slight recession as World War II ends.

1946 San Diego County Water Authority annexed to Metropolitan Water District and city of Coronado withdraws.

1947 San Diego Aqueduct brings Colorado River water to city.

1948 *San Diego Magazine* begins publication; the 200-inch Hale telescope completed on Palomar Mountain.

1949 University of San Diego receives its charter from state; San Diego broadcasts first television show on Channel 8; Mission Bay aquatic park formally dedicated; Portugal donates statue of Juan Rodríguez Cabrillo to stand at Cabrillo National Monument on Point Loma.

1950 San Diego's population reaches 334,387; San Diego County 556,808.

1951–1960

Harry Truman and General Dwight D. Eisenhower serve as US presidents; General Douglas MacArthur removed as far-east commander; US Supreme Court bans segregation in education; NASA organized; jet airline passenger service inaugurated; Fidel Castro takes over government of Cuba; Alaska and Hawaii admitted to Union; Edmund G. "Pat" Brown follows Goodwin J. Knight as California's governor; California's population reaches 15,717,204.

1951 John D. Butler becomes first native San Diegan elected mayor; conversion of tuna clippers to purse seiners begins.

1952 California Western University opens on Point Loma; Carlsbad incorporated as a city.

1953 Chamber of commerce urges forming a unified port district.

1954 University of San Diego Law School opens; Kearny Mesa industrial center established; FedMart opens a membership store in south San Diego.

1955 Bonds voted for construction of the Tenth Avenue Marine Terminal; Councilman Charles C. Dail elected mayor.

1956   General Dynamics takes over Convair; Fiesta del Pacifico begins as tourist attraction; Torrey Pines city park becomes California State Park Preserve; University of California campus proposed; city of Imperial Beach incorporated.

1957   First Atlas missile built at San Diego successfully testfired; Theodor Geisel (Dr. Suess) publishes *Cat in the Hat.*

1958   City council approves zone change to allow May Company department store to be built in Mission Valley; chamber of commerce leads successful bond issue to establish University of California, San Diego.

1959   City of Del Mar incorporated.

1960   A $1.75 billion bond issue for State Water Project approved statewide and supported 4 to 1 by San Diegans; military payroll reaches $280 million, making San Diego second-largest military establishment in US; city population reaches 573,224; county tops million mark at 1,033,011.

1961–1970

John F. Kennedy, Lyndon Johnson, and Richard Nixon serve as US. presidents; Peace Corps organized and space program launched; US. involvement in Vietnam and antiwar protests escalate across nation; civil rights movement gains steady ground; counterculture is born, and the Beatles cause a musical sensation; the UC Berkeley campus and others erupt with student demonstrations; John Kennedy, Martin Luther King, and Robert Kennedy assassinated; Neil Armstrong walks on moon; State Water Project makes headway on Feather River and Ronald Reagan elected governor of California.

1961   City council moves to acquire downtown land to centralize public buildings; San Diego Chargers open first season at Balboa Stadium.

1962   Salk Institute opens in La Jolla; Senator Hugo Fisher becomes secretary of State Resources Agency; voters approve $12.6 million in bonds for Mission Bay.

1963   Frank Curran elected mayor; Vista and San Marcos incorporated; chamber of commerce helps establish Economic Development Corporation.

1964   SeaWorld built on Mission Bay; University of California opens 1,000-acre campus at La Jolla.

1965   Charles Dail Community Concourse and Civic Auditorium opened.

1966   Voters approve $30 million to construct second pipeline for second San Diego aqueduct and approve construction of $27 million sports stadium in Mission Valley; Sports Arena completed in Midway area; Old Town becomes State Historic Park.

1967   San Diego's Opera company gives American premiere of Hans Weiner Henze's *The Young Lord*.

1968   Pennsylvania Railroad purchases 1,180 acre Scripps Miramar Ranch; United States International University opens.

1969   San Diego celebrates 200th birthday July 16; San Diego Coronado Bay Bridge connecting San Diego with Coronado completed; Major League San Diego Padres play in new Mission Valley stadium.

1970   San Diego County's worst brush fires to date blacken large areas of the back country; San Diego becomes fourteenth-largest city in United States (second largest in California) with 696,769 population; San Diego County numbers 1,357,854.

1971–1980

Richard Nixon, Gerald Ford, and Jimmy Carter are US presidents; Nixon successfully visits Red China; Watergate causes Nixon to resign; US withdraws from Vietnam; price of oil quadruples after organization of petroleum exporting countries (OPEC); steady inflation felt across nation; Jerry Brown, son of Pat, elected governor of California; Proposition 13 passes in state, severely limiting property taxes; California's population reaches 23 million by 1980.

1971   San Diego State College becomes a part of state university system; the Sherman-Gilbert House becomes first building moved to Heritage Park; Assemblyman Pete Wilson elected mayor of San Diego; National University founded in San Diego.

1972   University of San Diego merges its San Diego College for Women, College for Men and School of Law; Mayor Pete Wilson declares San Diego "America's Finest City."

1973   Point Loma College established by Church of the Nazarene; second pipeline of second San Diego Aqueduct (Pipeline 4) completed to Miramar Reservoir.

1975   Centre City Development Corporation founded; Vietnamese refugees housed at Camp Pendleton.

1976   San Diego participates in US Bicentennial celebration; restored *Star of India* sails on July 4; chamber of commerce establishes San Diego Motion Picture & Television Bureau; Morena Blvd. Price Club founded.

1977   City of Lemon Grove incorporated—fourteenth in county. Economic Development Corporation revitalized by chamber of commerce; University Town Center opens in La Jolla.

1978   Fires in Balboa Park destroy Aerospace Museum in Electric Building and Old Globe Theatre; chamber of commerce raises $110,000 to rebuild *Spirit of St. Louis* replica.

1979   San Diego Chargers win American Football Conference Western Division Championship; San Diego experiences heavy rains and flooding throughout city and county.

1980   The San Diego Trolley, first link in light-rail transit, dedicated; Poway and Santee incorporated; city population reaches 875,538 and the county numbers 1,861,846.

1981–1990

Ronald Reagan and George Bush serve as US presidents; Geraldine Ferraro in 1984 is the first woman nominated for vice president; US astronauts first humans to fly freely in space; Olympic games held in Los Angeles in 1984; San Francisco earthquake in 1989 measures 7.1; the Berlin Wall falls in 1989; the US slips into an economic recession.

1981   San Diego Stadium named after *San Diego Union* sportswriter Jack Murphy; San Diego Trolley connects city with Tijuana border; ground breaking for Horton Plaza downtown.

1982   San Diego becomes 8th-largest city in the nation; Mayor Pete Wilson elected to the United States Senate; San Diego offers first bilingual primary education classes in California.

1983   Queen Elizabeth in San Diego; Roger Hedgcock elected mayor.

1984   State coastal commission approves $125 million convention center; San Diego Padres win the National League Pennant.

1985   Horton Plaza opens on August 9; disasterous fire in Normal Heights; Roger Hedgcock resigns over alleged improper reporting of campaign funds.

1986   Maureen O'Connor elected first woman mayor; PSA acquired by US Air; Encinitas and Solana Beach incorporated; Lyceum Theater opens in Horton Plaza.

1987   Dennis Conner wins America's Cup; Father Joe Carroll opens St. Vincent de Paul Village with services for the homeless.

1988   Military population estimated at 344,000 or one-third of total in San Diego; Superbowl XXII played in San Diego on January 31; Pete Wilson reelected United States senator; congressional approval of Indian Gaming Regulatory Acts (IGRA) received for casinos in San Diego County.

1989   San Diego Sockers win their 4th straight MISL championship; downtown skyscrapers and San Diego Convention Center open.

1990   US Senator Pete Wilson becomes governor of California; California State University San Marcos opens; city population reaches 1,110,549; County numbers 2,498,016.

1991–2000

A crisis in the Persian Gulf in August 1990 erupts into war in January 1991; the USSR disbands; America commemorates the 500th anniversary of the 1492 arrival of Columbus in the New World; Democrats Bill Clinton and Al Gore capture the presidency and vice presidency of the United States in November 1992; Republicans regain control of Congress in November 1994; NAFTA Free Trade Agreement signed 1994; Bill Clinton and Al Gore retain their respective offices in 1996.

1991   San Diego begins its fifth year of drought; Lindbergh Field handles 9.4 million passengers; cross-border planning becomes a major priority.

1992   San Diego hosts the America's Cup yacht races; the Columbus Quincentenary celebrated with lectures at the Cabrillo Monument; Susan Golding is elected mayor; *The San Diego*

Union and San Diego *Evening Tribune* merge as *The San Diego Union-Tribune*; Major League All-Star Baseball Game is held at San Diego Jack Murphy Stadium.

1993   San Diego remains a major US Naval facility despite closures.

1994   Former San Diego mayor Pete Wilson elected governor of California for a second term; California Center for the Arts opens in Escondido.

1995   The San Diego Chargers win the American Football Conference Championship and play in the Miami Super Bowl; New Zealand takes the America's Cup from San Diego.

1996   The San Diego Padres win Western Division Championship; the Republican National Convention is held in San Diego in August; presidential candidates Bill Clinton and Bob Dole debate at the University of San Diego in October.

1997   Jack Murphy stadium renamed Qualcomm; San Diego Trolley expands to Mission Valley and Qualcomm Stadium.

1997–1998 Unusually heavy rainfall caused by El Niño weather conditions.

1998   Padres, led by Tony Gwynn, go to the World Series as National League Champions; Super Bowl XXXII hosted in San Diego betweed Denver Broncos and Green Bay Packers.

1999   China donates two pandas to the San Diego Zoo.

2000   Dick Murphy becomes 33rd mayor in December; summer MTV filmed in Mission Beach; San Diego City population reaches 1,223,400 and San Diego County is at 2,813,833.

2001–2010

Republicans George W. Bush and Dick Cheney take office in 2001 after Florida recount; California suffers an energy crisis; terrorist attacks on September 11, 2001, in New York and Washington, D.C., shock the nation; US attacks Iraq and captures Saddam Hussein in 2003; firestorms in southern California wreak havoc in fall 2003; Arnold Schwarzenegger becomes California governor after recall of Governor Gray Davis in October 2003 and retains office in 2006; Bush and Cheney reelected in 2004; Democrats Barack Obama and

Joe Biden elected president and vice president in 2008; California governor Jerry Brown elected in 2010.

2001   San Diego County experiences rolling blackouts; San Diego military units prepare for emergency duty after 9/11 attack; Camp Pendleton troops deployed to Afghanistan to combat terrorism; San Diego Padres baseball great Tony Gwynn retires October 7.

2002   Maritime Museum of San Diego hosts International Festival of Sail; Indian casinos become well established in San Diego County as a result of 9th District US Court approval for California; 400th anniversary of the naming of San Diego de Alcalá by Sebastián Vizcaíno on November 12, 1602.

2003   Super Bowl XXXVII hosted in San Diego; former US Naval Training Center becomes Liberty Station multiuse development; San Diego Philanthropist Joan Kroc dies; Firestorms destroy over 2,000 homes in Scripps Ranch, Ramona, Valley Center, and towns in East County.

2004   San Diego Padres ballpark, Petco Park, opens downtown in April; US Navy Aircraft Carrier *Midway* becomes a harborfront museum; a disputed November mayoral election between Dick Murphy and Donna Frye goes to Murphy.

2005   San Diego Chargers win American Football Conference West title; record rainfall causes flooding and mudslides; Mayor Murphy resigns over irregularities in pension funding; Michael Zucchet serves as acting mayor for three days; council member Toni Atkins serves until the election of Jerry Sanders on November 8.

2006   Republican mayor Jerry Sanders faces burden of an enormous pension debt; some 40,000 students rally against an act that restricts immigration; median annual income in San Diego reaches $69,539 while the median price for a home is estimated at $399,000; North Korea alarms the world by testing a nuclear weapon.

2007   Sycuan Indians buy landmark US Grant Hotel; Craig Venter is honored for his work in understanding the human genome; October wildfires kill 14, injure at least 160, and burn 970,977 acres at a cost of 1.4 billion dollars; Witch Creek and Cedar Fires are within San Diego County; the San Diego Chargers win the AFC West championship title.

2008   San Diego's population reaches 1,317,635 by January 1; median housing prices drop about 30 percent. Using mobile phones while driving is banned; Mayor Jerry Sanders reelected June 3 although the city's pension fund debt payments remain unpaid; the city introduces a multimillion dollar development plan for Horton Plaza Park.

2009   Barack Obama and Joe Biden inaugurated for country's highest offices on January 20; a serious drought continues in California; San Diego reaches 1,353,993 in 2009; wildfires devastate the state with 404,601 acres burned causing $135 million in damages; Chula Vista's Little League team wins the World Series in Pennsylvania.

2010–2015

World disasters in 2010 include an earthquake in Haiti and British Petroleum oil spill in the Gulf of Mexico; Democrat Jerry Brown elected as California governor in November 2010; Republicans pick up 63 House seats and 6 in the US Senate; Obamacare signed into law March 23, 2010; iPhone developer Steve Jobs, founder of Apple, dies in October 2011; Barack Obama and Joe Biden reelected in November 2012; Hurricane Sandy strikes the East Coast in October; Governor Brown reelected in 2014; November 2015 terrorist attacks kill 129 in Paris.

2010   San Diego expands its digital world through use of tablets; California reaches a resident population of 37,253, 956; Mayor Jerry Sanders promotes community service programs; San Diego feels a 7.2 earthquake centered in Mexicali and experiences power outages; San Diego's population climbs to 1,307,402.

2011   The San Diego Maritime Museum begins construction of the historically accurate replica of Cabrillo's *San Salvador*, first European ship to reach San Diego; an earthquake and tsunami in Japan cause damage and debris along the Pacific coast; San Diego creates a new ninth council district; a citywide blackout results from the failure of a high voltage line from Arizona to California; *The San Diego Union-Tribune* is sold to Doug Manchester's group for $110 million.

2012   Obamacare upheld by the Supreme Court; Bob Filner takes over the role of strong mayor; the San Ysidro border crossing at 30 million people is the largest in the world; severe drought continues; unruly celebrants damage Lily Pond in Balboa Park resulting in repairs costing $10,000.

2013   Mayor Bob Filner convicted on charges of harassment of women and is removed from office; Todd Gloria, president of the city council, becomes interim mayor; by 2013, county population reaches 3,211,252 with 32.9% listing themselves as Hispanic or Latino; the median household income drops to $63,373 with about 14% of San Diegans living at the poverty level.

2014   Council president Todd Gloria continues as interim mayor; another successful Comic-Con takes place in San Diego Convention Center in July bringing 130,000 patrons to downtown; Shelley Zimmerman appointed first woman chief of police; Republican Kevin Faulconer captures the mayor's race and Governor Jerry Brown wins another term in California.

2015   The centennial celebration of the 1915 Panama-California Exposition starts the new year with a concert in Spreckels Organ Pavilion reminiscent of the opening 100 years before; San Diego introduces a climate action plan to combat the continuing drought; city legalizes medical marijuana; Cross-Border Airport terminal completed between California and Tijuana; NFL Chargers remain in San Diego.

Communities of the San Diego Metropolitan Area

Map by W.J. Hermiston

Place Names in San Diego County

Agua Caliente: hot water

Agua Hedionda: stinking water

Barona: Padre José Barona

Ballena: whale

Bonita: pretty

Borrego: big horn sheep

Buena Vista: good view

Campo: field

Chula Vista: pretty view

Coronado: crowned (from Mexico's *Islas Coronados*)

Cuca: a root used as a substitute for coffee

Cuyamaca: (Kumeyaay) behind the clouds

Dehesa: pasture

Del Cerro: of the hill

De Luz: of light

Del Mar: of the sea

Descanso: resting place

Dulzura: sweetness

El Cajon: the box

El Camino Real: the principal road

Encanto: charm, enchantment

Encinitas: little live oaks

Escondido: hidden

Guajome: (Luiseño) home of the frog

Guatay: (Kumeyaay) big house

Jamacha: (Kumeyaay) wild squash

Jamul: (Kumeyaay) foam or lather

Jana: (Kumeyaay) rippling water

La Jolla: Hoya, a hollow (possibly on the coast worn by waves)

La Mesa: the plateau, tableland

La Presa: the dam

La Punta: the point

Las Flores: the flowers

Las Pulgas: the fleas

Linda Vista: pretty view

Loma: hill

Loma Portal: gateway to the hill

Los Peñasquitos: the little cliffs

Mesa Grande: large plateau

Miramar: view of the sea

Mira Mesa: view of the plateau

Morena: brown

Otay: (Indian) brushy

Pala: (Luiseño) water

Palomar: pigeon coop

Pauma: (Luiseño) little water

Potrero: pasture

Rincon del Diablo: Devil's corner

Solana: sunny place

Tierrasanta: holy land

Tijuana: from Tiguan or Tihuan, meaning unknown, original river name Río Tia Juana no longer in use

Valle: valley

Vallecito: little valley

Viejas: old women

Vista: view

Federally Recognized Tribal Bands in San Diego County

Barona Band of Mission Indians

Cahuilla Band of Mission Indians

Campo Kumeyaay Nation

Chemehuevi Indian Tribe

Ewiiaapaaup Band of Kumeyaay Indians

Inaja-Cosmit Band of Indians

Jamul Indians Village A Kumeyaay Nation

La Jolla Band of Luiseño Indians

La Posta Band of Mission Indians

Los Coyotes Band of Mission Indians

Manzanita Band of Band of the Kumeyaay Nation

Mesa Grande Band of Mission Indians

Pala Band of Cupeño Indians

Pauma Band of Mission Indians

Rincon Band of Luiseño Indians

San Pasqual Band of Diegueño Mission Indians of California

Iipay Nation of Santa Ysabel

Sycuan Band of the Kumeyaay Nation

Viejas Band of Kumeyaay Indians

Selected Bibliography

Abbott, Patrick *The Rise and Fall of San Diego: 150 Million Years of History Recorded in Sedimentary Rocks*. San Diego: Sunbelt Publications, 1999.

Account of the Voyage of Juan Rodríguez Cabrillo. San Diego: Cabrillo National Monument Foundation, 1999.

Adema, Thomas. *Our Hills and Valleys: A History of the Helix-Spring Valley Region*. San Diego: San Diego Historical Society, 1993.

Agelidis, Nick. *La Jolla: A Photographic Journey*. San Diego: Sunbelt Publications, 2014.

Amero, Richard. *Balboa Park and the 1915 Exposition*. Edited by Michael Kelly. Charleston: The History Press. 2013.

Anderson, Nancy Scott. *An Improbable Venture: A History of the University of California San Diego*. La Jolla, CA: UCSD Press, 1993.

Baldridge, Charlene. *San Diego: Jewel of the California Coast*. Flagstaff: Northland Publishing. 2003.

Barrus, Pamela, and Chris Stowers. *Top 10 San Diego*. DK Eyewitness Travel Guide. 2013.

Beauchamp, R. Mitchel. *A Flora of San Diego County, California*. National City: Sweetwater River Press, 1986.

Berger, Dan, Peter Jensen and Margaret C. Berg. *San Diego: Where Tomorrow Begins*. Northridge: Windsor Publications, 1987.

Beebe, Rose Marie and Robert M. Senkewicz. *Junípero Serra: California, Indians, and the Transformation of a Missionary*. Norman: University of Oklahoma Press. 2015.

Benson, Sara. *Lonely Planet Los Angeles, San Diego & Southern California*. Lonely Planet. 2015.

Blair, Tom and Bob B. Yarbrough and Ron Donoho. *San Diego: World-Class City*. Memphis: Towery Publishing, 1998.

Boudoin, Burt J. *Fortress on the Hill: Founding the University of San Diego and the San Diego College for Women, 1942–1963*. Mission Hills, CA: Saint Francis Historical Society, 2001.

Brandes, Ray. *San Diego: An Illustrated History*. Los Angeles: Rosebud Books, 1981.

Breed, Clara E. *Turning the Pages: San Diego Public Library History, 1882–1982*. San Diego: Friends of the San Diego Public Library, 1983.

Carlin, Katherine Eitzen and Ray Brandes. *Coronado: The Enchanted Island*. Coronado: Coronado Historical Association, 1987.

Carrico, Richard L. *Strangers in a Stolen Land: American Indians in San Diego, 1850–1880*. 2nd. Edition. San Diego: Sunbelt Publications, 2008.

Case, Thomas. "The Year 1588 and San Diego de Alcalá." *The Journal of San Diego History*. Winter 1988 (Vol. 34:1).

Christman, Florence. *The Romance of Balboa Park*. San Diego: San Diego Historical Society, 1988.

Crawford, Richard. *San Diego Yesterday*. American Chronicles. Charleston: The History Press. 2013.

_____. *The Way We Were in San Diego*. American Chronicles. Charleston: The History Press. 2011.

Crosby, Harry. *Antigua California: Mission and Colony on the Peninsular Frontier, 1697–1768*. Albuquerque: University of New Mexico Press, 1994.

_____. *Last of the Californios*. La Jolla: Copley Books, 1981.

_____. *Gateway to California: The Expedition to San Diego 1769*. San Diego: Sunbelt Publications, 2003.

Ciani, Kyle Emily. "A Passion for Water: Hans Doe and the California Water Industry." *The Journal of San Diego History*, Spring 1999, Vol. 45, No. 2.

Cutter, Donald and Iris Engstrand. *Quest for Empire: Spanish Settlement in the Southwest*. Golden, CO: Fulcrum Publishing, 1996.

Dana, Richard Henry Jr. *Two Years Before the Mast*. New York: Dodd, Mead & Co., 1946.

Davis, Mike, Kelly Mayhew and Jim Miller. *Under the Perfect Sun: the San Diego Tourists Never See*. New York: New Press, 2003.

Downs, Jim. *The Real World of Mission San Luis Rey*. Oceanside: Liebfrinck, 2015.

Engstrand, Iris H.W. *Serra's San Diego*. San Diego: San Diego

Historical Society, 1982.

_____. *San Diego: California's Cornerstone*. Tulsa: Continental Heritage Press, 1980.

_____. *San Diego: Gateway to the Pacific*. Houston: Pioneer Publications Inc., 1992.

_____. *Royal Officer in Baja California 1768–1770: Joaquín Velázquez de León*. Los Angeles: Dawson's Book Shop, 1976.

Engstrand, Iris H.W. and Ray Brandes. *Old Town San Diego 1821–1874*. San Diego: Alcalá Press, 1976.

Engstrand, Iris H.W. and Anne Bullard. *Inspired by Nature: The San Diego Natural History Museum after 125 years, 1874–1999*. San Diego: Conklin Litho, 1999.

Engstrand, Iris H.W. and Paul Campuzano. *Harley Eugene Knox: San Diego's Mayor for the People*. San Diego: San Diego Historical Society, 2003.

Engstrand, Iris H.W., Richard Griswold del Castillo and Elena Poniatowska, *Culture y Cultura: Consequences of the U.S.-Mexican War 1846-1848*. Los Angeles: Autry Museum of Western Heritage, 1998.

Engstrand, Iris H.W. and Kathleen Crawford. *Reflections: A History of the San Diego Gas & Electric Co. 1881–1991*. San Diego: San Diego Historical Society, 1992.

Engstrand, Iris H.W. and Cynthia Davalos. *A History of the San Diego Yacht Club 1886–2000*. San Diego: Conklin Litho, 2000.

Engstrand, Iris H.W. and Clare White. *The First Forty Years: A History of the University of San Diego 1949–1989*. San Diego: University of San Diego, 1989.

Estacio, Aldryn. *San Diego–Aerial Drone Photography*, Vol. 1. 2015.

Ewing, Nancy Hanks. *Del Mar: Looking Back*. Del Mar, CA: Del Mar History Foundation, 1988.

Fetzer, Leland. *San Diego County Place Names, A To Z*. San Diego: Sunbelt Publications. 2005.

Fletcher, Edward. *Memories of Ed Fletcher*. San Diego: Pioneer Printers, 1952.

Gamble, Adam, and Cooper Kelly. *Good Night San Diego*. San

Diego: Barnes & Noble. 2006.

Glassman, Bruce. *San Diego Brewery Guide*. 2nd Edition. San Diego: Georgia Bay Books. 2014.

Gould, Steve, and Sara Day. *San Diego, California: A Photographic Portrait*. Rockport: Twin Lights Publishers, Inc. 2015.

Halsey, Rick. *Fire, Chaparral, and Survival in Southern California*. San Diego: Sunbelt Publications, 2005.

Harlow, Neal. *California Conquered: War and Peace on the Pacific, 1846–1850*. Berkeley: University of California Press, 1982.

Harrison, Donald. *Louis Rose: San Diego's First Jewish Settler and Entrepreneur*. San Diego: Sunbelt Publications, 2004.

Heilbron, Carl H. *History of San Diego County*. San Diego: San Diego Press Club, 1936.

Hendrickson, Nancy. *San Diego Then and Now*. San Diego: Thunder Bay Press. 2003.

Hennessey, Greg. City Planning, Progressivism, and the Development of San Diego, 1908–1926. MA Thesis. San Diego State University, 1977.

Higgins, Shelly. *This Fantastic City—San Diego*. San Diego: City of San Diego, 1956.

Holle, Gena. *The San Diego Trolley*. Glendale, CA: Interurban Press, 1990.

Hopkins, H.C. *History of San Diego: Its Pueblo Lands & Water*. San Diego: City Printing Co., 1929.

Innis, Jack Scheffier. *San Diego Legends: The Events, People, and Places That Made History*. San Diego: Sunbelt Publications. 2005.

Kelsey, Harry. *Discovering Cabrillo*. Altadena: Liber Apertus Press, 2004.

_____. *Juan Rodriguez Cabrillo*. San Marino, CA: Huntington Library, 1986.

Killea, Lucy Lytle. "Political History of a Mexican Pueblo," *The Journal of San Diego History*. Spring and Fall 1966.

_____. *Colonial Foundations of Land Use and Society in San Diego, 1769–1846*. Doctoral thesis. San Diego: University of California, San Diego, 1975.

Kipen, David, editor. *San Diego in the 1930s: The WPA Guide to*

America's Finest City. Berkeley: University of California Press, 2013.

Kooperman, Evelyn. *San Diego Trivia*. San Diego: Silver Gate Publications, 1989.

_____. *San Diego Trivia II*. San Diego: Silver Gate Publications, 1993.

Lindsay, Diana. *Anza-Borrego A to Z*. San Diego: Sunbelt Publications, 2000.

Lindsay, Lowell, ed., *Geology of San Diego County: Journey Through Time*. San Diego: Sunbelt Publications, 2000.

MacPhail, Elizabeth C. *Kate Sessions: Pioneer Horticulturist*. San Diego: Silver Gate Publications San Diego Historical Society, 1976.

_____. *The Story of New San Diego and Its Founder Alonzo E. Horton*. San Diego: Pioneer Printers, 1969; rev. ed. San Diego: San Diego Historical Society, 1979.

Marshall, David. *Balboa Park*. Charleston: Arcadia Publishing. 2007.

Marston, Mary Gilman. *George White Marston: A Family Chronicle*. Los Angeles: Ward Ritchie Press, 1956.

Mathes, W. Michael. *Vizcaino and Spanish Expansion in the Pacific Ocean, 1580–1630*. San Francisco: California Historical Society, 1968.

McGaugh, Scott. *The Military in San Diego*. Charleston: Arcadia Publishing. 2014.

Meaney, Marian. *Spain–Culture Smart!: the essential guide to customs & culture*. London: Kuperard. 2006.

Mills, James R. *San Diego...Where California Began: A Brief History of the Events of Four Centuries*. 5th ed. revised. San Diego: San Diego Historical Society, 1985.

Montana, Maria Desiderata, and John Dole. *San Diego Chef's Table: Extraordinary Recipes From America's Finest City*. Lyons Press. 2013.

Morgan, Neil. *San Diego: The Unconventional City*. San Diego: Morgan House, 1972.

Moyer, Cecil. *Historic Ranchos of San Diego*. San Diego: Union-Tribune Publishing Co., 1966.

Naversen, Andrea. *San Diego: Coming of Age*. Carlsbad, CA: Heritage Media Corp, 2003.

Nolen, John. *A Comprehensive City Plan for San Diego, California.* San Diego: City Planning Department, 1926.

Palenske, Garner A. *Wyatt Earp in San Diego: Life After Tombstone.* San Diego: Sunbelt Publications. 2011.

Papageorge, Nan Taylor. "Role of the San Diego River in the Development of Mission Valley." *The Journal of San Diego History,* Spring 1971, Vol. 27, No. 2.

Pescador, Katrina, and Alan Renga. *Aviation in San Diego* Charleston: Arcadia Publishing. 2007.

Pescador, Katrina. *San Diego's North Island: 1911–1941.* Charleston: Arcadia Publishing. 2007.

Phillips, George Harwood. *Chiefs and Challengers: Indian Resistance and Cooperation in Southern California.* Berkeley: University of California Press, 1975; Norman: University of Oklahoma Press, 2014.

Pourade, Richard. Call to California: The Epic Journey Of the Portolá-Serra Expedition in 1769. San Diego: Copley Books, 1968.

_____. *City of the Dream.* San Diego: Copley Books, 1977.

_____. *Gold in the Sun.* San Diego: Union-Tribune Publishing Co., 1965.

_____. *The Explorers.* San Diego: Union-Tribune Publishing Co., 1961.

_____. *The Glory Years.* San Diego: Union-Tribune Publishing Co., 1964.

_____. *The Silver Dons.* San Diego: Union-Tribune Publishing Co., 1961.

_____. *Time of the Bells.* San Diego: Union-Tribune Publishing Co., 1966.

_____. *The Rising Tide.* San Diego: Union-Tribune Publishing Co., 1967.

Proffitt Jr., T.D. *Tijuana: The History of a Mexican Metropolis.* San Diego: San Diego State University Press, 1994.

Pryde, Phillip R. *San Diego: An Introduction to the Region.* 5th Edition. San Diego, CA: Sunbelt Publications, 2014.

Quinney Kimber M., and Thomas J. Cesarini. *San Diego's Fishing Industry*. Charleston: Arcadia Publishing. 2009.

Quinn, Ronald J. "Historians and the Spanish Occupation of San Diego." *The Journal of San Diego History*, Vol. 45, Summer, 1999: 117–120.

Ranchos of San Diego County. (multiple authors) Charleston: Arcadia Publishing. 2008.

Rebman, John, and Norman Roberts. *Baja California Field Guide*. 3rd. edition. San Diego: Sunbelt Publications, 2012.

Requa, Richard. *Inside Lights on the Building of San Diego's Exposition, 1935*. San Diego, 1935.

Rick, Glenn A. *San Diego, 1927–1955: Recollections of a City Planner*. San Diego: Published by William Rick, 1977.

Remeika, Paul, and Lowell Lindsay. *Geology of Anza-Borrego*: Edge of Creation. San Diego: Sunbelt Publications. 1992.

Robinson, Alfred. *Life in California*. Santa Barbara: Peregrine Press, 1970.

Rolle, Andrew, and Arthur C. Verge. *California: A History*. Hoboken: Wiley-Blackwell. 2014.

San Diego's Gaslamp Quarter. Gaslamp Quarter Association and San Diego Historical Society. Charleston: Arcadia Publishing. 2003.

Schaelchlin, Patricia A. *The Little Clubhouse on Steamship Wharf: San Diego Rowing Club, 1888–1983*. Leucadia, CA: Rand Editions, 1984.

———. *The Newspaper Barons: a Biography of the Scripps Family*. San Diego: San Diego Historical Society, 2003.

Schad, Jerry. *Afoot and Afield in San Diego County: A Comprehensive Hiking Guide*. Birmingham: Wilderness Press, 2007.

———. *50 Best Short Hikes San Diego*. Birmingham: Wilderness Press. 2011.

Showley, Roger. *Balboa Park—A Millennium History*. Carlsbad, CA: Heritage Media Corp. 1999.

———. *San Diego: Perfecting Paradise*. Carlsbad, CA: Heritage Media Corp. 1999.

Smythe, William E. *History of San Diego, 1542–1908*. San Diego: The

History Company, 1908.

Starr, Kevin. *Americans and the California Dream*. New York: Oxford University Press, 1973.

_____. *California: A History*. New York: Modern Library Chronicles, 2007.

_____. *The Dream Endures: California Enters the 1940s*. New York: Oxford University Press, 1997.

_____. *Material Dreams: Southern California Through the 1920s*. New York: Oxford University Press, 1990.

Starr, Raymond G. *San Diego: An Illustrated History*. Norfolk and Virginia Beach: Donning Company, 1986.

_____. *San Diego State University: A History in Word and Image*. San Diego: San Diego State University Press, 1995.

Steidel, Dave, and Lance Alworth. *The Uncrowned Champs: How the 1963 San Diego Chargers Would Have Won the Super Bowl*. New York: Skyhorse Publishing. 2015.

Swank, Bill. *Baseball in San Diego: From the Plaza to the Padres*. Charleston, SC: Arcadia Publishing, 2005.

Swank, Bill and Bob Chandler. *Tales from the San Diego Padres*. Foreword by Jerry Coleman. Champaign, ILL: Sports Publishing, 2006.

Tibesar, Antonine, ed. and trans. *Writings of Junipero Serra*. Washington, D.C.: American Academy of Franciscan History, 1955–1966.

Tobias, Todd. *Charging Through the AFL*. Turner Publishing Co., 2004.

Tyler, Jeff. *Campgrounds of San Diego County: Federal, State, County, Regional, Municipal*. San Diego: Sunbelt Publications, 2000.

Unitt, Philip, ed. *The Birds of San Diego County*. San Diego Society of Natural History, 1984.

Valley, David with Diana Lindsay. *The Jackpot Trail*. San Diego: Sunbelt Publications, 2003.

Walker, Dan. *Thirst For Independence: The San Diego Water Story*. San Diego: Sunbelt Publications, 2004.

Walshok, Mary Lindenstein and Abraham Shragge, *Invention and Reinvention: The Evolution of San Diego's Innovation Economy.* Stanford: Stanford University Press, 2013.

Van Dyke, Theodore S. *Millionaires for a Day: An Inside History of the Great Southern California "Boom."* New York: Fords, Howard & Hulbert, 1890.

Two comprehensive websites for San Diego history are:
www.sandiegohistory.org (San Diego History Center)
www.signonsandiego.com (*The San Diego Union-Tribune*).

Del Mar Thoroughbred Club. *Photo courtesy Del Mar Throughbred Club.*

San Diego's changing skyline looking east from Harbor Drive. ©*2016 Ted Walton.*

Index

Sunbelt's San Diego Booklist

Coast to Cactus: The Canyoneer Trail Guide to San Diego Outdoors......Diana Lindsay, Mgr. Ed. The new "bible" for really getting to know and appreciate San Diego County's biodiversity while exploring it firsthand on any one of over 250 trail guides. Written by the San Diego Natural History Museum Canyoneers.

Gateway to Alta California: The Expedition to San Diego, 1769......................Harry Crosby An account told through diary excerpts and the author's comments about the first overland journey of Spaniards and natives of Baja California to reach our present state of California as settlers and mission founders. Fully illustrated, it gives a colorful description of the hardships of a trail through the little-traveled wilderness from Loreto to San Diego.

Good Camp: Gold Mines of Julian..Leland Fetzer An informal history of the gold mines of the Cuyamacas, peopled with famous and not-so-famous Californians who made names for themselves on and in the rugged mountains of San Diego's backcountry. Includes a guide to the mines that can still be viewed today, plus those that offer guided tours.

Inspired by Nature: The San Diego Natural History Museum after 125 Years.....Iris Engstrand A colorful history of one of the oldest scientific institutions west of the Mississippi River. Founded in 1874, the museum focuses on the greater Southern California/ Baja California region—concentrating on the collection and identification of the area's fauna and flora, as well as the discovery and naming of the country's oldest fossils along with a variety of new species.

Louis Rose: San Diego's First Jewish Settler..Donald H. Harrison The story of a pioneer resident who was integral to San Diego's shaping as a city in 1850. President of the Board of Trustees for San Diego during 1853–1855, Louis Rose is remembered in the names of Roseville and Rose Canyon. He was also a founding member of the synagogue that eventually became Temple Beth Israel, San Diego's largest synagogue.

Old Magic: Lives of the Desert Shamans..Nicholas Clapp For a thousand generations, desert shamans of the far West sought order in the stars and in the mysteries and wonder of their grand, if unforgiving landscape. Drawing on the lore of a dozen tribes, Old Magic conjures the year-to-year life of a shaman—a life of service to his people, a life fraught with torment and danger.

San Diego: An Introduction to the Region, 5th edition..Philip Pryde This is the essential one-volume reference to the history, economics, demographics, natural features, and environmental issues of today's binational region on the Pacific borderlands, home to Native Americans for millennia with an insightful overview of San Diego County's first residents.

San Diego Legends, 2nd edition..Jack Innis
San Diego journalist Jack Innis describes the many fascinating people and events that influenced the development of San Diego, plus the colorful characters and groups that made headlines in the past century.

Strangers in a Stolen Land: History of Indians in San Diego County ....Richard Carrico
The story of the Native Americans of San Diego County from 1850 through the 1930s—including the Kumeyaay (Ipai/Tipai), Luiseño, Cupeño, and Cahuilla—from their prehistoric origins through the Spanish, Mexican, and American periods. Contains previously unpublished maps and illustrations.

San Diego County Place Names, A to Z..Leland Fetzer
From the earliest peoples of the county to the later settlers, the Spanish land grants, Mexican Ranchos, Indian Villages, and gold mines to family farms, tiny hamlets, and short-lived post offices—each has made a mark in history by putting a place name on a map. Here are over 1500 of these revealing portals into history.

San Diego's Finest Athletes: Five Exceptional Lives..Joey Seymour
These five athletes from San Diego each shattered barriers for future minority athletes, while accomplishing outstanding feats in their chosen sports. The talent, dedication, and spirit of Maureen Connolly (tennis), Charlie Powell (boxing and football), Greg Louganis (diving), Tiffany Chin (ice skating), and Adrian Gonzalez (baseball), make this book ideal for sports fans.

San Diego Specters .... John Lamb
Only the most authentic and plausible ghostly tales are included in this entertaining investigation into famous and obscure haunted sites throughout San Diego County. Ideal for ghost watchers.

Tom Hom, Rabbit on a Bumpy Road: A Story of Courage and Endurance................Tom Hom
This is Tom's memoir in meeting life's challenges to achieve "The American Dream." He was born into a Chinese family in the year of the Rabbit in the 1920s when much of American society was segregated, socially and economically. Today, Tom Hom is a respected elder whose journey and words of wisdom offer encouragement to a new generation of Americans.

Sunbelt Publications

Award-winning Sunbelt Publications, incorporated in 1988, produces and distributes natural science and outdoor guidebooks, regional histories, and stories that celebrate the land and its people. Sunbelt books help to discover and conserve the natural, historical, and cultural heritage of unique regions.

Our publishing program focuses primarily on the Californias—today three states in two nations sharing one Pacific shore. Our books, with an underlying theme of "journey," encourage readers to discover and conserve the wonders of this unique region. Sunbelt Publications has won over 50 major awards in various categories for its publications.

Visit us online at:
www.sunbeltpublications.com